FLAME IN
THE MOUNTAINS

Herbert Arthur Hodges
(1905–1976)

FLAME IN THE MOUNTAINS

Williams Pantycelyn, Ann Griffiths
and the Welsh Hymn

Essays and translations by H. A. HODGES
Edited by E. WYN JAMES

The generous contribution of Jewin Welsh
Presbyterian Church, London, towards the publication
of this book is gratefully acknowledged.

First impression: 2017

© Copyright: Anna Parsons Howard,
E. Wyn James and Y Lolfa, 2017

The contents of this book are subject to copyright, and may
not be reproduced by any means, mechanical or electronic,
without the prior, written consent of the publishers.

Cover design: Olwen Fowler

ISBN: 978 1 78461 454 6

Published and printed in Wales
on paper from well-maintained forests by
Y Lolfa Cyf., Talybont, Ceredigion SY24 5HE
website www.ylolfa.com
e-mail ylolfa@ylolfa.com
tel 01970 832 304
fax 01970 832 782

CONTENTS

Cover Illustrations	7
Introduction (E. Wyn James)	9
Acknowledgements	28
Vita Equina: The Life of H. A. Hodges (Anna Parsons Howard)	30
H. A. Hodges (1905–1976): A Bibliography (Anna Parsons Howard)	38

PART ONE: WILLIAMS PANTYCELYN AND THE WELSH HYMN

Flame in the Mountains: Aspects of Welsh Free Church Hymnody	47
Williams Pantycelyn: Father of the Modern Welsh Hymn	67
Over the Distant Hills: Thoughts on Williams Pantycelyn	94
Hymn Translations	108

PART TWO: ANN GRIFFITHS

Homage to Ann Griffiths: An Introduction	119
A Note of Introduction to 'Ann Griffiths: A Literary Survey'	133
'Ann Griffiths: A Literary Survey' (Saunders Lewis; translated by H. A. Hodges)	138

The Hymns of Ann Griffiths (edited by E. Wyn James; translated by H. A. Hodges)	161
The Letters of Ann Griffiths (translated by H. A. Hodges)	215
Notes on the Hymns of Ann Griffiths	235
Notes on the Letters of Ann Griffiths	283
Scriptural References and Allusions in the Hymns and Letters of Ann Griffiths (E. Wyn James)	303

Cover Illustrations

THE COVER DESIGN includes part of the hymn-tune, *Cwm Rhondda*, taken from the copy in Pontypridd Museum of the festival programme of 1907 in which it was first printed. *Cwm Rhondda* ('Rhondda Valley') by John Hughes (1873–1932) is one of the best known of all Welsh hymn-tunes. It was composed around the time of the Welsh Revival of 1904–05 and appears to have been first sung at a praise festival at the Baptist chapel, Capel Rhondda ('Rhondda Chapel'), in Hopkinstown, Pontypridd, in Glamorgan on 17 November 1907. At that hymn-singing festival it was sung to the words of Ann Griffiths' hymn, '*Wele'n sefyll rhwng y myrtwydd*' ('Behold standing among the myrtles'), and these are the Welsh words that are most frequently sung to that tune today. However, in English, the tune is almost invariably wedded to William Williams, Pantycelyn's 'Guide me, O thou great Jehovah'.

The image of Ann Griffiths (1776–1805) reproduced on the cover is from the carved corbel head in the Ann Griffiths Memorial Chapel in Dolanog, near her birthplace in Montgomeryshire. It is an imaginary likeness based on descriptions by contemporaries and influenced by the Arts and Crafts movement. The chapel was opened in 1904.

The image of William Williams (1717–91) of Pantycelyn was first published in an edition of his collected works in 1867. It is based on a sketch made by one John Williams (b. 1772) from the parish of Llanddarog in Carmarthenshire, who remembered Williams Pantycelyn coming regularly to preach near his home during his youth and who drew the resemblance from recollection many years after Pantycelyn's death.

INTRODUCTION

E. Wyn James

THE HYMN IS one of the great highlights of Welsh literature. The genre began to develop in earnest in the context of the Methodist Revival of the eighteenth century, and the second half of that century would witness a veritable 'hymn explosion' in Wales. It has been estimated that over three thousand hymns were composed in Welsh during that period, with over a quarter of them coming from the pen of William Williams (1717–91) of Pantycelyn, the man who H. A. Hodges rightly calls 'the creator of the modern Welsh hymn' and whose work has been described as 'central to Welsh literature because it contains such a powerful expression of a spiritual movement which brought about a radical change in the culture of the Welsh people'.[1]

Williams Pantycelyn paved the way for a 'golden age' of evangelical hymn-writing, stretching for a century between the powerful 'Llangeitho' Revival of 1762 and the widespread revival of 1859. This was a period which saw at least fifteen major religious revivals in Wales and which witnessed a phenomenal growth in evangelicalism, initially mainly among members of the established Anglican Church, but increasingly also among Nonconformists, with the result that by the mid-nineteenth century almost four out of every

---

1 Dafydd Johnston, *The Literature of Wales: A Pocket Guide* (Cardiff: University of Wales Press, 1994), p. 67.

five of those attending a place of worship in Wales frequented Nonconformist chapels.

A number of notable hymn-writers emerged from Williams Pantycelyn's shadow. Some of the earliest of these lived in fairly close proximity to Williams' farm in north Carmarthenshire, including the circulating schoolmaster, Morgan Rhys (1716–79), and Dafydd Jones (1711–77), the drover from Caeo; but as the revival movement spread gradually throughout Wales, significant hymn-writers began to emerge in other parts of the country, and none more remarkable than Ann Griffiths (1776–1805), or Ann Thomas as she was known until her marriage in 1804.[2]

Williams Pantycelyn and Ann Griffiths are very different in so many ways. The life of one of them spans much of the eighteenth century, while the other lived for only twenty-nine years at the end of that century and the beginning of the next, dying in 1805 following childbirth. Williams Pantycelyn had a prominent leadership role in the Methodist movement, travelling the length and breadth of Wales, covering over 2,500 miles on horseback each year for more than forty years, whereas Ann Griffiths lived her life in comparative obscurity on her family's farm, Dolwar Fach, in the parish of Llanfihangel-yng-Ngwynfa in north Montgomeryshire, and probably travelled not much further than the twenty-five-mile journey to Bala to sit at the feet of her mentor, Thomas Charles (1755–1814), the great Welsh Methodist leader of the second generation and one of the founders of the Bible Society. Williams was a prolific author who wrote around a thousand hymns, not to

---

2   For an overview of the development of the Welsh hymn down to the beginning of the twentieth century, see E. Wyn James, 'The Evolution of the Welsh Hymn', in *Dissenting Praise: Religious Dissent and the Hymn in England and Wales*, ed. Isabel Rivers and David L. Wykes (Oxford: Oxford University Press, 2011), pp. 229–68.

mention two epic poems, over thirty elegies and a number of substantial prose works, while all that has survived of Ann's work is just over seventy stanzas and eight letters. He wrote his hymns very consciously, not only to give expression to his own convictions, experiences and emotions, but also to give voice to the wide range of spiritual conditions found among members of the Methodist community which he served, in order that they might 'express and ... enrich their experience',[3] while she wrote her verses, often during periods of intense meditation, in order to encapsulate her deepest thoughts and feelings, and shared only some of them with a close circle of confidantes.

However, there are similarities. Although very different in style, they share an intensity of expression, as one might expect of evangelical hymn-writers who lived through periods of profound spiritual experience and fervent emotion. For both, the central source-text is the Bible; both were Calvinist in doctrine; and both return again and again to the same basic themes: an acute awareness of the majesty of God and of their own frailty and waywardness; the centrality of the cross of Christ in the plan of salvation; and a deep longing – a longing to be holy, a longing for heaven, and above all, a longing for Christ, the Beloved; for ultimately the hymns of both can be described as love-songs to God Incarnate.

Another similarity is that Williams Pantycelyn and Ann Griffiths are not only in a class of their own as the two most outstanding of all Welsh hymn-writers, but both also rank among the most prominent figures in the whole of Welsh literature. The eminent literary critic, R. Geraint Gruffydd,

---

[3] Brynley F. Roberts, 'The Literature of the "Great Awakening"', in *A Guide to Welsh Literature c. 1700–1800*, ed. Branwen Jarvis (Cardiff: University of Wales Press, 2000), p. 290. See also Kathryn Jenkins' chapter on Williams Pantycelyn in the same volume.

renowned for his expertise in all periods of Welsh literature, did not hesitate to place Williams Pantycelyn and Ann Griffiths among the most notable of all the poets in the 1,500-year history of that literature;[4] while another leading literary critic, Bobi Jones, has described Pantycelyn as 'the greatest Welsh writer between the end of the fifteenth and the beginning of the twentieth century' and Ann's work as 'unsurpassed in our literature'.[5] And William Williams and Ann Griffiths are not only giants of the literary, cultural and religious life of Wales, but, as demonstrated in this volume, they are also figures of international status and significance.

In 'Over the Distant Hills', the third essay in this volume, H. A. Hodges goes so far as to describe Williams Pantycelyn as 'no mere provincial notability', but rather one of the most 'compelling voices' in the history of Christianity in Britain – 'for those who can hear'; for as Hodges emphasises in that same essay, there are particular problems facing those who deserve international acknowledgement and attention if, like Williams Pantycelyn and Ann Griffiths, they write in a 'lesser-used' language. 'The world', he says, 'will never take a man seriously as a writer and teacher if he writes in a language which no one outside his own small country understands, and never finds a competent translator. How much influence would Kierkegaard have had if his works had existed only in Danish?' However, both Williams Pantycelyn and Ann Griffiths have been particularly fortunate to have in the persons of H. A.

---

4   E. Wyn James (ed.), *Y Ffordd Gadarn: Ysgrifau ar Lên a Chrefydd gan R. Geraint Gruffydd* (Pen-y-bont ar Ogwr: Gwasg Bryntirion, 2008), p. 189; R. Geraint Gruffydd, 'Ann Griffiths: Llenor', *Taliesin*, 43 (December 1981), p. 76.

5   R. M. Jones, *Highlights in Welsh Literature* (Swansea and Llandybïe: Christopher Davies, 1969), p. 62; idem, 'Ann Griffiths and the Norm', in *A Guide to Welsh Literature c. 1700–1800*, ed. Branwen Jarvis, p. 326.

Introduction

Hodges (1905–76) and his close friend and collaborator, A. M. ('Donald') Allchin (1930–2010), two passionate and well-informed advocates and interpreters in English and on an international stage; and indeed, not only for Pantycelyn, Ann Griffiths and the Welsh hymn, but also for Christian spirituality in Wales more generally.

As Hodges' granddaughter, Anna Parsons Howard, explains in her biographical essay on him in this volume, it was through the Fellowship of St Alban and St Sergius, founded in 1928 to foster ecumenical dialogue, especially between Anglican and Eastern Orthodox Christians, that Hodges and Allchin first came into contact and began working together. H. A. Hodges was a Yorkshireman who spent most of his career as Professor of Philosophy at the University of Reading, but who devoted himself increasingly to the study of theology and spirituality. He had been reared a Methodist, and although he became an Anglican in his twenties, in later life he took an increasing interest in Methodist hymnody. This led to a joint publication by him and A. M. Allchin in 1966 on the hymns of John and Charles Wesley. By then both he and Allchin had begun studying Welsh hymnody, and the work of Williams Pantycelyn and Ann Griffiths in particular. Those studies were sufficiently well advanced by 1967 for Hodges to venture to publish the first of his contributions on Welsh literature, namely his translation of Saunders Lewis' lecture on Ann Griffiths and 'Flame in the Mountains', his overview of the Welsh hymn which is included as the opening essay in this volume and which first appeared in the October 1967 issue of *Religious Studies*, an international journal for the philosophy of religion published by Cambridge University Press.

During the period from about the early 1960s until his death in 1976, H. A. Hodges devoted much time to the study of Welsh hymnody and poetry, working closely in these matters with A. M. Allchin. As we shall elaborate upon later in this introduction, the years from around 1966 onward saw them working on an edition of the hymns and letters of Ann Griffiths, including an extensive introduction, a task which was almost completed at the time of Hodges' death but which was never published. Increasingly during those years, Hodges also began to study the life and work of Williams Pantycelyn in depth, so much so that in his obituary for Hodges, published in *Sobornost*, the journal of the Fellowship of St Alban and St Sergius, Donald Allchin could say that Pantycelyn was the hymn-writer whose work Hodges came to love above all others. Hodges and Allchin also began studying Welsh Christian poetry of the twentieth century, especially that of Saunders Lewis, D. Gwenallt Jones, Waldo Williams and Euros Bowen.[6] Hodges made English translations of a number of their poems, some of which A. M. Allchin published in various volumes over the years. Hodges also published an article on D. Gwenallt Jones in 1970. However, most of his published work relating to Wales was on Williams Pantycelyn, Ann Griffiths and the Welsh hymn, and it is these publications that have been assembled in this volume, together with some parts of the unpublished edition of the work of Ann Griffiths.

In his essay, 'Flame in the Mountains', H. A. Hodges describes himself as a 'fortunate foreigner' who, in exploring Welsh literature, had found himself in a new world; and Donald Allchin reacts very similarly. Both learnt Welsh and immersed themselves in Welsh culture and history. Both were emphatic that Wales was not an extension of England. As Hodges says in 'Flame in the Mountains': 'Wales is a nation with its own life and culture, which merits study and demands respect. ... Even when it shares with England in a great mass movement like

---

6   See A. M. Allchin, *Praise Above All: Discovering the Welsh Tradition* (Cardiff: University of Wales Press, 1991), pp. 34–6.

the Evangelical Revival, still Wales has a voice of its own and something of its own to say.' Both also express astonishment at their discovery of this 'other' on their very doorstep, and bewail the ignorance in England of the Welsh language and its culture. A. M. Allchin could say, for example, in an address to the Honourable Society of Cymmrodorion in 1974, during the period in which he and H. A. Hodges were working on their edition of Ann Griffiths' hymns and letters:

> Like most of my fellow-countrymen, I grew up in almost total ignorance of the existence of all things Welsh. As one whose discovery of the existence of Wales dates back less than fifteen years, I still have much of the inexperience of a novice, and something of the fervour and indiscretion of a convert. I use such words as 'convert' and 'conversion' advisedly, in speaking of the change of attitudes and perspectives which the discovery of Wales involves for an Englishman, who is at all concerned with the history and culture of the island on which he lives. It means for him a voyage of exploration which requires the abandonment of national prejudices and blindness almost as old as the [English] nation itself. ...
>
> As an Englishman, I am more and more aware of the impoverishment of our understanding of our own history which follows from our ignorance of *y pethau Cymraeg* [things Welsh]. For our future, as well as for yours, the question of the [Welsh] language is of vital importance. May we look forward to the day when it will no longer be thought strange for an educated Englishman to have a knowledge of the history and language of Wales, when every school child in England will have access to the classics of your tradition, at least in translation, and when Welsh will be fully recognised as one of the major languages of *Prydain Fawr* [Great Britain].[7]

---

7   A. M. Allchin, 'Ann Griffiths: An Approach to Her Life and Work', *The Transactions of the Honourable Society of Cymmrodorion*, Sessions 1972 and 1973 (1974), pp. 170–1; cf. A. M. Allchin, *The World is*

Because they had both learnt Welsh and had not only immersed themselves in 'things Welsh' but had become enthralled by them, Williams Pantycelyn and Ann Griffiths, not to mention the riches of Welsh spirituality in general, found in H. A. Hodges and A. M. Allchin two enthusiastic ambassadors who could discuss their work sensitively, knowledgeably and perceptively. Because of their wide interest and expertise in Methodist, Anglican, Catholic and Orthodox spirituality, a particularly valuable contribution was the way Hodges and Allchin were able to place Welsh spirituality in an international context; and they were both extremely keen to promote Ann Griffiths and Williams Pantycelyn internationally. Donald Allchin could say, for example: 'As we worked together on the study of Ann's writings, Hodges and I found ourselves saying from time to time; here are things which belong not only to Welsh-speaking Wales but to the whole world.'[8] Interestingly, they would also argue that their work on Welsh-language literature, although being in English and aimed mainly at an international readership, had a contribution to make to the study of that literature in Wales itself and among Welsh-speakers;

---

a Wedding: Explorations in Christian Spirituality (London: Darton, Longman and Todd, 1978), p. 45: 'I have come to believe in the last fifteen years, in which I have gradually been coming to discover the existence of Wales, that our English inability to hear and learn Welsh, our unwillingness to acknowledge the existence of this language and this people, other than as an historical curiosity, is rooted in deep and unrecognised feelings of guilt dating back to the centuries of struggle during which our Anglo-Saxon ancestors conquered the greater part of Southern Britain and drove the earlier inhabitants back into the Western extremities of the island. Here we have the historical origins of some of the greatest weaknesses of our whole English-speaking world ... our inability to hear the other, our unwillingness to learn the language of the other, ... our insensitivity to things that are small ...'

8   Allchin, *Praise Above All*, p. 84.

Introduction

for just as in their experience, discovering another culture had helped them better discern their own, so also 'outsiders' can bring different insights and perspectives precisely because they are approaching a culture from the outside, which in turn can enrich the understanding of the indigenous members of that culture. That is not to say, of course, that their conclusions might not be challenged on occasions. Some of their emphases and interpretations are open to debate, and indeed, Hodges and Allchin modified their own approaches to some extent as their knowledge and understanding of Wales and Welsh language and culture developed; and regarding international comparisons, it is worth quoting from a chapter on A. M. Allchin by his friend, the Professor of Theology, D. Densil Morgan: 'Above all Donald was a synthesizer. Sometimes this led him into difficulties as he saw similarities and parallels that the evidence could not support.'[9] Having said that, one must hasten to add that both H. A. Hodges and A. M. Allchin have made an invaluable contribution to our understanding of the two outstanding Welsh hymn-writers under consideration here and of the wider Christian tradition in Wales.

A. M. Allchin is a constant background presence in this volume. Arthur Macdonald Allchin was born in London on Easter Sunday 1930. Educated in Oxford, where he read Modern History, he was awarded a BLitt for a history of the Anglican monastic movement in the nineteenth century. He was ordained an Anglican priest and spent four years as a curate in London before being appointed in 1960 to the staff of Pusey House, an Anglo-Catholic theological and pastoral centre in Oxford. In 1973 he became a residentiary canon at Canterbury

---

9   D. Densil Morgan, 'Donald Allchin and the Welsh Tradition', in *Boundless Grandeur: The Christian Vision of A. M. Donald Allchin*, ed. David G. R. Keller (Eugene, Oregon, USA: Pickwick Publications, 2015), p. 132.

17

Cathedral, returning to Oxford in 1987 as founding Director of the St Theosevia Centre for Christian Spirituality. Over the years his interest in Welsh spirituality expanded and deepened, to encompass not only the hymn-writers of the eighteenth century and Christian poets of the twentieth, but other figures and periods, concentrating increasingly on Welsh religious poetry of the medieval period. He was also drawn increasingly into the religious life of Wales, and following his retirement in 1994, he moved to live in Bangor in north Wales, where he was an Honorary Professor in Theology and Welsh at the university; and Bangor would be his base for the next fourteen years, until ill health led to his return to Oxford, where he died in 2010.

In his entry on Allchin in the *Oxford Dictionary of National Biography*, Densil Morgan could say:

> The most compelling thing about Donald Allchin was his childlike openness and infectious enthusiasm. A born reconciler, he delighted in bringing people together. The words 'praise', 'joy', and 'wonder' were forever on his lips, and in the titles of his books, and although he never depreciated the concepts of sacrifice and atonement, his spirituality was emphatically one of resurrection and hope.

Such sentiments are echoed constantly by all who have written about him. For example, when he presented Allchin for a Lambeth Doctor of Divinity in 2006, Archbishop Rowan Williams described him as 'a bridge-builder, one who connects and sees connections' and 'a one-man ecumenical movement', who had been enabled by his

> gift of compelling enthusiasm and imaginative sympathy ... to perceive illuminating likenesses between such unlikely pairs as Maximus the Confessor and Richard Hooker, Ann Griffiths

Introduction

and Elizabeth of Dijon, Solzhenytsyn and Pantycelyn, Evelyn Underhill and the Italian Sorella Maria. ... The man who learnt Welsh in order to bring the treasures of Ann Griffiths to a wider audience is the same man who tackled Danish to open up Grundtvig to us. The man who helped establish the Trust to preserve Bardsey Island as a place of prayer and pilgrimage is the man who could help you negotiate your way to the monasteries of the Wadi al Natroun or of Athos.

And given that A. M. Allchin was his doctoral supervisor when he studied modern Russian Orthodox thought at Oxford, it is perhaps not surprising that Rowan Williams' own English translation of one of the hymns of Ann Griffiths was sung at his enthronement as Archbishop of Canterbury in 2003.

I experienced Donald Allchin's 'infectious enthusiasm' at first hand, and in particular in the context of the bicentenary of the death of Ann Griffiths in 2005. He had written an introduction to the edition of Ann Griffiths' hymns and letters which I had edited for the fine press, Gwasg Gregynog, in 1998. Then, in October 2003, we met at his request to discuss some matters relating to Ann Griffiths and the impending bicentenary of her death. Among other things we discussed some possible publications, and at that meeting we agreed to co-edit a collection of H. A. Hodges' writings on Welsh hymnody, to be published in 2005 in order to commemorate not only the bicentenary of Ann's death, but also the centenary of Hodges' birth, since there is a strange correspondence in their dates, with Ann Griffiths being born in 1776 and dying in 1805, and H. A. Hodges being born in 1905 and dying in 1976. Unfortunately, although we proceeded to plan the contents of the volume and had begun editorial work, circumstances prevented us from completing the book in time for it to be published in 2005; and Donald Allchin's increasing ill health together with various pressures upon me in other directions, means that it is only now that the volume is at last seeing the light of day, to coincide with the three-hundredth anniversary of the birth of Williams Pantycelyn.

The contents of the present volume follow substantially that which Donald Allchin and I had originally planned in 2003, one of the main differences being that the essay, 'H. A. Hodges: An Appreciation', which Donald had intended contributing to the book was never written. The other main difference is the decision to include my own critical edition of the Welsh text of Ann Griffiths' hymns and my index to the scriptural references and allusions in her hymns and letters, so as to facilitate comparison between the English translations and the original Welsh and to provide essential tools for any in-depth study of Ann's work. The other significant addition is the section of hymn translations by H. A. Hodges of the work of Welsh hymn-writers other than Ann Griffiths.

The current volume falls into three parts. The first, introductory section includes a biographical essay on H. A. Hodges by his granddaughter, Anna Parsons Howard, which provides a portrait of the man, his career and interests, and the circles in which he moved. This is followed by a bibliography of publications by and about Hodges, again by Anna Parsons Howard, which will prove invaluable for anyone wishing to study H. A. Hodges and his work further. His publications are organised under subject headings, thereby providing a useful overview of his academic interests, activities and networks. The next section consists of three essays on Williams Pantycelyn and the Welsh hymn, together with some of Hodges' translations of hymns other than those by Ann Griffiths, while the final section is devoted to Ann Griffiths. This latter section is the most extensive as it includes not only Hodges' own writings on Ann Griffiths and his translation of a celebrated lecture on

Introduction

her by the eminent Welsh author and critic, Saunders Lewis (1893–1985), but it also contains English translations of the whole corpus of Ann's work, including both metrical and prose translations of her hymns, with the Welsh originals of the hymns placed opposite the metrical translations. Between the translations of her hymns and letters, the Welsh originals of the hymns and the index to scriptural references and allusions, the present volume will be vital for anyone wishing to study Ann Griffiths' work in any detail.

A further word of explanation is required regarding the section of the book on Ann Griffiths. As has already been noted, H. A. Hodges and A. M. Allchin had been working for a number of years on an edition of her hymns and letters, which was close to completion when Hodges died in early July 1976. As far as I can gather, the intention was to include in that volume an edited version of the original Welsh text of Ann's hymns and letters, together with English translations, an extensive introduction, and notes on the hymns and letters. Although Allchin fully intended completing the edition following Hodges' death and initially hoped to publish it in 1977, by the end of 1979 he could say in a Christmas letter that the 'big edition' of Ann's work 'still lingers'; and it was never finally completed.

In September 1997, Donald Allchin gave me typed copies of the notes on the hymns and letters which were to have been included in that 'big edition', for me to use in the context of the doctoral thesis on Ann Griffiths' hymns that I was preparing at the time. Subsequently, when planning the present volume, we agreed to include those unpublished notes. At all stages, they were always referred to as 'Hodges' notes', and not notes written jointly by Hodges and Allchin.

When I had the opportunity to consult the A. M. Allchin Archive in 2014, I was surprised to find fairly advanced drafts of their substantial introduction to the 'big edition' of Ann's work. That introduction consists of a chapter on Ann's family background and an overview of the history of the Methodist Revival in Wales and its nature, followed by chapters on Ann's life, on the textual history of her work and its literary qualities, and on 'Ann in Her Letters', concluding with a lengthy chapter on 'Ann, Contemplative and Theologian'. The discovery of this introduction placed me on the horns of a dilemma. There were parts of it that would need updating in the light of current scholarship, some of them substantially, but there were other parts, especially in the second half, that perhaps warranted inclusion in the present volume. Ultimately, I decided not to include them, partly because it would have changed the focus and balance of the book significantly and made it a very different volume from the one A. M. Allchin and I had envisaged at the planning stage, and partly because there is no clear indication of the authorship of the various parts of the introduction, in what was, after all, a joint venture between Hodges and Allchin.[10] I sense that much of the introduction, in its final draft at least, was by Hodges, and that the nature of Allchin's input was probably mainly by way of discussion and comments on earlier drafts. That would fit with Allchin's comment in 1974 that 'Professor Hodges's knowledge of the language and literature of Wales, and in particular of the hymns and writings of the Methodist revival, is far older and deeper than mine',[11] together with his acknowledgement in a Christmas letter in 1976 that 'the edition of Ann, which I hope

---

10   Another factor is that at no time in our conversations did Donald Allchin suggest that any part of the introduction to their 'big edition' of Ann's work be included in the present volume. It is also worth adding, perhaps, that much of the essence of the introduction is distilled in Hodges' discussions in this volume and in Allchin's various publications on Ann Griffiths.
11   Allchin, 'Ann Griffiths: An Approach to Her Life and Work', p. 170.

Introduction

will be ready next year ... [is] a collaboration in which I was very much the junior partner'. However, one cannot be sure.

More certain is the matter of the authorship of the English translations of Ann's work. The intention seems to have been to include prose translations of Ann's hymns in the 'big edition', and drafts of these together with draft English translations of Ann's letters are to be found in the A. M. Allchin Archive. However, the translations by H. A. Hodges of Ann's hymns which were included side by side with the Welsh originals in the volume, *Homage to Ann Griffiths* (1976), which was published almost on the day Hodges died, were not those literal prose translations, but rather metrical versions. Donald Allchin used the prose translations preserved in his archive in books and articles over the years, always acknowledging Hodges as the translator, and since those prose translations have never been published in their entirety, they have been included in this volume in addition to Hodges' metrical versions. In the case of the translations of Ann's letters, Donald Allchin stated clearly in a letter to me in August 2001 that they were made by H. A. Hodges. Therefore, one can say with some confidence that the English translations of Ann Griffiths' hymns and letters in this volume, together with the notes on her hymns and letters, are by H. A. Hodges, although undoubtedly, as in the case of the introduction to their 'big edition' of Ann's work, A. M. Allchin would have had an input by way of discussion and comment.

The items gathered in this volume appeared over a period of about ten years in a variety of publications, all with their different 'house styles', and with some material published here for the first time. The editorial aim, therefore, has been to create a consistency throughout the volume with regard to matters such as spelling, use of capitals, italics, etc. As regards substance, editorial changes have been kept to a minimum.

23

Revisions and corrections were called for occasionally in the light of current scholarship, and some explanatory material has been added here and there. Although the draft introduction to Hodges and Allchin's proposed edition of Ann's work has not been included here, some sections have been woven into Hodges' notes on her hymns and letters as appropriate.

As is inevitable in the case of items discussing similar matters in different publications over a number of years, there was some duplication. Much of this has been retained, since, rather than being unnecessarily repetitive, such material's use in one context often complements or further illuminates its use in another place. However, in the case of the second and third articles in this volume, in particular, there was considerable overlap of material in places, and those sections have been revised silently to avoid the more obvious examples of duplication.

Biblical quotations are from the 'traditional' Welsh translation of 1620, which Ann Griffiths knew like the back of her hand, and from the English Authorised Version of 1611, which Ann would have used had she written in English. In Hodges' English translations, his use of 'thy', 'thou', etc. has been retained, as they help to distinguish between the second persons singular and plural; and in contrast to English, that distinction is still in current usage in Welsh, as it was in Ann's day. Hodges' translations of the same Welsh texts varied somewhat from publication to publication; they have been revised in order to provide a uniform translation of the same text throughout the volume. Although Hodges' translations are generally very accurate, in some cases comparisons with the original Welsh texts have led to some minor editorial revisions. In the case of Ann Griffiths' hymns and letters, the texts used here are those of my critical edition, published in 1998, and

Introduction

this has also led to some editorial revisions.[12] In the case of the other Welsh hymns quoted in this volume, the text used is, in most cases, the one found in *Llyfr Emynau a Thonau*, the hymn- and tune-book of the Calvinistic and Wesleyan Methodists published in 1929, which is the hymn-book that H. A. Hodges seems to have used most frequently. In a letter to me in June 2003, his widow, Mrs Vera Hodges, told me that she remembered her husband saying that 'if he wanted *one* book to take into hospital, that book would be a Welsh hymn-book'; that hymn-book would almost certainly have been the Welsh Methodist hymn-book of 1929.

It is appropriate to close this introduction by quoting at length from H. A. Hodges and A. M. Allchin's introduction to their unpublished edition of the hymns and letters of Ann Griffiths, since it reinforces a number of the matters that have been touched upon here:

> It will be evident that the editors of this book feel like men who have discovered a large and imposing object. It will be equally evident that its size and significance is not a question of quantity. There are only eight letters and some thirty or so hymns in the works of Ann Griffiths. There is a brief life spent entirely within a limited area in mid-Wales. The greatness of this writer – and once having encountered her work it is difficult not to use this term – the greatness of this writer lies in another dimension, one which makes us think of depth and intensity rather than diffusion and extent, of quality of vision rather than spread of activity.

---

12 As H. A. Hodges' discussions on the textual history of Ann Griffiths' hymns and letters have been superseded in part by more recent scholarship, they have not been included in this volume. Those wishing to learn more of their textual history should consult my PhD thesis, 'Golygiad o Emynau Ann Griffiths' (University of Wales, 1998) and my edition of her work, *Rhyfeddaf Fyth… : Emynau a Llythyrau Ann Griffiths* (Gwasg Gregynog, 1998).

Looked at in this light, we would claim that the life and work of this Welsh farmer's wife is of universal significance. She is a voice in the great tradition of Christian spirituality, and only within the wholeness of that tradition can she be rightly understood. Her output is small, her means of expression limited. As a writer she cannot rank with such figures as St Teresa of Avila or St John of the Cross, who, besides expressing their insight in religious verse and in letter-writing, composed long and systematic treatises on the spiritual life. Yet in the small compass of what she did write one is constantly reminded of the quality of a St Teresa, a St John, a St Symeon the New Theologian. Saunders Lewis speaks of the finest of her hymns as one of the great religious poems of Europe, and he does not exaggerate. Indeed, in so far as the contemplative element within the religious traditions of mankind may prove to be a unifying factor between them, her importance, like that of other Christian contemplatives, may reach farther still. Those from outside the Christian world will perhaps, in the future, find in her things which we have not been able to perceive.

If there is any particular merit in this present work, its editors would hope that it lies at this point. In Wales, where Ann Griffiths' memory has always been loved and her hymns constantly studied and discussed, almost inevitably the commentators have been too close to her to see her in a full perspective. This is in no way to decry their work. Without the succession of writers from John Hughes to the present day, who have edited and pondered her work, not only would this edition have been impossible, the texts themselves would have been lost. Both editors come from outside Wales, and would therefore wish to pay tribute to the work of Ann's fellow-countrymen who have cherished her memory.

Our own desire, however, [has been] to compare Ann with the classical tradition of Christian East and West. ... [In this context] we have had to face the specific question of the relation of mysticism to the Protestant tradition, and that again has forced us to ask questions about the relationship of the Reformation, taken as a whole, to the traditional

Introduction

Churches of East and West. ... In the presence of the hymns of Ann Griffiths, we have felt ourselves to be in touch with a witness not only to the distinctive tradition of the Genevan reformation, but with one who can represent the catholic heritage in something of its wholeness. ...[13]

Our interests ... have been primarily, though not exclusively, theological and spiritual. But we have also been aware in the course of our work of the possibility of seeing Ann in another context, that of the history of her own nation and culture. Here is an early nineteenth-century representative of a Celtic nation which has maintained even to this day a strong, living literary language. ...

We could not but be conscious of the fact that the language in which she sang is at present struggling for its life, nor of the ignorance of all that pertains to the history and tradition of Wales, which is assumed as normal by the greater part of those who live in the southern part of this island called Britain. We look forward to a day when it may no longer be regarded as a matter of surprise that an educated Englishman should acquire at least some knowledge of the older literary language of our country. ... The discovery of Wales is part of the discovery of Britain. It is a necessary part of the rediscovery of England.

But the ultimate meaning of the life and work of Ann Griffiths lies in a different dimension from that of the relations between Wales and England. It lies rather in the affirmation which it makes that our life on this planet is not wholly without meaning, that truth can be seen and known and loved, that even in flesh and blood eternal realities are present and made known. The little unpretending farmhouse, Dolwar Fach, in the parish of Llanfihangel-yng-Ngwynfa in which Ann spent the whole of her brief life, is itself an eloquent sign of the presence of ultimate meanings at the heart of earthly existence. ...

---

13 For an extended discussion of this aspect, see the chapter, 'Ann Griffiths, Mystic and Theologian', in A. M. Allchin, *The Kingdom of Love and Knowledge: The Encounter Between Orthodoxy and the West* (London: Darton, Longman and Todd, 1979).

Acknowledgements

THANKS ARE DUE to a number of people for their help and cooperation in the production of this volume. I am grateful to the family of H. A. Hodges for their enthusiastic support and for their permission to reproduce his work in this book. A special thanks must go to Anna Parsons Howard, granddaughter of H. A. Hodges, for her assistance in that context and in particular for preparing the biographical essay on her grandfather and the bibliography of his publications. Thanks are also due to the publishers and editors of the books and journals in which the works by H. A. Hodges included in this volume appeared over the years, for their readiness to allow them to be republished here. Full details of the publishers and the publications in which those works appeared are included at the beginning of each item and in the bibliography. Thanks are due to Siwan Jones, the granddaughter of Saunders Lewis, for her permission to include the translation of his lecture, 'Ann Griffiths: A Literary Survey'.

I was honoured to be awarded a Cardiff University Research Leave Fellowship in 2013–14, which allowed me to spend time at Gladstone's Library researching into the A. M. Allchin Archive, and I am grateful to Louisa Yates, Director of Collections and Research at Gladstone's Library, and other members of the Library's staff for their welcome and assistance, and to the Warden of Gladstone's Library, Peter Francis, for permission to publish material from the A. M. Allchin Archive. I am also grateful to the staff of the Special Collections and Archives at Cardiff University Library for their help and to

Acknowledgements

Alan Vaughan Hughes, the Head of Special Collections and Archives, for permission to publish H. A. Hodges' translations of Ann Griffiths' letters and his metrical translations of her hymns, the copyright of which was transferred to Cardiff University by H. A. Hodges' family following their inclusion on Cardiff University Library's 'Ann Griffiths Website', which was launched under my editorship in 2003.

Thanks are also due to Olwen Fowler for her striking cover design, and to Pontypridd Museum and to Joseph Herl, Professor of Music at Concordia University, Nebraska, for their help regarding the first printed copy of the hymn-tune, *Cwm Rhondda*, which was used in the cover design. The generous contribution of Jewin Welsh Presbyterian Church, London, towards the publication of this book is gratefully acknowledged. I am also grateful to Huw Edwards of the BBC for his advice and help. Last, but not least, my thanks go to the publishers, Y Lolfa, for accepting the volume for publication, to their staff for their professionalism, and especially to Eirian Jones, the publishers' English-Language Editor, for steering the book with great care and efficiency through the various stages of production.

VITA EQUINA: THE LIFE OF H. A. HODGES

Anna Parsons Howard

HERBERT ARTHUR HODGES, or 'Horse' as he was known to his family and friends, was Professor of Philosophy at the University of Reading and considered to be 'one of the most distinguished lay theologians that the Church of England has known in the twentieth century'.[1] Born a Methodist, he later became an Anglican with a great interest in Eastern Orthodoxy. He was widely published, writing many books, articles and papers, principally in the field of theology. Later in life he developed his great interest in hymns, particularly those of the Wesleys and Welsh-language hymns, which he translated into English himself.

Hodges' fascination with hymnody had its roots in his Methodist upbringing. He was born in Sheffield on 4 January 1905, the only child of a teacher and a travelling salesman. His parents, Willis and Lily, met at their local Methodist church where Willis played the organ. His mother also played the harmonium at home, her repertoire apparently consisting mainly of hymns. Referring to the formation of his faith and his experiences at the Hanover Chapel in his teens, Hodges wrote that 'the strongest influence seems to me now, as I look

---

1 A. M. Allchin, 'The Epworth-Canterbury-Constantinople Axis', *Wesleyan Theological Journal*, 26:1 (Spring 1991), pp. 23–37.

back, to have been the hymn book. ... Watts was a strong influence, and so were some of the Pietist hymns translated by John Wesley, and a few other writers which set forth the overwhelming and incomparable majesty of God and his sole illimitable reality.'[2]

He was an exceptional student, winning scholarships first to King Edward VII School in Sheffield and later to Balliol College, Oxford (BA 1926). He gained a double first in Classics, but recalled that 'as my studies progressed, the subject in which I wanted to be a don changed, from Greek to Ancient History and at last to Philosophy'.[3] He spent a year as a lecturer at New College, Oxford, before being appointed lecturer in Philosophy at the University of Reading in 1928, at that point the newest university in Britain. In 1934, at the age of twenty-nine, he was appointed Professor and Head of Department. He remained at Reading for thirty-five years until his retirement in 1969, turning down repeated offers of chairs at Oxford and Edinburgh among other places.

Hodges won his doctorate[4] for research on Wilhelm Dilthey (1833–1911), the German philosopher, and subsequently published two books on this subject.[5] Hodges later described Dilthey as writing 'much to bring out the intimate connections between the study of language and literature, history, biography and the social sciences'.[6] Such concerns were echoed by Hodges himself who actively encouraged 'the

---

2 'Vita Equina Interior': personal papers of H. A. Hodges in the care of the author, dated 1972.
3 'A Question of Identity': personal papers of H. A. Hodges in the care of the author, undated *c*. 1970.
4 Magdalen College, Oxford (DPhil, 1932).
5 H. A. Hodges, *Wilhelm Dilthey: An Introduction* (London: Kegan Paul, Trench, Trubner & Co., 1944) and *The Philosophy of Wilhelm Dilthey* (London: Routledge & Kegan Paul, 1952).
6 'A Question of Identity'.

intermingling of disciplines' during his time at Reading.[7] He had been introduced to Dilthey's work by his tutor, the political and moral philosopher A. D. Lindsay (1879–1952), during his time at Balliol. Lindsay likewise followed the ideal of 'making visible the unity and interdependence of all the different branches of learning' in his role as founding Principal of the University of Keele.[8]

Hodges was widely acknowledged to be an excellent teacher but, while he kept abreast of developments in his field, he published relatively few contributions to his own discipline beyond his work on Dilthey. His published works were on the whole books and articles within the sphere of theology and, later, hymnology. He was invited to deliver the Gifford Lectures in Aberdeen in 1956–57 and, in his final years, reworked the material which was then published posthumously.[9] He wrote of himself, perhaps too modestly, that it 'was my allotted work; not to be a scholar working to extend the range of human knowledge, but to use such modest scholarship as I could command to extend the light of understanding among the people I met'.[10]

After going up to Oxford he was, for a short period, a lay Methodist preacher in neighbouring villages. At the age of nineteen, however, he 'departed from the Christian Faith ... and was for a year or two professedly an atheist'.[11] When he returned to Christianity it was in 'a distinctly Anglican and Catholic form',[12] something which paralleled the experience

---

7 Ibid.
8 Ibid.
9 H. A. Hodges, *God Beyond Knowledge*, ed. W. D. Hudson (London: Macmillan, 1979).
10 'A Question of Identity'.
11 Dewi Morgan (ed.), *They Became Anglicans: The Story of Sixteen Converts and Why They Chose the Anglican Communion* (London: Mowbray, 1959), p. 64.
12 Allchin, 'The Epworth-Canterbury-Constantinople Axis'.

of his friend and contemporary, the Anglican theologian and philosopher, Austin Farrer (1904–68), who played a part in the rekindling of his faith.

Hodges joined the Church of England in 1928; but while he remained an Anglican for the rest of his life, he had a vision of Catholicism as understood by the Greek East.[13] He believed that 'the Orthodox possessed a true and full expression of faith, but he never followed up this conviction by becoming Orthodox'.[14] He was long interested in church unity and was an Anglican representative at the first General Assembly of the World Council of Churches in Amsterdam in 1948. He was later a member of Archbishop Ramsey's Commission on Intercommunion and was involved in the creation of the subsequent report which was presented to the Lambeth Conference in 1968. He much regretted the breakdown of union talks between the Methodist Church and the Church of England in 1972.[15]

It was Hodges' interest in Eastern Orthodoxy and the family's long association with the Fellowship of St Alban and St Sergius that first brought him into contact with A. M. Allchin, resulting in a long and successful working relationship and friendship. They collaborated on various projects, the first of which was a selection of the hymns of John and Charles Wesley with a theological commentary on them. It was published to coincide with conversations between the Anglican and Methodist churches in 1966.[16]

In his obituary of Hodges, Allchin described him as a 'rare

---

13 H. A. Hodges, *Anglicanism & Orthodoxy: A Study in Dialectical Churchmanship* (London: SCM Press, 1955).
14 Stephen Parsons, Foreword to H. A. Hodges, *God Be in My Thinking* (Leominster: Orphans Press, 1981).
15 Alan P. F. Sell, *Four Philosophical Anglicans* (Farnham: Ashgate, 2010), p. 211.
16 H. A. Hodges and A. M. Allchin, *A Rapture of Praise: Hymns of John and Charles Wesley* (London: Hodder & Stoughton, 1966).

phenomenon, an Englishman with a deep love and knowledge of the language and tradition of Wales'.[17] Hodges' interest in Wales had grown out of his annual childhood holidays in Colwyn Bay. Already a talented linguist, he taught himself Welsh and became very interested in Welsh hymnody. He had a particular interest in William Williams of Pantycelyn, producing translations of his hymns and articles on his work which are reproduced in this volume. His translation of Williams' hymn, '*Yn Eden, cofiaf hynny byth*' ('Can I forget bright Eden's grace'), is included in the Methodist hymn-book, *Hymns and Psalms* (1983).

Following Hodges and Allchin's collaboration on the hymns of the Wesleys, their main project was a study of the Welsh hymn-writer, Ann Griffiths. The two men planned to produce an edition of her hymns and letters, together with English translations, a lengthy introduction, and notes on the hymns and letters. Their intention had been to publish that edition in 1976, to coincide with the bicentenary of Ann Griffiths' birth, but although the work was in an advanced stage at the time of Hodges' death in the July of that year, it was never completed, and parts of it are finally published in the present volume for the first time. However, both Hodges and Allchin published a volume each on Ann Griffiths in 1976. Hodges published his metrical translations of her hymns in the volume *Homage to Ann Griffiths*, along with an introduction by him and his translation of a lecture on Ann Griffiths by the renowned Welsh scholar, Saunders Lewis (1893–1985).[18] For his part, A. M. Allchin published a study of the life and work of Ann Griffiths in the 'Writers of Wales' series in the same year.

---

17 A. M. Allchin, Obituary of H. A. Hodges, *Sobornost*, series 7, no. 4 (Winter–Spring 1977), pp. 306–8.
18 *Homage to Ann Griffiths*, ed. James Coutts (Penarth: Church in Wales Publications, 1976).

When quoting from Ann Griffiths' hymns and letters in that book, Allchin used Hodges' prose translations of her hymns and his translations of her letters, and he subsequently included Hodges' translations of her letters in their entirety, together with his metrical translations of her hymns, in the American edition of the book, published in 1987.[19]

In addition to collaborating in the study of Williams Pantycelyn, Ann Griffiths and other Welsh hymn-writers, Hodges and Allchin shared a keen interest in a group of Welsh-language poets of the mid-twentieth century who 'in their very different ways, wrote out of a deep, if often hard won, commitment to the historic Christian faith';[20] and Allchin included in his publications a number of Hodges' English translations of their poems.[21]

In 1939 Hodges married one of his students, Vera Joan Willis, the daughter of an Anglican clergyman. They had two sons and two daughters, one of whom died in infancy. Allchin wrote in his obituary that Hodges was 'a very reticent man by nature, [who] had at the same time a genius for friendship'.[22]

---

19 A. M. Allchin, *Ann Griffiths*, 'Writers of Wales' (Cardiff: University of Wales Press, 1976); revised edition, *Ann Griffiths: The Furnace and the Fountain* (Cardiff: University of Wales Press, 1987). The American edition in which Hodges' translations of her letters were first published is entitled *Songs to Her God: Spirituality of Ann Griffiths* (Cambridge, Mass.: Cowley Publications, 1987).

20 A. M. Allchin, *God's Presence Makes the World: The Celtic Vision Through the Centuries in Wales* (London: Darton, Longman and Todd, 1997), p. 89.

21 For example, a poem by Bobi Jones in A. M. Allchin, *The World is a Wedding: Explorations in Christian Spirituality* (London: Darton, Longman and Todd, 1978); poems by D. Gwenallt Jones and Waldo Williams in *Threshold of Light: Prayers and Praises from the Celtic Tradition*, ed. A. M. Allchin and Esther de Waal (London: Darton, Longman and Todd, 1986); poems by D. Gwenallt Jones in A. M. Allchin, *Resurrection's Children* (Norwich: Canterbury Press, 1998); see also the discussion on the work of Euros Bowen in A. M. Allchin, *The Joy of All Creation: An Anglican Meditation on the Place of Mary*, second, enlarged edition (London: New City, 1993).

22 Allchin, Obituary of H. A. Hodges.

Perhaps not the easiest of characters, some people found him to be rude and taciturn, but his daughter recalls that once people got past his curtness they often found him a very good and informed conversationalist. He loved music and played the piano well, though he would only play in front of an audience at the family's annual Christmas carol parties. He had a keen interest in art, and from 1954 to 1973 he was Master of the Guild of St George, established by John Ruskin in the 1870s 'to right some of the social wrongs of the day and make England a happier and more beautiful place in which to live and work'.[23] Hodges was actively concerned with social problems and with adult education. As W. D. Hudson could say of him: 'He spent his youth in the Yorkshire steel town [of Sheffield]. Not only was there evidence of this in the traces of a Yorkshire accent which he retained throughout his life, but also in his strong and lasting sympathy with the aspirations of the underprivileged for education and a better environment.'[24]

Hodges retired early because of ill health, his final years being beset by a series of illnesses. He died in Reading on 2 July 1976, a week after finishing his final book.[25]

Since this current volume owes much to Hodges' friendship and collaboration with A. M. Allchin, it is perhaps fitting that the last word be given to Allchin in the words of his 1977 obituary:[26]

> To characterise H. A. Hodges is particularly difficult. He was a shy and elusive character, not giving himself easily, but giving himself whole-heartedly when he felt a response. Archbishop Anthony speaks of 'total integrity of heart and

---

23 See the Guild of St George website (http://www.guildofstgeorge.org.uk/).
24 W. D. Hudson, 'H. A. Hodges (1905–1976)', in H. A. Hodges, *God Beyond Knowledge*, ed. W. D. Hudson (London: Macmillan, 1979), p. vii.
25 H. A. Hodges, *God Be in My Thinking*, published in 1981.
26 Allchin, Obituary of H. A. Hodges.

mind'. There was something translucent about him and his work. There is a phrase from the Buddhist Scriptures which he particularly relished, 'Gone beyond'. Those who read his pages of introduction to *Homage to Ann Griffiths*, almost the last thing he wrote, will glimpse something of the meaning of his delight in those words. He speaks there of her astonishment before 'the inherent wonders of the Faith'. 'First comes wonder in the sense of sheer surprise ... But second, wonder may mean a mingling of awe and admiration, such as we feel on contemplating the divine wisdom, love and power ... And third, wonder may mean the recognition of a mystery, an incomprehensibility, such as we always find in the long run when we look into the being of God and his actions towards us. Ann is filled with wonder in all these three senses, even in this life; and heaven to her means living in the midst of a sea of wonders.' In this life, the pilgrimage of heart and mind is something which has only been begun.

★ ★ ★

Dr Anna Parsons Howard is the granddaughter of H. A. Hodges. Born a few months after the publication of Homage to Ann Griffiths, *she was named in memory of the hymn-writer. She wrote her doctoral thesis on late medieval liturgy and plainsong.*

H. A. HODGES (1905–1976): A BIBLIOGRAPHY

Anna Parsons Howard

Archives
H. A. Hodges, Personal papers in the care of Anna Parsons Howard, Johnby Hall, Cumbria.

A. M. Allchin Archive, Gladstone's Library, Hawarden, Flintshire.

Literature about H. A. Hodges
A. M. Allchin, Obituary of H. A. Hodges, *Sobornost*, series 7, no. 4 (Winter–Spring 1977), pp. 306–8.

A. M. Allchin, 'The Epworth-Canterbury-Constantinople Axis', *Wesleyan Theological Journal*, 26:1 (Spring 1991), pp. 23–37.

Anne Beacock, 'H. A. Hodges: *The Pattern of Atonement* in its Context', MA thesis, Durham University, 1978. http://etheses.dur.ac.uk/10127/.[1]

Anna Parsons Howard, 'Herbert Arthur Hodges', in *The Canterbury Dictionary of Hymnology*, eds J. R. Watson and Emma Hornby, 2013. http://www.hymnology.co.uk/h/herbert-arthur-hodges.

---

[1] I am indebted to Beacock's thesis for much of this bibliography, which was compiled with the assistance of Hodges' widow.

W. D. Hudson, 'H. A. Hodges (1905–1976)', in H. A. Hodges, *God Beyond Knowledge*, ed. W. D. Hudson (London: Macmillan, 1979), pp. vii–x.

Christopher M. Jones, 'HODGES, Herbert Arthur (1905–76)', in *Dictionary of Twentieth-Century British Philosophers*, ed. Stuart Brown (Bristol: Thoemmes Continuum, 2005).

Alan P. F. Sell, *Four Philosophical Anglicans* (Farnham: Ashgate, 2010).

Works by H. A. Hodges

Hymnology and Poetry:

'Methodism, A Lost Anglican Doctrine of the Spiritual Life', *Sobornost*, series 3, no. 12 (Winter 1952), pp. 545–55; revised version, 'The Doctrine of Perfection in Charles Wesley's Hymns', *CR Review (Quarterly Review of the Community of the Resurrection)*, 237 (1962), pp. 5–10.

H. A. Hodges and A. M. Allchin, *A Rapture of Praise, Hymns of John and Charles Wesley* (London: Hodder & Stoughton, 1966).

'Ann Griffiths: A Note of Introduction', *Sobornost*, series 5, no. 5 (Summer 1967), pp. 338–41, followed by Hodges' English translation of Saunders Lewis' lecture, 'Ann Griffiths: A Literary Survey', pp. 341–55.

'Flame in the Mountains: Aspects of Welsh Free Church Hymnody', *Religious Studies*, 3 (1967–68), pp. 401–13.

'Gwenallt', *Sobornost*, series 6, no. 1 (Summer 1970), pp. 25–33; republished as 'Gwenallt: An English View of the Poet', *Planet*, 29 (October 1975), pp. 24–9.

'Williams Pantycelyn, Father of the Modern Welsh Hymn', *Bulletin of the Hymn Society of Great Britain and Ireland*, 135 (February 1976), pp. 145–52; 136 (June 1976), pp. 161–6.

'Over the Distant Hills: Thoughts on Williams Pantycelyn', *Brycheiniog*, 17 (1976–77), pp. 6–16.

'Introduction', in *Homage to Ann Griffiths*, ed. James Coutts (Penarth: Church in Wales Publications 1976), pp. 5–13. The volume also includes Hodges' metrical translations of Ann Griffiths' hymns and his translation of Saunders Lewis' lecture, 'Ann Griffiths: A Literary Survey'.

'Part Two: Letters and Hymns', in A. M. Allchin, *Songs to Her God: Spirituality of Ann Griffiths* (Cambridge, Massachusetts, USA: Cowley Publications, 1987), pp. 77–126; namely Hodges' metrical translations of Ann Griffiths' hymns and his translations of her letters.

Theology and Church Studies:
'The Meaning of Moral Rearmament', *Theology*, 38 (January–June 1939), pp. 322–32.
'What Difference Does Christianity Make?', *Christian News-Letter*, Supplement, 27 (1940), pp. 260–3.
'Social Standards in a Mixed Society', *Christian News-Letter*, Supplement, 43 (1940).
'Christianity in an Age of Science', in *Real Life is Meeting*, ed. J. H. Oldham (London: Sheldon Press, 1942), pp. 44–51.
'How Far Will Science Take Us?', *The Listener*, 3 December 1942, p. 722.
'What is Religion?', Discussion with Sir Frederick Whyte, *The Listener*, 22 April 1943, pp. 482–3.
'The Problem of Archetypes', *Christian News-Letter*, Supplement, 2 June 1943.
'Some Questions for the Fellowship', *Sobornost*, series 2, no. 27 (June 1943), p. 5.
'The Integration of Heathenism and Unbelief into the Life of the Christian Church', *Sobornost*, series 2, no. 29 (June 1944), pp. 7–9.
'The Secularisation of Thought', *Christendom*, 59 (1945), pp. 75–7.

'A Neglected Page in Anglican Theology', *Theology*, 48 (May 1945), pp. 104–10.
The Christian in the Modern University (London: SCM Press, 1946).
'Christianity in the Battle of Doctrines', *The Student World*, 40 (1946), pp. 11–12.
'Christian Obedience in the University', *The Student World*, 41 (1947–48), pp. 126–43.
'Things and Persons', in *Logical Positivism and Ethics*, Proceedings of the Aristotelian Society, Supplementary Volume XXII (London: Harrison and Sons, 1948), pp. 190–201.
'Art and Religion', *Church Quarterly Review*, 146 (July–September 1948), pp. 131–49.
Christianity and the Modern World View (London: SCM Press, 1949).[2]
'Introduction', in *Man and His Nature: Broadcast Talks in Religion and Philosophy* (London: SCM Press, 1949).
The Way of Integration (London: Epworth Press, 1951).
'Introduction', in Lorenzo Scupoli, *Unseen Warfare*, trans. E. Kadloubovsky and G. E. H. Palmer (London: Faber & Faber, 1952).
Languages, Standpoints and Attitudes (London: OUP, 1953).
'Angels and Human Knowledge', in *The Angels of Light and the Powers of Darkness*, ed. E. L. Mascall (London: Faith Press, 1954).

---

2 This publication was based on a paper prepared for the 'Moot', a study and discussion group set up by J. H. Oldham (1874–1969), which met twice or three times a year from 1938 to 1947 and included T. S. Eliot, John Baillie, John Middleton Murry, Karl Mannheim, Alec Vidler, Walter Moberly and H. A. Hodges among its most regular members. Hodges could say of the 'Moot' that 'it occupied my best energies for a period of years from 1942 onwards'. See Keith Clements (ed.), *The Moot Papers: Faith, Freedom and Society 1938–1947* (London: T. & T. Clark, 2010).

Anglicanism & Orthodoxy: A Study in Dialectical Churchmanship (London: SCM Press, 1955).

The Pattern of Atonement (London: SCM Press, 1955).

'Herbert Arthur Hodges', in *They Became Anglicans: The Story of Sixteen Converts and Why They Chose the Anglican Communion*, ed. Dewi Morgan (London: Mowbray, 1959), pp. 63–71.

Review of V. Lossky, *The Mystical Theology of the Eastern Church*, in *Sobornost*, series 3, no. 24 (Spring 1959), pp. 648–50.

'In a Son', in *God and the Universe: A Course of Sermons Preached in the Chapel of Pusey House, Oxford* (London: Mowbray, 1960), pp. 47–53.

'Holiness, Righteousness, Perfection', *Sobornost*, series 4, no. 5 (Summer 1961), pp. 229–41.

Review of N. Cabasilas, *La Vie en Jésus-Christ*, in *Sobornost*, series 4, no. 8 (Winter 1963), pp. 467–9.

Death and Life Have Contended (London: SCM Press, 1964).

'Methodists, Anglicans and Orthodox – II', in *We Belong to One Another: Methodist, Anglican and Orthodox Essays*, ed. A. M. Allchin (London: Epworth Press, 1965), pp. 30–47.

(with V. Hodges), 'Obituary: The Revd Gilbert Shaw', *Sobornost*, series 5, no. 6 (Winter–Spring 1968), pp. 451–4.

'Filioque?', *Sobornost*, series 5, no. 8 (Winter–Spring 1969), pp. 559–62.

God Beyond Knowledge, ed. W. D. Hudson (London: Macmillan, 1979).

God Be in My Thinking (Leominster: Orphans Press, 1981).

Philosophy:

'Phenomenology – II', in *Phenomenology, Goodness and Beauty*, Proceedings of the Aristotelian Society, Supplementary Volume XI (London: Harrison and Sons, 1932), pp. 84–100.

'Nicolai Hartmann's Ethics', *Laudate*, 11 (1933), pp. 173–83; 230–41.

'Idealism', *Laudate*, 14 (1936), pp. 83–90; 138–51.

'A Study of Wilhelm Dilthey's Philosophy', *Laudate*, 17 (1939), pp. 23–7; 80–99; 165–8; 218–23; 18 (1940), pp. 25–45.

'British Philosophy, 1689–1830', in *Augustans and Romantics 1689–1830*, ed. H. V. D. Dyson and John Butt (London: Cresset Press, 1940), pp. 109–21.

'The Task of the Universities in Time of War', *The Student Movement*, 42 (1940), pp. 74–6.

'Science and Ethics: What is the Real Voice of Philosophy?', *The Guardian* (Church), 1 January 1943, p. 4.

Wilhelm Dilthey: An Introduction (London: Kegan Paul, Trench, Trubner & Co., 1944).

'What's the Point of Philosophy?', *The Listener*, 24 May 1945, pp. 573, 577.

'The Meaning of Synthesis', in *Synthesis in Education*, ed. D. M. E. Dymes, Reports of the Annual Conferences of the Institute of Sociology, vol. 5 (Malvern: Le Play House Press, 1945), pp. 4–12.

'The Lesson of Nietzsche', *Laudate*, 23 (1945–46), pp. 50–66.

Objectivity and Impartiality (London: SCM Press, 1946).

'The Crisis in Philosophy', in *Reformation Old and New: A Tribute to Karl Barth*, ed. F. W. Camfield (London: Lutterworth Press, 1947), pp. 184–98.

'Our Culture: Its Thought', in *Our Culture: Its Christian Roots and Present Crisis*, ed. V. A. Demant (London: SPCK, 1947), pp. 17–34.

'Philosophy', in *The Individual in Contemporary Society: The Contribution of Adult Education*, Report of the 21st Annual Conference of the British Institute of Adult Education (London: British Institute of Adult Education, 1947).

The Philosophy of Wilhelm Dilthey (London: Routledge & Kegan Paul, 1952).

'The Thought of Karl Marx', in *Christian Faith and Communist Faith*, ed. D. M. Mackinnon (London: Macmillan, 1953), pp. 3–20.

'What is to Become of Philosophical Theology?', in *Contemporary British Philosophy: Personal Statements (Third Series)*, ed. Hywel D. Lewis (London: George Allen & Unwin, 1956), pp. 209–33.

PART ONE

Williams Pantycelyn and the Welsh Hymn

FLAME IN THE MOUNTAINS:

Aspects of Welsh Free Church Hymnody[1]

I

Everyone knows that Wales is a land of scenery. It is also known to have local customs and usages, and a peculiar language; in fact it has also its own history and historical memories. By virtue of these things Wales is a nation with its own life and culture, which merits study and demands respect.

Chapels are well known to be a feature of the scenery, and chapels are places where people sing. A moment's thought will remind us that there must be something which is sung. Somewhere in these chapels there must be hymn-books, and in these a hymn-literature must exist, which it might be of interest to explore. The fortunate foreigner who does explore this literature finds himself in a new world, of which I propose to say something here. It is especially the hymnody of the chapels which concerns me; for it is Nonconformity which has been the distinctive voice of Wales in religious matters in the last three centuries.

The chapels made a central contribution to the spiritual and cultural life of the nation in the nineteenth century. Today

---

1   First published in *Religious Studies*, 3 (1967–68), a journal published by Cambridge University Press.

47

they are in decline. Their world of thought and feeling, though intense and deep, was narrow, and their discipline came to be felt to be constricting. Something similar has happened in England. The long rows of houses interspersed with chapels in the Rhondda Valley, and those chapels converted to secular uses or not in use at all, are not unlike what may be seen in places in Yorkshire. In Wales, as in England, we have witnessed the decline of a once flourishing culture.

This does not mean that we can afford to forget the chapels. The record of their power and influence is clearly inscribed on the pages of history, even if it is now past history. And is it only past history? The achievement of the chapels at their best was to combine deep feeling with an ethic of self-discipline, and a biblical vision of human life and history with a deep metaphysical intuition. Something of this tradition will surely live on in some form, though the place of the chapels themselves in the life of the nation will not be what it once was.

The tradition of chapel hymnody has its origin in the Evangelical Revival of the eighteenth century, as has the parallel tradition in England. Near the source of both stands Isaac Watts, many of whose hymns and metrical psalms were rendered into Welsh by Dafydd Jones of Caeo. But it was the Methodist movement which at once created the societies for which so many of the hymns were written, and trained the people who wrote them. The older Dissenting bodies caught fresh fire from the movement, and came to share a common tradition of hymnody with it, to which all alike contributed.

II

The first things one notices about these hymns are naturally those which lie nearest the surface: metre and versification, qualities of style, imagery.

Metre: much the same varieties as one is used to in England.

Aspects of Welsh Free Church Hymnody

In fact the Welsh tradition here is largely based on English models. The tradition of mediaeval Welsh poetry finds no succession here. For the purposes of a popular religious movement something simpler and more direct was needed, and was found.

Style: this differs, of course, from author to author, but yet the reader who comes to it from the hymn-literature of England will find in it a narrower range of variation, a greater homogeneity. There is little here of the English freedom in borrowing from other countries. But the rich possibilities of the Welsh language are fully exploited. These authors are capable of vivid rhetoric and majestic declamation, but they are also capable sometimes of a breath-taking simplicity of statement.

Imagery: here each will find different things to interest him. To me it is pleasant to see how in various ways the Welsh landscape asserts itself. All Christians conceive the Christian life as a journey through difficult country. There is biblical backing for this conception in Israel's journey through the desert, or in the return of the exiles from Babylon to Jerusalem; and there is also the conception of the pilgrimage to Zion, crystallised for English and Welsh readers in Bunyan's famous story, *The Pilgrim's Progress*. The Bible gives warrant for deserts and seas and rivers to be crossed. It seems, however, that the pilgrim meets with steeper slopes and higher hills in Wales than in other parts of Christendom. It is the scenery of daily life inserting itself into the traditional mythology. One sees how natural it is when one of the hymn-writers, Ann Griffiths, says in a letter to a friend: 'I have had some very smart trials, and strong winds, so that I almost lost my breath on the slopes.' This could have happened to her often enough in physical fact on her hill farm, or on the rough journey to and from her Methodist meeting-house three miles away. At the same time in one or two of the writers one finds a tendency to heighten the imagery even to the point of violence. The pilgrim travels over rough crags, with the sound of mountain torrents in his ears. We hear of wind and storm, clouds and darkness, sometimes thunder and lightning and even earthquake. One finds the same imagery of violence when 'the windows of heaven were opened' (Genesis 7:11) is transmuted into *'torrodd holl argaeau'r nefoedd'* ('all the dams of heaven burst').[2] And where else would the Rock of Ages become a refuge against fire and flood, and a place of safety amid the ocean of eternity?[3] The powerful rhetoric of wind and water and rock is never far away from these people.

Let us not pause to illustrate these points at length. Let us pass on to weightier matters – to the theological and spiritual content of the hymns.

III

There is nothing in the theology and spirituality of the hymns that is in principle new. It is orthodox evangelical theology and evangelical piety. Yet to some English readers a certain difference of feeling will slowly become perceptible; and if we enquire into its source, we shall ultimately find it to be theological. What we have here is not merely evangelical, but Reformed; and we remind ourselves that Welsh Methodism, from which the chief inspiration of this whole tradition came, was and has always continued to be Calvinistic Methodism. In its origins slightly senior to the movement inspired by the Wesleys, and in its development independent of them, it grew to maturity under its own teachers and guides, all of whom held firmly to the Calvinist line, though without excessive dogmatism or party spirit.

---

2   [In the hymn, '*Dyma gariad fel y moroedd*', by William Rees ('Gwilym Hiraethog'; 1802–83). – *Ed.*]

3   [In the hymn, '*Arglwydd Iesu, arwain f'enaid / At y Graig sydd uwch na mi*', by S. J. Griffith ('Morswyn'; 1850–93). – *Ed.*]

It is easy to score controversial points against Calvinism. The Wesleys showed the way and one need only follow it. Mention predestination; explain that it means an arbitrary decree of God whereby some human beings are elected to salvation and others assigned to damnation before they are even born, and irrespective of what they may think or do when they have been born; work yourself into a state of moral indignation at the imputation of such conduct to God – and there you are. A kind of case can be made out, by a none-too-subtle reasoner, for saying that Calvinist principles lead to this conclusion, and that therefore Calvinists are logically bound to hold it. But, as a later Welsh writer has remarked, 'it was wholly unfair to attribute to the Calvinists the opinions which other people supposed were necessary conclusions from their doctrines'. The Wesleys' rhetoric was so splendid that it hid the weaknesses and inconsistencies of their own position, and Calvinism was given a bad name and hanged. Yet it remains true that this 'Calvinism' of theirs is not what was preached in Wales, and certainly not what inspired these hymns.

What did inspire them? In the last resort, I should say, a vision of the majesty of God; not merely power, not even supreme and unconditional power, but something far higher and deeper – a metaphysical intuition of the sheer Godness of God.

Next to this, a vision like that expressed in the first chapter of the Epistle to the Ephesians, of a world whose first creation and final destiny are governed by the wisdom of God, for our good and 'to the praise of his glory'. This same chapter inspired the young French Carmelite, Elizabeth of the Trinity,[4] who changed her name to 'Praise of Glory' and dedicated her life to the mysteries of the divine infinity and the divine

---

4   [See A. M. Allchin, *Women of Prayer: Ann Griffiths & Elizabeth of the Trinity* (Oxford: SLG Press, 1992). – *Ed.*]

predestination. Here in Wales, something of this vision runs through a whole movement. It finds voice in a well-known hymn in praise of God's providence:

> *Rhagluniaeth fawr y nef,*
>   *Mor rhyfedd yw*
> *Esboniad helaeth hon*
>   *O arfaeth Duw:*
> *Mae'n gwylio llwch y llawr,*
> *Mae'n trefnu lluoedd nef,*
> *Cyflawna'r cwbwl oll*
>   *O'i gyngor Ef.*[5]

(The great providence of heaven, how wondrous is this wide exposition of God's design: it watches over the dust of the earth, it orders the hosts of heaven, it fulfils the whole of his counsel.)

Next to this again, the doctrine of the eternal Covenant. By this is meant not any covenant made by God with men, but the covenant of God with God, made in eternity before the world was. There is an eighteenth-century Welsh poem – *Golwg ar Deyrnas Crist* ('A Prospect of the Kingdom of Christ') by William Williams of Pantycelyn – which describes the making of this covenant. In it the Father explains his plans to the Son before the creation of the world. He is going to create a world in which there will be human beings, and they shall be 'capable of falling, or of standing and living', and he will 'suffer them to fall'. But he does this in order that grace may abound.[6] The Son is to take flesh and suffer and die, and so

---

5   [The first verse of a hymn by David Charles (1762–1834) of Carmarthen, brother of Thomas Charles, one of the founders of the British and Foreign Bible Society. – *Ed.*]

6   ['*Efe arfaethodd grëu rhieni dynol-ryw / Mewn cyflwr gall'sent gwympo, neu sefyll fyth a byw; / A diodde' iddynt gwympo, fel trwy eu cwymp y bai / Gras yn cael ei ddatguddio, a gras yn amalhau*': Gomer M. Roberts (ed.), *Gweithiau William*

win salvation for all who shall believe in him. A Covenant on these terms is made between the Persons in eternity. God's successive covenants with men are merely the working out of this, they are part of the provisions of this prior Covenant in heaven.

There is a hymn which states the doctrine clearly and well:

Cyn llunio'r byd, cyn lledu'r nefoedd wen,
Cyn gosod haul, na lloer, na sêr uwchben,
Fe drefnwyd ffordd yng nghyngor Tri yn Un
I achub gwael golledig euog ddyn.

Trysorwyd gras, ryw annherfynol stôr,
Yn Iesu Grist cyn rhoddi deddf i'r môr;
A rhedeg wnaeth bendithion arfaeth ddrud
Fel afon gref lifeiriol dros y byd.[7]

(Before the world was formed, before the bright heavens were spread out, before sun or moon or stars above were set in place, a way was planned in the council of Three in One to save wretched, lost, guilty man.

Grace was treasured up, an endless store, in Jesus Christ before a law was given to the sea; and the blessings of the precious design ran like a strong river flooding through the world.)

Again we can look outside the British Isles for a parallel. It is not unfair to see a reflection of this Covenant in the famous icon of the Old Testament Trinity by Andrei Rublev. Three men visit Abraham to announce the coming birth of Isaac. Abraham kills a calf and gives them a meal. According to the eastern Fathers these three men are a theophany, a manifestation of the

---

Williams Pantycelyn. Cyfrol 1 (Cardiff: University of Wales Press, 1964), p. 9. – *Ed.*]

7 [The first two verses of a hymn by Peter Jones ('Pedr Fardd'; 1775–1845). – *Ed.*]

Trinity. Rublev paints them as three figures of identical build and feature, with robes whose colours symbolise the relation between the Persons. They are seated at a table, and on this table between them is a dish containing the head of the slain calf. It signifies the sacrificial death which Christ is to die. The Father and the Spirit are pointing towards it, and the Son, with his face towards the Father, reaches out his hand to take it. Rublev has here given us the Trinity not in being but in action, with the Son accepting his Passion at the instigation of the Father and the Spirit. This is not the actual making of the Covenant, which was before time, but it is a shadowing forth of it in the mode of prophecy. We may remember that Isaac is himself a son who became a victim, foreshadowing the true and only Victim.

This doctrine gives to Christian belief and experience a peculiar depth and stability and assurance. I do not mean the personal assurance of ultimate salvation; the question, how the individual can know that he is himself within the Covenant, is a different question. What I mean is that the whole business of man's spiritual life and commerce with God is no mere accident in the world process, that God's own action for the salvation and final glorification of man is no addition or afterthought, no mere device to meet a sudden crisis, but flows from nothing less than the pre-temporal will of the changeless Creator.

Cyfamod cry' – pwy ato ddyry ddim?
Nid byd na bedd all dorri'i ryfedd rym:
Diysgog yw hen arfaeth Duw o hyd;
Nid siglo mae, fel gweinion bethau'r byd.[8]

(A strong covenant – who shall add anything to it? Not the world

---

8 [A verse from the hymn, '*Cyfamod hedd, cyfamod cadarn Duw*', by Edward Jones (1761–1836) of Maes-y-plwm. – *Ed.*]

nor the grave can break its wondrous power: unmoveable for ever is God's ancient design; it never shakes, like the feeble things of this world.)

And so the knowledge of it is a joy and a privilege: '*Melys gofio y cyfamod / Draw a wnaed gan Dri yn Un*' ('Sweet it is to remember the covenant made yonder by Three in One'). Or, as the same writer, Ann Griffiths, has it in one of her letters: 'Let us magnify our privilege that we have known something of the effects of the eternal covenant decreed above.' And again she refers to 'the free covenant and the counsel of the Three in One regarding those who are the objects of the primal love'. There it is: God loved us before we were, before the world was, and our status as his children has therefore something of the timeless in it. A powerful idea. Another writer, William Williams of Pantycelyn, shows us how one can plead the Covenant in prayer:

> *Nac aed o'th gof dy ffyddlon amod drud,*
> *Yn sicir wnaed cyn rhoi sylfeini'r byd;*
> *Ti roist im yno drysor maith di-drai;*
> *Gad imi heddiw gael dy wir fwynhau.*

(Forget not thy precious faithful covenant, that was made firm before the world's foundations were laid; there thou gavest me a great unfailing treasure; grant me today truly to enjoy thee.)

I do not mean to suggest that every page of a Welsh hymn-book will be found to contain some lines on the Covenant. Far from it. These things remain mostly in the background. But they have shaped an attitude and an atmosphere which subtly pervades the whole tradition. They embody the distinctive way in which this tradition apprehends and experiences the relation between human life and the timeless reality of God.

IV

What great names stand out in this tradition?

At the source of the whole stream is Pantycelyn (William Williams of Pantycelyn, 1717–91). Son of a farming family near Llandovery in Carmarthenshire, he at first trained for a medical career, but underwent a conversion in consequence of which he turned to preaching and threw in his lot with the Methodists. During the first half-century of the movement he was one of its principal leaders. He published several prose works on religious subjects and two long religious poems in the epic manner; but his best-known contribution lies in some eight or nine hundred hymns, which make him as it were the Charles Wesley of Wales.

The parallel with Wesley is imperfect. Williams has not Wesley's classical scholarship or his command of the techniques of rhetoric, though he has a fine lyrical gift, a turn for the telling phrase and a power of declamation, which developed steadily with use and experience. Nor is his theology as systematic as Wesley's. Wesley wrote deliberately in order to make available a body of theology in verse. Williams Pantycelyn wrote without any such overall plan, singing of what was in his mind and heart, so that in the sequence of his works one can trace the gradual maturation of his Christian understanding and experience. One admires Wesley, one rejoices in his splendour and is stunned by his power, but one is at ease and at home with Pantycelyn.

Some of the great themes of theology are scantily represented in his hymns. There is little directly on the Trinity, or on the doctrine of the Spirit, little about the Church or the fellowship of believers (a great theme in Wesley), and nothing of any concern for society or the world at large. Nevertheless, for one who is not trying to cover the ground systematically, his range is wide and his expressions are stimulating.

It goes without saying that, in a writer of the Evangelical Revival, the themes of sin and guilt, repentance and forgiveness, are constantly present, and are linked with that of the saving work of Christ on the cross. It is natural too that, in the eighteenth century, much should be heard of the blood and the wounds. Amid a great deal that is of no special merit certain hymns stand out, such as this one, where he dramatises the whole story of Fall and Restoration in one brief stanza:

Yn Eden, cofiaf hynny byth,
Bendithion gollais rif y gwlith;
   Syrthiodd fy nghoron wiw.
Ond buddugoliaeth Calfari
Enillodd hon yn ôl i mi;
   Mi ganaf tra fwyf byw.

(In Eden – I shall always remember this – I lost blessings in number as the dew; down fell my fair crown. But the victory of Calvary won this back for me; I shall sing as long as I live.)

Here one sees, first, how firmly he has grasped the Pauline idea of the solidarity of all mankind in Adam. The Fall in Eden is no mere episode of past history for him; he was there himself, he remembers. And then the Restoration – where Wesley would call upon his reader to 'shout' his joy and triumph, and Watts would summon rocks and hills to join in the jubilation, Williams says simply, 'I shall never stop singing.' It is not less effective.

From rejoicing in the work of Christ one passes naturally to the contemplation of his Person, in wonder, adoration and love. Pantycelyn is aware of the metaphysical mystery of the Incarnation:

> *Ymhlith holl ryfeddodau'r nef,*
> *Hwn yw y mwyaf un –*
> *Gweld yr anfeidrol ddwyfol Fod*
> *Yn gwisgo natur dyn.*

(Among all the wonders of heaven, this is the greatest one – to see the infinite divine Being wearing the nature of man.)

His characteristic attitude, however, is the more affective one expressed in the Song of Songs. The Beloved is white and ruddy, fair of form, wholly beyond compare. Pantycelyn is in the Puritan tradition of devotion which makes free use of the Song. Charles Wesley for some reason stood outside it, but Isaac Watts wrote a series of thirteen hymns based on passages in the Song. Pantycelyn wrote twenty-seven hymns in the same vein, besides the numerous allusions to the Song which we find throughout his other hymns. One can hold a roll-call of hymns whose first lines are so many declarations of love:

> *'Rwy'n dy garu, addfwyn Iesu.* (I love thee, gentle Jesus.)
> *'Rwy'n dy garu, Ti a'i gwyddost.* (I love thee, thou knowest.)
> *'Rwy'n dy garu er nas gwelais.* (I love thee though I never saw thee.)
> *Anweledig, 'rwy'n dy garu.* (Invisible One, I love thee.)

In some of these hymns Pantycelyn reaches his greatest heights. Take these four verses from one of them:

> *Os yw tegwch d'wyneb yma*
> *Yn rhoi myrdd i'th garu'n awr,*
> *Beth a wna dy degwch hyfryd*
> *Yna'n nhragwyddoldeb mawr?*
> *Nef y nefoedd*
> *A'th ryfedda fyth heb drai.*

Pa fath uchder fydd i'm cariad,
   Pa fath syndod y pryd hyn,
Pryd y gwelwyf dy ogoniant
   Perffaith llawn ar Seion fryn?
     Anfeidroldeb
   O bob tegwch maith yn un.

Pa feddyliau uwch eu deall
   A gaf ynof fi fy hun,
Wrth ystyried bod y Duwdod
   Perffaith pur a minnau'n un?
     Dyma gwlwm
   Nad oes iaith a'i dyd i maes.

Cwlwm wnaed yn nhragwyddoldeb,
   Sicir, cadarn, mawr ei rym;
Ni all myrddiwn o flynyddoedd
   Dorri hwn, na'i ddatod ddim:
     Gwna, fe bery
   Tra parhao Duw mewn bod.

(If here the beauty of thy face makes myriads love thee now, what will thy fair beauty do yonder in eternity? Heaven of heavens will wonder at thee ceaselessly for ever.

What height will my love reach, what marvelling then, when I shall see thy full perfect glory on Mount Zion? Infinity of the whole range of beauties in one.

What thoughts above understanding shall I have within me as I consider that the perfect pure Godhead and I are one? Here is a bond which there is no language to express.

A bond that was made in eternity, sure, strong, very powerful; a myriad years cannot break it or undo it at all: it abides and will abide while God remains in being.)

Here we have a synthesis; we have not only the beauty of Christ and the love which it kindles, but the mystery of the union of God and man through him, and behind that again the mystery of the eternal Covenant.

Toward that consummation, in this life, the Christian treads his toilsome way. Williams Pantycelyn is, above all other hymn-writers, the Christian pilgrim. That theme is prominent in his work at all periods, from first to last. The journey is always through difficulties. Most often it is through a desert, like the journey of Israel from Egypt. A variety of Old Testament images are brought in: we hear of the pillar of cloud and fire, the waters of Marah that are to be made wine, the manna, the fruits of Canaan that lie ahead, the vision of Mount Zion in the distance. We also hear much of the hostile tribesmen who surround the traveller; his journey is a running battle with them. As will be seen from these instances, no regard is paid to historical or geographical accuracy; the images are not visualised realistically; they are like counters which can be combined at will.

There are difficulties of terrain and difficulties made by enemies along the road. But occasionally another note makes itself heard. The things of this world are not merely hard and challenging; they are unstable and in the last resort unreal. Pantycelyn is not only moving through a world of sin and suffering to the home of perfect holiness and joy; he is also moving through a world of unrealities to the invisible, incomprehensible Reality which is God. It is true that when he speaks of this aspect of the truth he usually puts it in an experiential form: not that God is in fact beyond comparison with any of his creatures, but that when he fills a man's mind he drives all created things out of it:

Aspects of Welsh Free Church Hymnody

Mae haul a sêr y rhod
  Yn darfod oll o'm blaen;
Mae twllwch dudew'n dod
  Ar bopeth hyfryd glân:
Fy Nuw ei Hun sy'n hardd, sy'n fawr,
Ac oll yn oll mewn nef a llawr.

(The sun and stars in the sky all pass away from before me; thick black darkness comes over every bright and pleasant thing: my God himself is beautiful, is great, and all in all in heaven and earth.)

V

Williams Pantycelyn has no rival but one, and that a very different kind of person. Ann Griffiths (1776–1805) was a farmer's daughter and a farmer's wife in Montgomeryshire. Her literary remains comprise some thirty hymns and eight letters, in which a highly individual mind finds utterance. She has not the literary skill of the mature Pantycelyn, but she has an outstanding power of using biblical imagery, with all its associations, in ways which make a fresh and lasting impression on the mind. She has not Pantycelyn's background of reading, and the range of her ideas is narrower than his; but within that limited range she makes certain points with unsurpassed force and clarity.

Her prevailing attitude of mind is that of one contemplating, with joy and perpetual wonder, the great mysteries of the Faith. That is her aspiration in this life: '*Mewn môr o ryfeddodau, / O! am gael treulio f'oes*' ('O to spend my life in a sea of wonders'). It is her expectation for the hereafter:

O! ddedwydd awr tragwyddol orffwys
  Oddi wrth fy llafur yn fy rhan,
Ynghanol môr o ryfeddodau
  Heb weled terfyn byth, na glan.

(O blessed hour of eternal rest from my labour in my lot, in the midst of a sea of wonders with never a sight of a boundary or a shore.)

Chief among these wonders are the eternal Covenant, the Incarnation, and the Atonement; and in her mind the wonder of the Incarnation seems in a manner to absorb and contain both the others. Like Pantycelyn, she gazes with adoring love and joy upon the Incarnate God; but, far more openly and explicitly than Pantycelyn, she wonders at the sheer paradox of the two natures in one Person. She marvels at Christ and worships him even more for what he is than for what he has done – which he anyhow could not have done if he had not been what he is. See how she brings out the paradox of the death of the Creator:

> O! f'enaid, gwêl y fan gorweddodd
> Pen brenhinoedd, Awdwr hedd,
> Y greadigaeth ynddo'n symud,
> Yntau'n farw yn y bedd.

(O my soul, behold the place where lay the chief of kings, the Author of peace, the creation moving in him, and he dead in the tomb.)

Compare what she says in one of her letters:

> No wonder the sun hid its rays when its Creator was pierced by nails. To my mind it is a marvel who was on the cross: he whose eyes are as a flame of fire piercing through heaven and earth at the same moment unable to see his creatures, the work of his hands. My mind is too overwhelmed to say anything more on the matter.

Together with this keen eye for the paradoxes, and the mysteries of which they are the phenomenal manifestation,

Ann has also a strong sense of the absoluteness of God. He is absolute in the infinity and eternity of his being, but he is also absolute in righteousness, and his law is the expression of what that means for any creature who would approach him. The gulf between the righteous God and sinful man is infinite. But then, infinite too is the merit of the Atonement which God has himself eternally purposed and carried out at a moment in time. God's law is perfect, and in Christ it receives perfect satisfaction, so that righteousness not merely allows, but demands, the release of the guilty whose debt has been fully paid. As Ann says in a letter:

> I never before knew so much reverence towards and love for the law, not in spite of the fact that it brings a curse, but because it brings a curse in every place outside of a Mediator. Thus it shows its purity.

The greatest wonder of the Atonement is that it is wrought without the least relaxation of the law's demands. It is a lawful way (*ffordd gyfreithlon*) for sinners to grace and favour with God. And finally, as God has so signally vindicated his own honour both in the fact and in the manner of his redemption of man, it follows that the redeemed are kindled to an insatiable desire for purity of heart, so that God may be honoured in them also:

> That word is on my mind: 'And the blood of Jesus Christ his Son cleanseth us from all sin.' I have never had a greater longing to be pure.

VI

If one wished to set a third name beside these two, on grounds of popularity it would probably have to be that of Elfed (the Rev. H. Elvet Lewis, 1860–1953). But that brings us into a very different age and atmosphere. Elfed belongs to a time when the fire of the movement which created these hymns was burning low. The last of the great Welsh revivals came and went in the middle years of his life. It was the time when the Free Church mind, in England and Wales alike, was breaking out of its obsession with personal experiences and personal ethics and looking both hopefully and critically at the wider social scene. Men began to cry out for social justice, for world peace and unity and progress; and it seemed possible for a generation or two to see these things as the realisation of the Kingdom of God on earth. The energies thus diverted outwards were no longer available for that inner life of which Pantycelyn and Ann had sung.

Elfed himself is much more than a merely religious figure. As poet and critic he has a significant place in the history of Welsh literature. He did much to help Wales to look beyond its narrow nineteenth-century interests and find its place in relation to the modem European literary tradition. As a hymn-writer he has the practised skill of the poet, his lines move easily, his phrases are direct and clear; but he has none of that vivid experience and inward struggle out of which his predecessors sang. One cannot point to any distinctive and compelling theological vision to which he gives voice; one can only say that he sings easily and beautifully and sometimes memorably, but never disturbingly, of different aspects of the Christian story, and of various activities, ecclesiastical, social and national. He is in the spirit of his time when he tells us that we are God's fellow-workers, engaged in building his house – the same theme which T. S. Eliot explored in his play *The Rock*. Elfed says that God's fellow-workers must never be downcast at the difficulties they meet; God is in control and all will come out right. But he knows that the obstacles are real and the danger of discouragement is to be taken seriously. And it is here that he turns inward to the quiet paths of prayer:

Pan fyddo achos Iesu
　Yn eiddil a di-glod,
Pan losgo'r lamp yn isel
　Wrth ddisgwyl iddo ddod,
A thwrf y rhai annuwiol
　Fel sŵn ystormus li –
Ar dawel lwybrau gweddi
　O! cadw, cadw fi.

(When the cause of Jesus is weak and inglorious, when the lamp burns low while we await his coming, and the tumult of the ungodly is like the sound of a stormy flood – O keep me, keep me on the quiet paths of prayer.)

Did Elfed ever know that his prayer was being answered in the widespread recovery of the doctrine and discipline of contemplative prayer which is a feature of Christianity in the twentieth century?

VII

And the conclusions from all this? Only a few points.

1. Wales has a voice of its own, and has something to say. Even when it shares with England in a great mass movement like the Evangelical Revival, still Wales has a voice of its own and something of its own to say.

2. One of the channels through which it speaks is the hymn-tradition which we have been considering. The development of this tradition was determined to a great extent by two outstanding personalities which appeared in the early days, namely Williams Pantycelyn and Ann Griffiths. In them the meaning of the tradition is brought to a point.

3. Both are enthusiasts, and in both the enthusiasm is a response to a definite body of beliefs. These beliefs are expressed in a set of dogmatic formulae, but these are only important

because behind and beyond them is an intuitive apprehension of the Invisible and of our relation to it. It is a complex and astonishing relation, and the formulae bring this out. So do the hymns. This is especially true of Ann Griffiths, whose mind, we may well say, dwells in the Absolute and in the Paradox.

4. In a Christian and Evangelical movement, the consciousness of human sin and guilt and of what are believed to be the facts of the Atonement must of course play a central part. But it is not the ultimate thing. What is ultimate is the Primal Love, which is altogether prior to sin and guilt and suffering, and makes them occasions for its own more brilliant unfolding. To this ultimate, by a kind of metaphysical tropism, minds penetrate, and live in the contemplation of it.

5. The tide of this metaphysical vision and responsive utterance has receded in Wales just as it has in England. But whether we consider it as a thing altogether of the past, or as an abiding possibility of human experience which might some day be reactivated, in either case the study of the Welsh variant has an interest of its own.

WILLIAMS PANTYCELYN:

Father of the Modern Welsh Hymn[1]

I

If we seek a figure to represent and typify the tradition of modern Welsh hymn-writing, beyond doubt that figure must be William Williams, commonly called Pantycelyn (= Holly Dell) after the farm where he lived. He had significant predecessors, and there were strong singers among his contemporaries. Yet it is true to say that the whole tradition of Welsh hymn-writing from his time onward is marked with his stamp.

Williams was born in 1717 and died in 1791. His father was an elder in an Independent congregation at Cefnarthen, near Llandovery. He studied at an academy run by one Vavasor Griffiths, an Independent minister, at Llwyn-llwyd near Hay-on-Wye, and was intent on becoming a doctor. While there, however, he underwent a conversion through the preaching of Howel Harris, and on his advice sought Anglican orders. He was ordained deacon, and served as curate under Theophilus Evans, vicar of Llangamarch, in charge of the districts of

---

1 A paper read at the Hymn Society of Great Britain and Ireland's Annual Conference in Cardiff, July 1975, and subsequently published in the Society's *Bulletin*, no. 135, vol. 8:9 (February 1976) and no. 136, vol. 8:10 (June 1976).

Llanwrtyd and Abergwesyn.[2] Williams was soon in trouble with the authorities for a variety of offences, which ranged from preaching outside the parish to omitting the sign of the cross in baptism. He was never ordained a priest. In 1743 he resigned his curacies to become a full-time Methodist preacher. For the rest of his life he travelled the length and breadth of Wales preaching, teaching, organising and counselling. He is buried in the churchyard at Llanfair-ar-y-bryn, his parish church.

By these activities over more than forty years he takes rank with Howel Harris and Daniel Rowland among the founding fathers of the Calvinistic Methodist Connexion in Wales. Like them, he was in some sense an Anglican to the end, for he died twenty years before the Separation.[3] It would be hard, however, to find anything distinctively Anglican in his theology or his spirituality. He stands firmly in the Puritan tradition.

Williams published several hymn collections in Welsh and two in English. The principal Welsh collections are *Aleluia*, *Hosanna i Fab Dafydd* ('Hosanna to the Son of David'), *Caniadau y rhai sydd ar y Môr o Wydr* ('Songs of those who are on the Sea of Glass'), *Ffarwel Weledig, Groesaw Anweledig Bethau* ('Farewell to things seen, welcome to things unseen'), and *Gloria in Excelsis*. His total product in Welsh is in the neighbourhood of 850 hymns. Besides these he wrote two long religious poems: *Golwg ar Deyrnas Crist* ('A Prospect of the Kingdom of Christ'), which is an epic treating of the life of Christ from the moment when he was appointed King and Redeemer of the yet-to-be-created world to the moment of the still-future

---

2   [Theophilus Evans (1693–1767) wrote a very popular book on early Welsh history entitled *Drych y Prif Oesoedd* ('A Mirror of the Early Ages'). He also wrote *The History of Modern Enthusiasm*, which was a scathing attack on all forms of religious nonconformity, including Methodism. – *Ed.*]

3   [The Welsh Calvinistic Methodists, also known by now as the Presbyterian Church of Wales, began ordaining their own ministers in 1811, thus completing the process of separating from the Anglican Church. – *Ed.*]

Williams Pantycelyn: Father of the Modern Welsh Hymn

Consummation; and *Bywyd a Marwolaeth Theomemphus* ('The Life and Death of Theomemphus'), a kind of *Pilgrim's Progress* in epic verse. Some passages from these poems are in use today as hymns. There are also other poems on sacred and secular subjects, and some prose writings on subjects theological and pastoral.

The *Môr o Wydr* book has a special interest because of its effect on the Methodist cause in Wales. The movement had been grievously weakened and discouraged by the feud between Harris and the other leaders in the years after 1750. The publication of *Môr o Wydr* in 1762 put new heart into the movement. At Llangeitho for instance, on the Sunday when the new book was first used, it produced nothing less than a fresh revival.[4]

Williams is the creator of the modern Welsh hymn. His mastery of language and of poetic form, imperfect at first, grew continually throughout his writing life. He has not Wesley's classical scholarship and he does not seem to have known much about the Welsh poetic tradition; which is perhaps just as well, for it sets him free to develop his own style, marked by a great simplicity and directness of expression. He stands in succession to Rhys Prichard, Edmwnd Prys and others, who gave the Welsh psalms, hymns and devout meditations in simple metres and in simple phrases which all could understand. But he enriches this tradition by a considerable variety in his choice of metres. The Rev. Gomer M. Roberts has listed thirty-four different stanza forms which occur in his hymns and thinks that he may be the inventor of the powerful 2.88.888 metre, which

---

[4] [See R. Geraint Gruffydd, 'The Revival of 1762 and William Williams of Pantycelyn', in Emyr Roberts and R. Geraint Gruffydd, *Revival and Its Fruit* (Bridgend: Evangelical Library of Wales, 1981). The small village of Llangeitho in Cardiganshire was a focal point for the Methodist movement in the eighteenth century, with thousands flocking there from all parts of Wales to sit under the powerful ministry of Daniel Rowland. – *Ed.*]

is not used in English.[5] As with Wesley, however, some of the hymns are very long and are in use now only in a shortened form.

I have mentioned Wesley; and Williams is indeed in some respects the Charles Wesley of Wales. Both were men of high poetic gifts, who placed them in the service of the Methodist movement, and both left a lasting mark on the piety of that movement. There is, however, one notable difference. Wesley, though capable of splendid outbursts of spontaneity, at other times wrote to a plan. In his hymns, as collected and arranged by his brother in the 'Large Hymn Book' of 1780, is set forth systematically the characteristic spiritual doctrine of Methodism. Not so Williams. He writes as he thinks and feels, and has not the scholar's urge to paint a full and articulated and well-balanced picture. As a result his hymns, even more than Wesley's, are an intimate personal document. In the sequence of his publications we can trace not only the growing maturity of a poetic talent, but also the deepening and widening experience of a Christian soul.

Looking in detail, we miss some of the characteristic Wesley emphases. The doctrine of sin and forgiveness is of course well to the fore, and Williams himself is known to have undergone a typical evangelical conversion in 1737 or 1738. But in his hymns we do not find any concentration upon the circumstances and feelings of the actual conversion experience or upon the doubts and struggles which may precede it; nothing about 'legal night' or about the 'mourner brought to the birth', as the Wesleys put it. Another Wesley emphasis which is missing is the sense of the fellowship of believers in the Christian community. It would be absurd to suggest that Williams' religion was a solitary or individualistic one; he

---

5 [See Gomer M. Roberts, *Y Pêr Ganiedydd (Pantycelyn)*, vol. 2 (Gwasg Aberystwyth, 1958), chapter 3. – *Ed.*]

devoted his life to setting up small Methodist societies (*seiadau*) through the length and breadth of Wales and fostering their community life. But he does not sing about it as Wesley does. As for total sanctification, he knows that it must come one day, and prays that it may come to him in this life; but there is nothing of Wesley's argumentative and heaven-storming eagerness; rather a quiet but insistent longing. In any case earthly perfection is overshadowed in his vision by heaven, the goal of his pilgrimage, the place of rest, of song and praise and feasting.

Williams belonged, like all the Welsh Methodist leaders, to the Calvinist side of the Revival. One naturally looks for signs of this in his hymns, but they are not very clearly there. With Wesley it is otherwise. The doctrine of the unlimited atonement, which was his main point in the doctrinal controversy, was also a chief point in the gospel he preached; so it is everywhere in his hymns, it could not be kept out. There seems to be no point of corresponding importance on the Calvinist side, which is correspondingly important in Pantycelyn's hymns.

A student of the Wesleys is bound to be tempted to see Calvinism through their eyes, which means identifying it with the doctrine of double predestination and a limited atonement. No doubt this doctrine can be found in the total Calvinist complex, and no doubt, if it is picked out and presented by itself as a theological theorem, there is a plausible case against it. If, however, one asks what Calvinism is, not as stated for reasons of controversy by its opponents, but as seen and felt and lived by its adherents, the answer may be different. The Calvinists thought the Arminian doctrine made a man's salvation insecure, because dependent on his own response to the gospel; whereas in fact the security of the redeemed rests upon nothing less than the pre-temporal will of the changeless

God. It is on this side of the matter that Calvinist devotion concentrates. In Pantycelyn we find no speculation on the number of the lost, and no theory as to why they are lost, except that it is due to lack of faith. All the attention is fixed on the redeemed, on their vast numbers, on the wonder of the fact of redemption and the splendour of the means by which it was wrought. So in the well-known hymn, '*Marchog, Iesu, yn llwyddiannus*' ('Ride, Jesus, triumphantly'):

> *Tyn fy enaid o'i gaethiwed,*
>   *Gwawried bellach fore ddydd,*
> *Rhwyga'n chwilfriw ddorau Babel,*
>   *Tyn y barrau heyrn yn rhydd;*
> *Gwthied caethion yn finteioedd*
>   *Allan, megis tonnau llif,*
> *Torf a thorf, dan orfoleddu,*
>   *Heb na diwedd fyth na rhif.*

(Draw my soul out of its captivity, let the dawn now break, smash to splinters the gates of Babel, draw the iron bars free; let captives in multitudes thrust their way out, like the waves of a flood, throng upon throng, in exultation, without ever an end or number.)

II

It is commonplace that the Christian life is a progression, and it is interesting to observe the various ways in which the progression is conceived. Sometimes it is the climbing of a holy mountain (Sinai perhaps, or Carmel) or of a spiritual ladder. Very often it is a journey by land or sea, and this aspect of it is overwhelmingly to the fore in Pantycelyn's hymns. But again there is variety in his conception of the journey.

Sometimes it is a desert journey, conceived on the model of Israel's exodus from Egypt. The only one of Pantycelyn's hymns which is well known in an English version is 'Guide me, O thou great Jehovah', and it illustrates very well his way of dealing with the theme. It is indeed the exodus, but where is Israel? Pantycelyn writes as an individual having an exodus on his own, with pillars of cloud and fire and a miraculous supply of water and a guided crossing of Jordan all to himself. And in general the individual traveller is the norm in Pantycelyn's writing, and he is constantly called a 'pilgrim'. Sometimes he has companions, though it is a group of friends rather than an embattled nation on the move. In moments of darkness and fear he hears the voices of others who are ahead of him on the way. Sometimes he has a glimpse of the shining goal which others have reached; and sometimes this is Canaan, sometimes Mount Zion, sometimes 'my Father's house'. Meanwhile he is often bewildered and under frequent attack. It is in fact a composite picture to which Bunyan contributes quite as much as the Old Testament.

The combination is seen very well in the following popular hymn:

> *Pererin wyf mewn anial dir,*
>   *Yn crwydro yma a thraw;*
> *Ac yn rhyw ddisgwyl bob yr awr*
>   *Fod tŷ fy Nhad gerllaw.*
>
> *Ac mi debygaf clywaf sŵn*
>   *Nefolaidd rai o'm blaen,*
> *Wedi gorchfygu a mynd trwy*
>   *Dymhestloedd dŵr a thân.*
>
> *Tyrd, Ysbryd Sanctaidd, ledia'r ffordd,*
>   *Bydd imi'n niwl a thân;*
> *Ni cherdda' i'n gywir hanner cam*
>   *Oni byddi Di o'm blaen.*

Flame in the Mountains

> *Mi ŵyraf weithiau ar y dde,*
> *Ac ar yr aswy law;*
> *Am hynny, arwain, gam a cham*
> *Fi i'r Baradwys draw.*

(I am a pilgrim in a desert land, wandering hither and thither, and somehow expecting every hour that my Father's house is close by.

And I think I hear the sound of heavenly ones before me, who have overcome and gone through storms of water and fire.

Come Holy Spirit, lead the way, be to me cloud and fire; I shall not walk half a step correctly unless thou be before me.

I shall veer sometimes to the right, and to the left; therefore lead me step by step to yonder paradise.)

A third source for the travel imagery is undoubtedly the landscape of Wales. Pantycelyn knew it as few men could. For forty years he rode long distances on preaching assignments, over hills and through valleys, in all seasons and in all weathers. In his hymns we constantly see him scaling mountains and steep crags, with the sound of mountain torrents in his ears. We hear of wind and storm, dark clouds, thunder and lightning, fire and flood. There is a whole family of hymns in which the theme is the coming of morning after a night journey, or the clearing of the sky after a storm. Reading these hymns, one receives a vivid picture of their author as he rides abroad, one hears the beat of his horse's hooves as he breasts the slopes, one sees him stand for a moment as he tops the hill, to look across further hills and valleys towards his destination, or to observe a change in the wind.

I shall have more to say about this group of images later on.

III

The hymns of the Christian pilgrimage tell us something that is true and important, but they need translating. The pilgrim's way, which is the Christian life, has a starting-point, a succession of later incidents, and a goal. What, in plain English or Welsh, are these?

The starting-point is the evangelical conversion, when the soul becomes for the first time vividly aware of its perilous state, and then receives the assurance of pardon and acceptance through the work of Christ. This experience is powerfully described in a group of Wesley's hymns, to which nothing altogether corresponds in Pantycelyn, though we know he had the experience. But what comes afterwards? Pantycelyn's answer to that question is best seen in a passage in his poem *Theomemphus,* where the hero, soon after his conversion, is catechised about his present spiritual state and his experiences.

We learn that he has been granted a clear vision of Christ as Mediator, as saving Victim, and as the King in his beauty. This vision weakens sometimes but is constantly renewed, and its effects on Theomemphus' mind have settled into a fixed disposition. He is at peace with God, secure in Christ against guilt and fear, free and bold to approach the throne. He rests with joy and wonder upon the eternal Covenant, in which his own blessedness and God's glory are seen to coincide. He struggles against self-esteem, strives to negate himself and to think only of God's glory. True, he is often beset by sins and fears, wave upon wave, so that he almost loses his wits; but even when temptation is at its strongest he still loves the law of God, and still looks to Christ for deliverance. He sorrows for sin, but it is a sorrow without fear, like that of the returned prodigal. He cannot doubt his election. He looks forward with longing to the time when he shall wake up satisfied in God's likeness, to sin no more.

Such is the state of a converted but not yet perfected soul. There is a real and constantly renewed vision of Christ and intimacy with God in him; but there is also a constantly renewed conflict with the forces of evil without and within the soul. This alternation of light and darkness is reflected in Pantycelyn's hymns. There is no lack of hymns of penitence and appeals for grace. He writes as one in great danger, even as one trembling on the verge of hell; and yet he makes his appeal in confidence, because the shoulders that carry the world can and will carry his burden, and because 'there is talk everywhere of how thou dost raise up the weak'.[6] There is an interesting hymn in which he pleads for a word of peace in the name of the Covenant:

> *Nac aed o'th gof dy ffyddlon amod drud,*
> *Yn sicir wnaed cyn rhoi sylfeini'r byd;*
> *Ti roist im yno drysor maith di-drai;*
> *Gad imi heddiw gael dy wir fwynhau.*
>
> *O! cofia'r hedd rai prydiau roist i lawr*
> *I'm henaid trist mewn cyfyngderau mawr;*
> *O! edrych eto, mae fy enaid gwan*
> *Gan syched mawr ar drengi yn y fan.*
>
> *Nid rhaid it ond dywedyd gair o hedd,*
> *Fy syched a dry'n dawel nefol wledd ...*

(Forget not thy precious faithful covenant, that was made firm before the world's foundations were laid; there thou gavest me a great unfailing treasure; grant me today to truly enjoy thee.

O remember the peace thou hast sometimes sent down to my sad soul in great tribulations; O look again, my feeble soul is near to death from great thirst.

---

6 ['*Mae sôn amdanat ym mhob man / Yn codi'r gwan i fyny*', from the hymn '*Darfu fy nerth, 'rwy'n llwfwrhau*'. – Ed.]

Thou needest but to speak a word of peace, and my thirst will turn into a quiet heavenly feast ...)

The experience of forgiveness is sometimes conceived as a vision of Christ crucified; the sinner is to see Christ, and feel according to his ability some hint of what Christ suffered for him, and so gain peace and life and joy. Elsewhere we hear of him washing himself clean in the stream that flows from Calvary, 'rising and flooding through the plains of the land of Salem';[7] he will cast off ten thousand sins in the powerful stream. Or again it is a question of throwing off his burden, as in Bunyan's story. This conception is combined with that of the vision of Christ in the hymn '*Mi dafla' 'maich oddi ar fy ngwar*':

Mi dafla' 'maich oddi ar fy ngwar
　Wrth deimlo dwyfol loes;
Euogrwydd fel mynyddoedd byd
　Dry'n ganu wrth dy groes.

(I shall cast my burden off my shoulders as I feel the divine suffering; guilt like the world's mountains will turn to song at thy cross.)

Christ is incomparable:

Os edrych wnaf i'r dwyrain draw,
　Os edrych wnaf i'r de,
Ymhlith a fu neu ynteu ddaw,
　'Does debyg iddo Fe.

(If I look over to the east, if I look to the south, amid all that has been or is to come, there is none like him.)

7　['*Y mae'n llanw ac yn llifo / Dros wastadedd Salem dir*', from the hymn '*Heddiw'r ffynnon a agorwyd*'. – Ed.]

We are shown briefly his crucifixion and ascension and his present work as intercessor in heaven, where Pantycelyn will shortly join him:

Ac yna caf fod gydag Ef
  Pan êl y byd ar dân,
Ac edrych yn ei hyfryd wedd,
  Gan' harddach nag o'r blaen.

(And there it will be mine to be with him when the world goes up in flames, and gaze into his delightful countenance, a hundred times fairer than before.)

'There is none like him'; and yet hereafter he will be seen 'a hundred times fairer than before'. It is in the development of these thoughts that Pantycelyn is most characteristically himself. The figure of the Crucified fills his field of vision and holds him in loving admiration. We are shown the initial paradox of who it is that does the work: God, the infinite divine Being, the Prince of Heaven, the Prince of Life, becomes man and suffers and dies, and even as he dies he forgives and prays the Father to forgive. He does all this for us, and for each of us, who deserve nothing better than everlasting flames and darkness. He does it that we may receive pardon and grace, that we may have life, that we may enter heaven. As for the means by which these benefits were purchased and secured to us, Pantycelyn's doctrine is in no way original, nor on the whole is the manner of its expression. We find the standard ideas and phrases, though there are a few turns of phrase that are characteristic of our author. One such which occurs over and over again is the observation, perfectly true but not usually made except by Welshmen, that Christ's great work was done in an afternoon. Nay rather, since the work is not done until it is finished, and he finished it by his death, the work was done in a brief moment: '*Gwnaethost fwy mewn un munudyn / Nag a wnaethai'r byd o'r bron*' ('Thou didst more in one short minute than all the world had done before'). The drama of that day is the drama of two suns:

> *Ar Galfari, rhwng daer a nef,*
> *Llewyrchodd ei ogoniant Ef;*
> *Un haul ymguddiodd y prynhawn,*
> *A'r llall a wnaed yn eglur iawn.*

(On Calvary, between earth and heaven, his glory shone out; one sun was eclipsed that afternoon, and the other became very bright.)

All the world hangs on the work of that day:

> *Yr hoelion geirwon caled,*
>   *Gynt a'i trywanodd E',*
> *Sy'n awr yn dal y nefoedd*
>   *Gwmpasog yn ei lle.*

(The rough hard nails which once pierced him now hold the whole compass of heaven in place.)

Again, much is heard of the stream which flows from Calvary, a stream in which we can wash ourselves clean, or from which we can drink; but here is a less usual development of the image:

> *Gwêl ar y croesbren acw*
>   *Gyfiawnder mawr y ne',*
> *Doethineb, a thrugaredd,*
>   *Yn gorwedd mewn un lle,*
> *A chariad anfesurol,*
>   *Yn awr i gyd yn un,*
> *Fel afon fawr lifeiriol*
>   *Yn rhedeg at y dyn.*

(See, on the cross yonder, the great righteousness of heaven, wisdom, and mercy, lying in one place, and measureless love, all these now together, running manwards like a great river in flood.)

In two hymns the story of our salvation involves that Power which in the English Bible is called the Serpent, but which in Pantycelyn's Welsh is also the Dragon (*y Ddraig*). In one hymn it is a fight between him and Christ:

Y ddraig a 'sigwyd gan yr Un,
Cans clwyfwyd dau, concwerodd un
    A Iesu oedd Efe.

(The Dragon has been crushed by the One; for two were wounded, One was victorious, and he was Jesus.)

Elsewhere it is different:

Fe ddaeth i wella'r archoll
    Trwy gymryd clwyf ei Hun –
Etifedd nef yn marw
    I wella marwol ddyn:
Yn sugno i maes y gwenwyn
    A roes y sarff i ni,
Ac wrth y gwenwyn hwnnw
    Yn marw ar Galfari.

(He came to heal our wound by receiving a wound himself – the heir of heaven dying to heal mortal man; sucking out the poison which the Serpent had injected into us, and dying of that poison on Calvary.)

Pantycelyn has many fine things to say about the cross, but at last there comes a moment when he is reduced to silence:

Bendithion ar fendithion,
  Trysorau angau loes,
Grawnsypiau mawrion aeddfed
  Yn hongian ar y groes,
Sydd yn cwmpasu f'enaid,
  Rhinweddau mawr eu grym;
A minnau yn eu canol
  Heb allu dwedyd dim.

(Blessings upon blessings, treasures of the pains of death, big ripe grape-clusters hanging upon the cross, are all around my soul, virtues great in their strength; and I am left speechless in their midst.)

IV

Wondrously though our pardon was purchased, pardon alone is not enough, nor is it the whole of what was purchased for us. There remains a work of grace to be wrought in us, the work of sanctification. It is a lengthy process, bringing, as we advance in it, an ever closer likeness to God and an ever deeper intimacy with him.

Pantycelyn as a Calvinist believes in the total depravity of human nature. But as a man with the training of a doctor and the experience of a counsellor he has his own interpretation of that formula. He shows no trace of the crypto-Manichaeanism which is the bane of so many puritan movements. Human nature, corrupt and defaced as it may be, is to be restored, not abolished. The passions, unruly though we now find them, can and shall be brought back to the orderly functioning which is theirs in the plan of creation. They are to be reintegrated in subordination to one overmastering affection, namely the love of God. This love is a fire which we cannot kindle in ourselves, it must come as a gift from God, and as we grow in this love we also grow in likeness to God, and become in a sense endowed with something of his nature. When that happens, God will be glorified not in spite of our passions, but in and through them, which after all is what they were created for. That is what Pantycelyn asks for explicitly in one hymn:

> O! sancteiddia f'enaid, Arglwydd,
>   Ym mhob nwyd, ac ym mhob dawn;
> Rho egwyddor bur y nefoedd
>   Yn fy ysbryd llesg yn llawn;
>   N'ad im grwydro,
>   Draw nac yma fyth o'm lle.
>   ......
> Planna'r egwyddorion hynny
>   Yn fy enaid bob yr un,
> Ag sydd megis peraroglau
>   Yn dy natur Di dy Hun:
>   Blodau hyfryd
>   Fo'n disgleirio daer a nef.

(O sanctify my soul, Lord, in every passion, and in every gift; put the pure principle of heaven in its fullness into my drooping spirit; let me not wander far or near out of my place. ...

Plant those principles in my soul, every one of them, which are like sweet odours in thine own nature; pleasant flowers which brighten earth and heaven.)

As Pantycelyn is no enemy to the passions, but looks for their transfiguration by divine love, so too he is not afraid of pleasure as so many puritans are. It is noticeable how often he uses the word *mwynhau* (to enjoy). We are free to enjoy all the pleasures of this world except where they are corrupted. What were they created for, but to be enjoyed? But (he goes on) there is one pleasure which is so overpowering that it blots out all the rest from our consciousness; it is the enjoyment (yes, enjoyment!) of God himself.

> *Melysach nag yw'r diliau mêl*
> *Yw munud o'th fwynhau;*
> *Ac nid oes gennyf bleser sydd*
> *Ond hynny yn parhau.*

(Sweeter than the honey-comb is a minute's enjoyment of thee; and I have no lasting pleasure but that.)

So we come back to the continually renewed God-vision; but now for the first time we can see it in its full amplitude and feel its full intensity.

Pantycelyn has an overwhelming sense of God as infinite being and infinite beauty. In the long poem *Golwg ar Deyrnas Crist* ('A Prospect of the Kingdom of Christ') he shows us God as creator, giving a magnificent roll-call of God's works in all their splendour. But in the hymns he speaks of what God is to him in personal experience, and how when God comes into view he eclipses all lesser lights. So in one hymn he dismisses the sun, moon and stars; a greater light has dawned, by which he can see his way 'through every ditch and stream'.[8] Elsewhere, it is as if the vision of God renders all finite things first pale and at last invisible:

> *Mae'r ddaear a'i holl swyn*
> *Oll yn diflannu'n awr;*
> *A'i themtasiynau cry'*
> *Sy'n cwympo'n llu i'r llawr;*
> *Holl flodau'r byd sydd heb eu lliw;*
> *'Does dim yn hyfryd ond fy Nuw.*

---

8 ['*trwy bob ffos a nant*', from the hymn '*Mae tywyll anial nos*'. – Ed.]

> *Mae haul a sêr y rhod*
> *Yn darfod oll o'm blaen;*
> *Mae twllwch dudew'n dod*
> *Ar bopeth hyfryd glân:*
> *Fy Nuw ei Hun sy'n hardd, sy'n fawr,*
> *Ac oll yn oll mewn nef a llawr.*

(The earth with all its charm wholly vanishes now, and the host of its strong temptations falls to the ground; all the world's flowers have lost their colour; nothing is pleasant but my God.

The sun and stars in the sky all pass away from before me; thick black darkness comes over every bright and pleasant thing: my God himself is beautiful, is great, and all in all in heaven and earth.)

This, be it noted, is not the mystical doctrine of the dark contemplation of God; Pantycelyn does not belong to that tradition. God takes all the light and colour out of finite things, but he is not himself apprehended as darkness. Though his nature is in itself incomprehensible to us, it is revealed in sovereign splendour in Christ, and the sight of that splendour is what blinds Pantycelyn to everything else. In the hymn '*Anweledig, 'rwy'n dy garu*' ('Invisible One, I love thee') we are shown the identity of the victor of Calvary, who did more in one short minute than the whole world before, and the invisible God who in his essential nature is beyond all human thought, while yet accessible to love and intimately present in the loving soul. Here we have the whole Christ-mystery blazoned forth, and Pantycelyn pursues the theme in a rich series of hymns in which he rises to the full height of his poetic power.

His soul's delight is to gaze upon Christ in his beauty:

Iesu yw tegwch mawr y byd,
 A thegwch penna'r nef;
Ac y mae'r cwbwl sydd o werth
 Yn trigo ynddo Ef.

(Jesus is the great beauty of the world and the highest beauty of heaven; and everything that is precious dwells in him.)

Nor does he only see the beauty of his Lord; he hears his voice:

O! llefara, addfwyn Iesu:
 Mae dy eiriau fel y gwin,
Oll yn dwyn i mewn dangnefedd
 Ag sydd o anfeidrol rin;
Mae holl leisiau'r greadigaeth,
 Holl ddeniadau cnawd a byd,
Wrth dy lais hyfrytaf tawel,
 Yn distewi a mynd yn fud.

(O speak, gentle Jesus: thy words are like wine, all bringing with them a peace which is of infinite virtue; all the voices of creation, all the attractions of flesh and world, at the sound of thy most delightful quiet voice, are muted and fall silent.)

From the contemplation of this beauty springs love; yet not a love of earthly origin but a flame that strikes down from heaven and has the promise of eternity in it:

Fflam o dân o ganol nefoedd
 Yw, ddisgynnodd yma i'r byd,
Tân a lysg fy natur gyndyn,
 Tân a leinw f'eang fryd:
  Hwn ni ddiffydd
 Tra parhao Duw mewn bod.

(It is a flame of fire from midmost heaven that came down hither into the world, fire that will burn my stubborn nature, fire that will fill the breadth of my mind: it will not be extinguished while God remains in being.)

Infinite beauty and unquenchable love; that is Pantycelyn's joy, that is what is meant by the 'enjoyment' of God. But the life of the Christian pilgrim is not wholly filled by the splendour of the God-vision. The alternation of light and darkness, which Theomemphus experienced after his conversion, continues through the years, and perhaps, while the light grows sometimes brighter, the darkness thickens in contrast with it. The pilgrim may at times experience peace and joy in the beauteous vision of God and in his felt presence, but at other times will come doubts of his condition, a feeling of the absence of God, a sense of his own utter nothingness. The author of the *Theologia Germanica* describes these alternating states as a kind of heaven and hell which the mature Christian soul must expect to meet. It is as safe in hell as in heaven, but when it is in the state of hell it cannot believe it is safe. Certainly Pantycelyn experienced these alternations and has expressed them with complete honesty, concealing neither the heights nor the depths. He loves to describe his experiences in terms of his physical adventures on the rough Welsh mountain roads. Always he is climbing hills, under alternations of rain and shine, storm and fair weather, cold north wind and warm south wind, clouded hills and wide clear prospects. These things are a parable of the Christian's course.

The darkness, when it comes, can be very deep. The initial joy of evangelical conversion, the discovery of how many sins can be covered by the merits of Christ, is now far in the past, and the soul is still deeply infected with sin. God knows it and the soul knows it, and feels naked before the throne. It still waits to be clothed in a genuine righteousness. It is like a man in darkness, behind bars, crying for release. It is a torture to itself, tyrannised over by pleasures which it hates. Sometimes even the original sense of pardon and acceptance through Christ comes under threat. How can it not, when one goes on sinning all the time?

> *Dwed i mi, a wyt yn maddau*
>   *Cwympo ganwaith i'r un bai?*
> *Dwed a ddeui byth i galon*
>   *Na all gynnig 'difarhau?*
> *Beth yw pwysau'r beiau mwyaf*
>   *A faddeui? – o ba ri'?*
> *Pa un drymaf yw fy mhechod*
>   *Ai griddfannau Calfari?*

(Tell me, dost thou forgive one who falls a hundred times into the same fault? Tell me, wilt thou yet come to a heart that cannot even attempt to repent? What is the weight of the greatest faults that thou forgivest? – what their number? Which weighs heavier, my sin or the groans of Calvary?)

Or again:

> *Y mae arnaf fil o ofnau,*
>   *Ofnau mawrion o bob gradd,*
> *Oll yn gwasgu gyda'i gilydd*
>   *Ar fy ysbryd, bron fy lladd:*
> *Nid oes allu a goncweria*
>   *Dorf o elynion sydd yn un –*
> *Concro ofn, y gelyn mwyaf,*
>   *Ond dy allu Di dy Hun.*

Ofni'r wyf na ches faddeuant,
  Ac na chaf faddeuant mwy;
Ofni'n fynych na ches olwg
  Eto ar dy farwol glwy';
Ofni bod fy meiau'n taro
  Yn erbyn iechydwriaeth rad,
Ac na chaiff fy enaid egwan
  Fyth ei olchi yn y gwaed.

Deuwch, yr awelon hyfryd,
  Deuwch dros y bryniau pell,
Dan eich adain dawel rasol,
  Dygwch y newyddion gwell:
Dygwch newydd at fy enaid –
  F'enw innau yno a gad,
Dedwydd enw'n argraffedig
  Yn yr iechydwriaeth rad.

(A thousand fears are upon me, great fears of every degree, all together pressing upon my spirit, all but killing me: there is no power that can conquer the banded host of enemies, that can conquer fear, the greatest enemy, but thine own power.

I fear that I have never received forgiveness and never shall receive it; I often fear that I have not yet beheld thy death-wound; I fear that my sins strike against the free gift of salvation, and that my feeble soul will never be washed in the blood.

Come, ye pleasant breezes, come over the far-off hills, under your quiet gracious wings bring the better news: bring news to my soul that my name is also to be found yonder, a blessed name inscribed in the free salvation.)

These are not routine confessions of sin; they are evidence of a threat to the very basis of the spiritual life, to the virtue of hope. But amid all these fears, that virtue is not lost, and Pantycelyn is always able to end with a trustful appeal for a renewal of his peace of mind.

The virtue of hope survives even the darkness, and in due course the God-vision returns, sometimes widening out into a kind of preview of heaven. For example, the flame of love, the beauty and infinity of the Object and the foreseen eternity are combined effectively in these verses:

> *Bydd dy degwch fyth yn newydd,*
>   *Fyth o newydd ennyn dân,*
> *Trwy holl oesoedd tragwyddoldeb,*
>   *Fyth heb flino yn y blaen;*
> *Fflam angerddol, heb un terfyn,*
>   *Trwy holl raddau'r nef yn un,*
> *Hi barha i losgi'n olau*
>   *Tra parhao Duw ei Hun.*
>
> *Nid oes ond dy fawredd dwyfol,*
>   *Yn y nef nac ar y llawr,*
> *Allsai ennyn y fath gariad*
>   *Ag wyf yn ei brofi'n awr;*
> *Pwy sefydlai f'ysbryd gwamal,*
>   *Pwy'm gosodai yn fy lle,*
> *Ond yr Hwn, heb derfyn arno,*
>   *Sy'n berffeithrwydd daer a ne'?*

(Thy beauty will be ever new, ever freshly kindling a fire, through all the ages of eternity, evermore without fail; a fervent flame without end, through all the degrees of heaven together, it will continue to burn brightly as long as God himself shall last.

There is nothing in heaven or earth but thy divine greatness that could kindle such love as I now feel; who could settle my unquiet spirit, who could establish me in my place, but he, the Illimitable, who is the perfection of earth and heaven?)

V

'While God remains in being'[9] – that is a preview of eternity; and here one might be tempted to end on a high note of climax. But that would be both doubtful theology and bad scholarship. Pantycelyn does reach these heights, but he is not permanently installed there. That is not the message which his work holds for us. For man cannot become permanently possessed of the God-vision until he is totally and permanently freed from sin. And that brings us to a question eagerly debated in Pantycelyn's time, the question of the possibility of Christian perfection.

Charles Wesley accepted his brother's doctrine that Christian perfection, involving the total eradication of sin, is a real possibility for serious Christians in this life. He wrote numerous hymns pleading to receive the great gift; and though he never believed himself to have received it, he tried to imagine what it would be like to be in that happy state. The picture of the Christian's spiritual journey which is set forth in the 'Large Hymn Book' ends with a delineation of the soul which has been brought right through to the goal.

For myself, after years of trying to say whatever can be said for Wesley, I was relieved to find in Pantycelyn what seemed a more realistic view. Wesley, I think we must say, sacrificed empirical truth to a theological theory. The theory may indeed be true for a few chosen souls; authoritative Catholic spiritual writers support it in that sense. But it gives a misleading picture of the experience of most Christians, even of most devout Christians, in later life, and it should not have been made part of the teaching of a mass movement, such as Methodism was. The hymns in which Pantycelyn reveals his own experience tell a different and a more recognizable story.

Because even the deepest darkness does not kill hope, and

---

9 ['*Tra parhao Duw mewn bod*', the last line of the hymn '*Os yw tegwch d'wyneb yma*'. – *Ed.*]

Pantycelyn's trust in the Covenant remains steady, his fears are always in the last resort vain. He cannot really doubt that the God-vision in its splendour represents the goal to which he will one day attain. But when? That becomes for him a question and the expression of a longing; yet a quiet longing and in no way an obsession. There is a group of hymns in which he hopes and prays that it may happen in this life, 'before evening' as he says once, or 'before sunset', or more plainly 'this side of the grave'. He asks, 'O why may I not begin my heaven now in the world?',[10] and dwells upon the thought of living in perpetual sunlight.

O! am nerth i dreulio 'nyddiau
    Yng nghynteddoedd tŷ fy Nhad;
Byw yng nghanol y goleuni,
    Twllwch obry dan fy nhraed;
Byw heb fachlud haul un amser,
    Byw heb gwmwl, byw heb boen,
Byw ar gariad anorchfygol
    Pur y croeshoeliedig Oen.

(O for strength to pass my days in the courts of my Father's house; to live in the midst of the light, darkness down under my feet; to live without ever a sunset, to live without a cloud, to live without pain, to live on the invincible pure love of the crucified Lamb.)

But that, he says, must be when God wills. In the meantime, like the Bride in the Song of Songs who calls to her Beloved to come to her over the hills of Palestine, Pantycelyn looks out with longing over the hills of Wales. So we see him in this hymn from one of his later publications, *Gloria in Excelsis* (1772):

---

10 ['*O! pam na chaf i ddechrau'n awr / Fy nefoedd yn y byd*', from the hymn ''*Rwy'n chwennych gweld ei degwch Ef*'. – Ed.]

'Rwy'n edrych, dros y bryniau pell,
    Amdanat bob yr awr;
Tyrd, fy Anwylyd, mae'n hwyrhau,
    A'm haul bron mynd i lawr.

Trodd fy nghariadau oll i gyd
    'N awr yn anffyddlon im;
Ond yr wyf finnau'n hyfryd glaf
    O gariad mwy ei rym.

Cariad na 'nabu plant y llawr
    Mo'i rinwedd nac mo'i ras,
Ac sydd yn sugno'm serch a'm bryd
    O'r creadur oll i maes.
            ......
Fe ddarfu blas, fe ddarfu chwant
    At holl bosïau'r byd;
Nid oes ond gwagedd heb ddim trai
    Yn rhedeg trwyddo i gyd.

(I am looking over the distant hills for thee every hour; come, my Beloved, it is getting late, and my sun is about to set.

All my loves together have now turned faithless to me, but I am happily sick of a more powerful love.

A love whose virtue or grace earth's children have not known, which sucks all my affection and my mind away from the created. ...

Gone is the taste, gone the desire for all the world's posies; there is nothing but changeless vanity running through the whole of it.)

Here we have neither the full glory of the God-vision nor the highest majesty of Pantycelyn's rhetoric. The mood is quieter, perhaps one might say a little weary; but the vision has clearly been with him and has left indelible traces upon him. Even in its temporary absence he is lastingly disenchanted with all finite things. Even so the seer of Patmos, after the glories of the vision of the heavenly city, ends his book quietly with the Bride's cry of longing: 'Come, Lord Jesus.'[11]

---

11 [Revelation 22:20. – *Ed.*]

OVER THE DISTANT HILLS

Thoughts on Williams Pantycelyn[1]

WILLIAM WILLIAMS (1717–91), sometime curate of Llanwrtyd, called Pantycelyn after the farm where he lived, called also the Sweet Singer (*Y Pêr Ganiedydd*), is one of three men who stand out as leaders in the Methodist Revival in Wales. The others were Howel Harris of Trefeca and Daniel Rowland of Llangeitho. Rowland was a powerful preacher and exercised his influence in that way. Harris was also a powerful preacher; it was his preaching which first set Williams on the road of evangelical experience; but he was much else besides, and became the founder of a remarkable religious and industrial community known as the Trefeca Family. Williams did not compare with the other two as a preacher, though he did preach regularly, travelling long distances to do so. But it was as a poet and hymn-writer that he won his fame. He more than anyone else gave the growing Methodist movement a voice, made it conscious of itself, showed it its soul. All in all he wrote some 850 hymns in Welsh, besides a considerable number in English (but these are relatively insignificant). Through these hymns, with their rich content of experience and their outstanding lyrical power, he has cast a spell over the mind of Welsh-speaking Wales which endures to this day.

It was not only as the singer of the movement that Williams

---

1 First published in *Brycheiniog*, 17 (1976–77), the journal of the Brecknock Society.

won recognition. He was also known as a guide of souls, a wise spiritual counsellor and a writer on the spiritual life. Much of his wisdom is manifest in the hymns, which are no mere emotional outpourings (though they often are that) but expressions of deep Christian experience. But it finds expression also in two long poems, of which I shall have to speak, and in a modest but valuable body of prose writing. His insights are deep, his judgments prudent, and he says what he thinks, without the false delicacy which reduced the nineteenth century to silence on certain matters.

The world will never take a man seriously as a writer and teacher if he writes in a language which no one outside his own small country understands, and never finds a competent translator. How much influence would Kierkegaard have had if his works had existed only in Danish? Yet Pantycelyn is no mere provincial notability, but one who is part of the history of Christianity in this island, and one of its compelling voices for those who can hear.

He had been trained as a doctor, and was well read in the physical science of his time, in geography and anthropology. He tried to see Christianity, and to make his public see it, in a broad context. Of course too he was well read in theology, though he was not himself a systematic theologian; he was the poet and analyst of the spiritual life. And even here he is not the author of a systematic doctrine; there is no distinctive Pantycelyn school of spirituality. His spirituality is in essentials that of the movement which he served, as seen and expressed and illuminated by him. In poetic narrative, in prose dialogue and in lyric expression he gives us a graphic portrayal of what it is like to live the Christian life.

I propose to take up three key points in his doctrine, and to show how his characteristic insights bear upon them.

1. *Pilgrimage*

It is a commonplace that the Christian life may be seen as a journey. The Bible and Christian tradition provide a wealth of images under which this journey may be portrayed. Prominent among them is that of a desert march, as of the Israelites proceeding from Egypt to Canaan, or from exile in Babylon back to Judaea. Often the goal is said to be Jerusalem, or Mount Zion. One may speak of a company of travellers, or of an individual braving the journey alone as in Bunyan's famous work. In either case it is a fighting journey; Israel has to contend with hostile tribesmen, and the individual pilgrim meets a series of friends and seducers. And there is an ever-present danger of losing the way.

The journey from Egypt is to the fore in many of Pantycelyn's hymns, notably in 'Guide me, O thou great Jehovah', the only one of his hymns which has become well known in an English version. Yet though Israel marched out of Egypt as a body, Pantycelyn here speaks as an individual, as if he were doing the pilgrimage alone, with a pillar of cloud and fire, a miraculous supply of food and drink, and a guided crossing of Jordan all to himself. And that is his general habit. In fact, however much the Old Testament precedent may count for on the surface, one is led to conclude that deep down in Pantycelyn's mind Bunyan's model was the determining one. Then too one finds that besides the enemies who beset him with their fiery darts, and the general description of the terrain as desert, he also meets with streams and floods, and with a succession of steep hills and threatening crags which belong unmistakably to the landscape of Wales. Indeed, tradition associates one passage in a hymn with a particularly dangerous mountain track, in the gorge of the Tywi just north of Ystrad-ffin, which he must often have passed, and that in all weathers, on his frequent journeys to and from Llangeitho.

It is not however in the pilgrimage hymns, but in the long poem *Theomemphus*, that Pantycelyn gives us his fullest and most systematic chart of the Christian's way through life. The poem was conceived and executed in conscious rivalry with Bunyan. Unlike *The Pilgrim's Progress,* which picks up its hero's story only at the moment of his conversion, *Theomemphus* traces its hero's spiritual history from the cradle to the grave; and whereas Bunyan's pilgrim is separated from his family and neighbours, a solitary traveller whose only friends or enemies are those whom he meets on his way, Theomemphus is shown experiencing the vicissitudes of sin and grace in the bosom of a Christian community, undergoing its discipline, rising to a position of influence within it, having an unhappy love affair and later on an unhappy marriage, but always as a real man and living in real circumstances. Pantycelyn says he has tried to make him a typical representative of the New Testament Christian, in the light of Scripture but also of contemporary experience. And whereas, in *The Pilgrim's Progress*, Christian's spiritual conflicts are all shown as conflicts with external enemies, Pantycelyn lets us follow the internal conflicts in Theomemphus' soul. In a word, his account of the spiritual life is fuller, more realistic and more intimate than Bunyan's.

If the pilgrimage is thus in sober fact a man's life lived in society, what becomes of the incidents of the journey, the enemies who beset the road and the physical difficulties which obstruct it? The enemies will include both spiritual assailants, the host of hell, and also human opponents or tempters. The physical difficulties will mean both external circumstances and conflicts internal to the soul. Pantycelyn's account of these things of course takes a slant from his own beliefs and experiences and those of his associates; but it shows also a breadth of view which transcends sect and party, and a grasp of essentials which is not outdated by the lapse of more than two centuries. Naturally so, for after all the tradition of evangelical belief and evangelical experience is still vigorous. The modern convert, just as much as Theomemphus, may have trouble with conflicting doctrines and theories, sometimes even the same ones, as for instance antinomianism. Like Theomemphus too, he may have to learn to distinguish between an erotic infatuation and a genuine Christian love. He may have to learn to disarm bitter opposition and prejudice. There have of course been some changes of emphasis. We tend nowadays not to be obsessed with a crushing sense of guilt associated with a fear of hell, as earlier generations were. But we are very conscious of our psychological tangles, and here at least we may find some common ground with Pantycelyn.

Calvinism had its doctrine of the total corruption of our fallen human nature, and offsetting that a doctrine of sanctification, i.e., the gradual victory of grace in subduing unruly passions and bringing order into the soul. Pantycelyn has no thought of challenging this doctrine; he fully accepts it; but as one who might have been a physician and who was in fact a skilful analyst and counsellor, he writes as much like a psychologist as a theologian. What is wrong with the human soul is that its passions are in disorder. There is nothing wrong with the passions in themselves. God created them. But they can only work in harmony when governed and integrated by a firm attachment to God, and in fallen human nature that does not happen. The meaning of sanctification is precisely to put the love of God in control and to integrate all the other affections around it. So Pantycelyn prays in one hymn: '*O! sancteiddia f'enaid, Arglwydd, / Ym mhob nwyd, ac ym mhob dawn*' ('O sanctify my soul, Lord, in every passion, and in every gift'). He goes on to recognize that this can only happen if he is made somehow a partaker in the divine nature: '*Planna'r egwyddorion hynny / Yn fy enaid bob yr un, / Ag sydd megis peraroglau ...*' ('Plant those principles in my soul, every one of them, which are like sweet odours ...'). But to receive the divine nature is not to lose his own. The soul is to be sanctified not by the removal of the passions, nor by their stern subjection; it is to be sanctified *in* all the passions, by their being brought into the fragrant harmony for which they were originally meant. Similarly Pantycelyn is not afraid of pleasure as so many nineteenth-century Christians were. It has been remarked how frequently the word *mwynhau* (to enjoy) occurs in his writings. The saints, he says (in *Theomemphus*), have enjoyed all sorts of pleasures and there is nothing wrong in that: '*Mae pleser yn gyfreithlon, – pam cafodd nwydau eu rhoi / Os rhaid oddi wrth wrthrychau yn wastad inni ffoi?*' ('Pleasure is lawful, – why were passions given if we have to be constantly in flight from objects?') Pantycelyn can say this without for a moment forgetting that the pleasure which overwhelms all others is the enjoyment of God.

2. *The goal of the pilgrimage*

The goal of the Christian's journey is heaven, and we conventionally picture it under the image of the heavenly city, golden, gem-adorned, conjubilant with song. Pantycelyn knows this imagery as well as the rest of us. But he knows too that behind all this hard, sensuous glitter there is something far deeper and of mysterious import. He knows that in reality heaven is the place – any place – where God is seen and possessed and enjoyed; and it is thus that he prefers to speak of his goal. Here again we find the word *mwynhau*. And when an old hand in spirituality, like Pantycelyn, talks in this way of enjoying God, it is not the emotionalism of the convert or the sentimentalism of the conventional worshipper that is finding expression. Talk like this is characteristic of the mystical strain in religion, and its constant recurrence in Pantycelyn marks his devotion as belonging to that strain. He is one of God's most passionate lovers. He looks towards him, even in this life, with a contemplative ardour which heaven will enhance and make perfect; at the same time he knows that the object of his loving gaze is incomprehensible, yet in spite of (or rather, because of) its incomprehensibility it is irresistibly attractive.

Pantycelyn has an overwhelming sense of God, and of God in Christ, and of Christ as God. This comes out strongly in the hymns, and is the whole substance of his long poem *Golwg ar Deyrnas Crist* ('A Prospect of the Kingdom of Christ'). This is a poem on a truly cosmic scale, describing the career of Christ from the moment in eternity when he was appointed to become Creator of the world, and then to become its Saviour and King, until the moment at the end of time when, having obtained an unchallenged kingship over all creation, he will hand it over to the Father. This is not the 'man for others' in whom our anaemic moralisers would have us put our trust. This is the God-Man for God and for man, the Victor over death and hell, the Pantokrator. In him Pantycelyn sees the source and end of his own being.

Of course he sings the praises of the Saviour and the work that was done on Calvary. With eager devotion he contemplates the cross, the blood and wounds, the death-stroke, the crucified but victorious Lamb. If I do not dwell upon this aspect of his writing, it is because he celebrates the same themes, and in the same language, as all the evangelical hymn-writers of his time. He has nothing distinctive except an interesting turn of phrase or imagery now and then.

Where he stands forth as splendidly himself is in his paeans of praise to Christ in glory. Outstanding among his themes is the all-surpassing beauty of Christ, and he sings of it in terms which often echo the Song of Songs: '*Rhosyn Saron, / Ti yw tegwch nef y nef*' ('Rose of Sharon, thou art the beauty of the heaven of heaven'). Or again:

Gwyn a gwridog yw fy Arglwydd,
　Gwyn a gwridog yw ei wedd;
Brenin y brenhinoedd ydyw
　Yma a thu draw i'r bedd;
　　Mae dy degwch
　Wedi f'ennill ar dy ôl.

(White and ruddy is my Lord, white and ruddy is his countenance; King of kings is he, here and beyond the grave; thy beauty has drawn me after thee.)

And it is not only Christ's visible appearance that holds Pantycelyn spellbound. He hears the voice of the Beloved calling him out from the world and its pleasures. The words of Jesus are like wine, and when he speaks all the voices of creation fall silent. Elsewhere again, with a renewed echo of the great Song, Christ is likened to a fruit tree; and Pantycelyn adds the touch that its root is on earth and its branches in bright heaven. Under this tree he will eat and drink:

Yno boed fy mwyd a'm diod,
　Dan ganghennau gwych y pren
Sydd â'i wreiddyn ar y ddaear,
　Ei frigau yn y nefoedd wen;
Dyn â'r Duwdod ynddo'n trigo,
　Ffrwythau arno'n tyfu'n llawn;
Cysgod dano i'r ffyddloniaid
　O foreddydd hyd brynhawn.

(There let my food and drink be under the fine branches of the tree whose root is on the earth and its branches in bright heaven; a man in whom the Godhead dwells, fruit growing upon him in abundance; under him is shade for the faithful from morning until evening.)

Pantycelyn, who as we know is no despiser of pleasure, does not hesitate to speak of the pleasure (*pleser*), delight (*difyrrwch*) and enjoyment (*mwynhau*) that he finds in the contemplation of Christ; but the key word to describe his response to the vision is of course love (*cariad*). It is a flame that is kindled in him by God's own eternal love: '*Fflam o dân o ganol nefoedd yw ...*' ('It is a flame of fire from midmost heaven ...'). He says that it 'beats all loves down' and 'swallows up all the base names of earth in his name':

Wel dyma'r cariad sydd yn awr
Yn curo pob cariadau i lawr,
Yn llyncu enwau gwael y llawr
  Oll yn ei enw'i hun.

Here again we find Christ eclipsing every object in the world. And of course he must, being who he is. Christ, being God, is not just very beautiful, but infinite in beauty. That is why his voice silences all the voices of creation and his name swallows up every name. Total eclipse comes over all created beauties when God appears: '*Mae twllwch dudew'n dod / Ar bopeth hyfryd glân ...*' ('Thick black darkness comes over every bright and pleasant thing ...'). God alone 'is beautiful, is great, and all in all in heaven and earth'. Though his nature is in itself incomprehensible to us, it is revealed in sovereign splendour in Christ, and the sight of that splendour is the heart of Pantycelyn's religion.

3. *The approach to the goal*

The recent convert starting out on his pilgrimage knows his goal, and knows that he will meet difficulties on the way; but through sheer lack of experience, in the face of all warnings he is apt to underestimate the difficulties of the journey and the time it will take. What happens to him as he progresses through the years into later life? Distant though the goal is, and fully attainable only in heaven, can he hope to find himself in this life drawing perceptibly nearer to it? Yes, sometimes and to some extent; but there will be discouragements and paradoxes, and he may often feel as if no progress is being made.

Let us consider. In order that the pilgrim may be conscious of drawing nearer to his goal, two conditions must be satisfied, and there are difficulties attached to both.

(a) He must be conscious of a growing recollection, an awareness of God which becomes gradually more habitual and more intimate. Now, the pilgrim may indeed have such an experience. But he will also be apt to find that his communications with God become less verbalised and tend towards silence and stillness; also that the terms in which he has been used to thinking of God begin to lose their power as he more and more sees their inadequacy. And so he may be tempted to think he is losing God just when he is finding him.

(b) Full communion with God is not possible while sin remains in us, and the Christian life is a continual struggle, first to avoid sinful actions, and then to kill their roots in our nature; not the passions, of course, but the self-assertive principle which has thrown the passions into disorder. The pilgrim may have some real success in the struggle and yet may fail to know it; for as time goes by he is constantly discovering greater depths of evil in himself, of which he had not previously been aware. Such growing awareness of one's own evil nature is a sign of progress, but the pilgrim may be so discouraged by what he sees that he overlooks the significance of the fact that he has gained the power to see it and the grace to hate it.

Here is paradox; here are conflicting trends. The Christian pilgrim, confident that in heaven he will live amid light and joy perpetual, is tempted to hope that he may obtain a foretaste even here, that as he approaches the end of his earthly course there may be for him a settled state of light at eventide. But the record of the actual experience of Christians shows rather a chequered picture of alternating light and darkness.

Pantycelyn knows the extremes of light and darkness. While his mind is fixed on God, all is well; but when he turns and looks at himself, all is darkness and guilt and fear. He complains that his sin is keeping God at a distance from him; he laments that he cannot refrain from sin, and sometimes that he cannot even truly repent. Consequently '*Y mae arnaf fil o ofnau, / Ofnau mawrion o bob gradd*' ('A thousand fears are upon me, / Great fears of every degree'). He speaks of 'fear, the greatest enemy' – '*Concro ofn, y gelyn mwyaf*' – which nothing short of God's own power can overcome. In his blackest moment he even fears that he has never really received the forgiveness of sins, and never will. Elsewhere he pleads for assurance that God's forgiveness is equal to dealing with 'one who falls a hundred times into the same fault'.

> *Beth yw pwysau'r beiau mwyaf*
>   *A faddeui? – o ba ri'?*
> *Pa un drymaf yw fy mhechod*
>   *Ai griddfannau Calfari?*

(What is the weight of the greatest faults that thou forgivest? – what their number? Which weighs heavier, my sin or the groans of Calvary?)

These are the extremes of darkness, although the virtue of hope survives even in the darkness. Striking though their expression is in the hymns, these extremes do not represent the general run of Pantycelyn's experience. The dominating fact is still his vision of the goal, the goal of total sanctification, a state of total adherence to God and total absorption in the vision of him. He wonders whether a foretaste of the splendour may not be possible in this life. Thus in one hymn he asks, '*O! pam na chaf i ddechrau'n awr / Fy nefoedd yn y byd*' ('O why may I not begin my heaven now in the world?'), and elsewhere:

> *O! am nerth i dreulio 'nyddiau*
> *Yng nghynteddoedd tŷ fy Nhad;*
> *Byw yng nghanol y goleuni,*
> *Twllwch obry dan fy nhraed ...*

(O for strength to pass my days in the courts of my Father's house; to live in the midst of the light, darkness down under my feet ...)

But this can only happen when final victory is won over sin. And when may that be? There is a group of hymns in which he hopes and prays that it may happen in this life. 'This side of the grave', he says once, and again 'before evening' and 'before sunset'. And there is a fine hymn in which he says the same thing in an indirect way. Like the Bride in the Song of Songs, he looks for the Beloved to come leaping upon the mountains, bounding over the hills:

> *'Rwy'n edrych, dros y bryniau pell,*
> *Amdanat bob yr awr;*
> *Tyrd, fy Anwylyd, mae'n hwyrhau,*
> *A'm haul bron mynd i lawr.*

(I am looking over the distant hills for thee every hour; come my Beloved, it is getting late, and my sun is about to set.)

In such ways Pantycelyn expresses his longings, but he leaves the time of their fulfilment, here or hereafter, to God. He knows that victory can never be his own achievement, but must come as a gift. So let it come when it will, he says; he will be found ready and waiting.

Behind all these hymns of long-deferred hope, the Welsh landscape perpetually asserts itself, the hills and the changeful weather. Often we find that the pilgrim is travelling by night, perhaps a stormy night with chilly adverse winds. One hymn is devoted entirely to praying for the coming of daylight and a change in the wind. Or perhaps it is not night, but he is journeying through stormy weather, under black clouds; and we hear his joy as he sees a break in the cloud and feels the wind changing:

> *Mi wela'r cwmwl du*
>   *Yn awr ymron â ffoi,*
> *A gwynt y gogledd sy*
>   *Ychydig bach yn troi;*
> *'N ôl tymestl fawr, daw yn y man*
> *Ryw hyfryd hin ar f'enaid gwan.*

(I see the black cloud now about to flee, and the wind from the north is veering just a little; after a great storm, there will shortly come pleasant weather upon my feeble soul.)

The hills are everywhere in these hymns. Those which he has to scale are of course the difficulties of life. But the goal of the journey, the heavenly city, is also a city on a hill, and sometimes it is glimpsed far, or not so far, ahead. Or again it is over the hills that the Beloved is to come, as the Bridegroom over the hills of Palestine; Pantycelyn desires to see the hill tops which the Beloved haunts, and he loves 'the wind which flies over my pleasant Canaan': *''Rwyf yn caru'r gwynt sy'n hedeg / Dros fy Nghanaan hyfryd wiw'*. To me at any rate, the thought of Pantycelyn is inseparable from that of the hills and the changeable weather upon them. I picture him at home in his

Over the Distant Hills

farm on the slope of a valley, reading and writing in his upstairs room or taking a hand in the work of the farm. I see him riding forth on his preaching journeys, through narrow gorges and over dizzy heights. I hear the beat of his horse's hooves as he breasts the slope, and hails the break in the black cloud, and feels the first breath of the south wind, and pauses a while to look longingly over the distant hills.

HYMN TRANSLATIONS

H. A. HODGES translated a number of Welsh hymns into English. Some were literal prose translations, while others were metrical adaptations. They include the following, given here with their Welsh originals.[1]

1. The first and last verses of a three-stanza hymn by William Williams (1717–91) of Pantycelyn, published in 1758. The translation appeared in the booklet published for the 'Act of Praise' held by the Hymn Society of Great Britain and Ireland at Tabernacle Welsh Baptist Chapel, The Hayes, Cardiff, during the Society's Annual Conference in July 1975, when H. A. Hodges lectured on Williams Pantycelyn. The translation was subsequently included in *Hymns and Psalms: A Methodist and Ecumenical Hymn Book* (London: Methodist Publishing House, 1983).

Yn Eden, cofiaf hynny byth,
Bendithion gollais rif y gwlith;
  Syrthiodd fy nghoron wiw:
Ond buddugoliaeth Calfari
Enillodd hon yn ôl i mi;
  Mi ganaf tra fwyf byw.

---

[1] In his volume, *Participation in God: A Forgotten Strand in Anglican Tradition* (London: Darton, Longman and Todd, 1988), A. M. Allchin says that most of the English translations of Williams Pantycelyn's hymns which are included in the chapter 'Man as God and God as Man: Charles Wesley and Williams Pantycelyn' were by 'the late Professor H. A. Hodges, a pioneer of Pantycelyn studies in England'. However, since he does not specify which of those translations were by Hodges, it has been decided not to include them here.

Ffydd, dacw'r fan, a dacw'r pren
Yr hoeliwyd arno Dwysog nen
   Yn wirion yn fy lle:
Y ddraig a 'sigwyd gan yr Un,
Cans clwyfwyd dau, concwerodd un,
   A Iesu oedd Efe.

Can I forget bright Eden's grace,
My beauteous crown and princely place,
   All lost, all lost to me?
Long as I live I'll praise and sing
My wondrous all-restoring King,
   Victor of Calvary.

Lo! Faith, behold the place, the tree
Whereon the Prince of Heaven, for me,
   All innocent, was nailed;
One here has crushed the dragon's might;
Two fell, but One has won the fight;
   Christ Jesus has prevailed.

2. The last two verses of the hymn, *''Rwy'n dy garu er nas gwelais'* ('I love thee although I have not seen thee'), by William Williams (1717–91) of Pantycelyn, first published in 1763. The translation appeared in *Threshold of Light: Prayers and Praises from the Celtic Tradition*, ed. A. M. Allchin and Esther de Waal (London: Darton, Longman and Todd, 1986).

Nid oes yno ddiwedd canu,
   Nid oes yno ddiwedd clod,
Nid oes yno ddiwedd cofio
   Pob cystuddiau a fu'n bod:
      Byth ni dderfydd
   Canmol Duw yn nhŷ fy Nhad.

Dechrau canu, dechrau canmol
  (Ymhen mil o filoedd maith)
Iesu, bydd y pererinion
  Hyfryd draw ar ben eu taith:
    Ni cheir diwedd
    Byth ar sŵn y delyn aur.

Yonder there is no end of singing,
  Yonder there is no end of praise,
Yonder there is no end of remembering
  Every past trouble:
    Never will it cease,
    The praise of God in my Father's house.

A beginning of song, a beginning of praise
  (At the end of a thousand long ages)
To Jesus, will be the joy of the pilgrims
  Yonder at the end of their journey:
    There will never be an end
    To the sound of the golden harp.

3. The first three and the last verse of a six-stanza hymn by William Williams (1717–91) of Pantycelyn, published in 1771. The translation appeared in *Threshold of Light: Prayers and Praises from the Celtic Tradition*, ed. A. M. Allchin and Esther de Waal (London: Darton, Longman and Todd, 1986).

Mi wela'r cwmwl du
  Yn awr ymron â ffoi,
A gwynt y gogledd sy
  Ychydig bach yn troi;
'N ôl tymestl fawr, daw yn y man
Ryw hyfryd hin ar f'enaid gwan.

Ni phery ddim yn hir
  O'r ddu dymhestlog nos;
Ni phwyntiwyd oesoedd maith
  I neb i gario'r groes;
Mae'r hyfryd wawr sy'n goleuo draw
Yn dweud bod bore braf gerllaw.

Mi welaf olau'r haul
  Ar fryniau tŷ fy Nhad,
Yn dangos imi sail
  Fy iechydwriaeth rad;
Fod f'enw i fry ar lyfrau'r nef,
Ac nad oes dim a'i blotia ef.

Melys fel diliau mêl,
  A maethlon er iachâd
Yw holl geryddon nef
  A gwialenodau 'Nhad:
Pob croes, pob gwae, pob awel gref
Sydd yn aeddfedu saint i'r nef.

I see the black cloud
  Now about to flee,
And the wind from the north
  Is veering just a little;
After a great storm, there will shortly come
Pleasant weather upon my feeble soul.

Nothing will remain long
  Of the black stormy night;
Long ages have not been appointed
  For anyone to carry the cross;
The fair dawn that shines yonder
Says that a fine morning is on the way.

I see the sunlight
    On the hills of my Father's house,
  Showing me the foundation
    Of my free salvation;
That my name is on high on the books of heaven,
And that there is nothing that can blot it out.

Sweet as the honeycomb,
    And nourishing for healing,
  Are all heaven's chastisements
    And the strokes of my Father's rod:
Each cross, each woe, each strong breeze
Matures saints for heaven.

4. The first verse is by the Calvinistic Methodist exhorter and almanack publisher, John Roberts ('Siôn Robert Lewis'; 1731–1806) of Holyhead. The other two verses were published anonymously in 1795 in a hymn-book prepared for the use of the Welsh Calvinistic Methodists. The second verse is sometimes attributed to the Independent minister, Dr George Lewis (1763–1822) of Llanuwchllyn. The translation appeared in *Threshold of Light: Prayers and Praises from the Celtic Tradition*, ed. A. M. Allchin and Esther de Waal (London: Darton, Longman and Todd, 1986). In his lecture on William Williams of Pantycelyn to the Hymn Society of Great Britain and Ireland in 1975, H. A. Hodges refers to the metre of this hymn as 'the powerful 2.88.888 metre, which is not used in English' and which was possibly devised by Williams Pantycelyn.

  Braint, braint
Yw cael cymdeithas gyda'r saint
Na welodd neb erioed ei maint;
  Ni ddaw un haint byth iddynt hwy;
Y mae'r gymdeithas yma'n gref,
  Ond yn y nef hi fydd yn fwy.

Hymn Translations

Daeth trwy
Ein Iesu glân a'i farwol glwy'
Fendithion fyrdd – daw eto fwy:
    Mae ynddo faith ddiderfyn stôr;
Ni gawsom rai defnynnau i lawr;
    Beth am yr awr cawn fynd i'r môr.

Gwledd, gwledd
O fywyd a thragwyddol hedd
Sydd yn y byd tu draw i'r bedd;
    Mor hardd fydd gwedd y dyrfa i gyd
Sy'n byw ar haeddiant gwaed yr Oen
    O sŵn y boen sy yn y byd!

Bright, bright
The fellowship of saints in light,
Far, far beyond all earthly sight.
    No plague can blight, no foe destroy.
United here they live in love:
    O then, above how deep their joy!

Set free
By Jesu's mortal wounds are we,
Blest with rich gifts – and more shall be.
    Blessings has he in endless store:
Some drops are showered upon us here;
    What when we hear the ocean's roar?

Deep, deep
The feast of life and peace they keep
In that fair world beyond death's sleep.
    Our hearts will leap their joys to see
Who, with the Lamb's dear merits graced,
    All sorrow past, reign glad and free.

5. The following three verses appeared at various points in the collection of 1806 in which Ann Griffiths' hymns were first published. All three were attributed to her at one time, but that attribution is now generally rejected. H. A. Hodges was particularly dubious regarding the attribution to Ann of the third, as it 'conspicuously lacks the crispness of thought and expression which we associate with her work'. His metrical translations of the three were published in *Homage to Ann Griffiths* (Penarth: Church in Wales Publications, 1976).

Ni eill y moroedd mawrion llydain
  Guddio pechod o un rhyw;
Ac ni allodd dylif cadarn
  Ei foddi'n wir, mae'n awr yn fyw;
Ond gwaed yr Oen fu ar Galfaria,
  Haeddiant Iesu a'i farwol glwy',
Ydyw'r môr lle caiff ei guddio,
  Byth ni welir mono mwy.

Not the great wide-rolling oceans
  E'er can hide man's sin away;
Not the mighty flood could drown it,
  It is living still today;
But the precious blood and merits
  Of the Lamb that once was slain –
There's the ocean that can hide it;
  It will ne'er be seen again.

Nid oes gwrthrych ar y ddaear
  A leinw'm henaid gwerthfawr drud;
Fy unig bleser a'm diddanwch
  Yw hyfryd wedd dy wyneb-pryd;
Gwedd dy wyneb dyr y clymau
  Â phob creadur ar y llawr,
Ac a wna enw câr a chyfaill
  Yn ddim, er mwyn ei Enw mawr.

There is not on earth an object
    That can bring content to me;
My sole pleasure, my sole comfort,
    Is thy glorious face to see;
This can break the bonds that bind me
    To all creatures here below;
Friends and kinsfolk shrink to nothing
    If but his great Name I know.

O! Arglwydd Dduw rhagluniaeth
    Ac iachawdwriaeth dyn,
Tydi sy'n llywodraethu
    Y byd a'r nef dy hun;
Yn wyneb pob rhyw g'ledi
    Y sydd, neu eto a ddaw,
Dod gadarn gymorth imi
    I lechu yn dy law.

Lord God, from whose deep counsels
    Salvation had its birth,
Thou only art the ruler
    Of all in heaven and earth;
In face of tribulation,
    Whatever may betide,
Let thy strong grace assist me
    Beneath thy hand to hide.

PART TWO

Ann Griffiths

HOMAGE TO ANN GRIFFITHS: AN INTRODUCTION[1]

I

In paying homage to Ann Griffiths (1776–1805) we celebrate an outstanding figure in the literary and religious history of Wales. Yet at first sight this farmer's daughter and farmer's wife, who spent the whole of her short life in one place on the southern slopes of the Berwyn range in north-east Wales, may not appear so very remarkable.

She is chiefly known as a hymn-writer, a few of whose verses are among the best-loved hymns of Wales, though others are not so well known. But behind the hymns is a person, a character, a spiritual vision of a distinctive quality. The life which she lived at Dolwar Fach won for her a reputation for personal wisdom and sanctity which even to this day draws visitors (or should I say pilgrims?) to Dolwar.

Her maiden name was Thomas. The Thomases of Dolwar Fach were a farming family, prosperous by the standards of the place and the time, and of good standing in the local community. During the first twenty years or so of Ann's life they were keen Church-people, assiduous in attendance at the parish church and regular in family prayers. But there came a time when they were converted, one by one, to the vigorous and growing Methodist movement. They turned from the parish church and joined a Methodist group whose chapel

---

1   First published as the 'Introduction' in *Homage to Ann Griffiths* (Penarth: Church in Wales Publications, 1976), a volume under the editorship of James Coutts, which contained H. A. Hodges' translation of Saunders Lewis' lecture, 'Ann Griffiths: A Literary Survey', followed by the Welsh texts of Ann's hymns opposite Hodges' metrical English translations.

can still be seen at Pontrobert. The family prayers at Dolwar were thrown open to Methodists in the neighbourhood, and the house became a centre of worship and of hospitality for travelling preachers.

Ann's mother died when she was only eighteen and, her elder sisters having married and gone off to form homes of their own, Ann became the mistress of Dolwar Fach and remained so to the end of her life. With her in the house were her brother Edward and his wife (until 1801), her father (until his death in 1804) and her brother John (who outlived her). There was also Ruth Evans, Ann's maid and spiritual confidante, through whom Ann's hymns have been preserved for posterity; Ruth came in 1801 and left in 1805 when she married John Hughes.[2] In 1804 Ann took a husband, Thomas Griffiths of Meifod, who also came to live at Dolwar. In 1805 Ann died after giving birth to a daughter; the child lived only a fortnight, and Ann herself died a fortnight later.

Such was the household at Dolwar Fach during the years of Ann's brief flowering. Running the house was a demanding occupation, and she is not known to have travelled much except for her frequent visits to the chapel at Pontrobert and to other Methodist centres in the neighbourhood. The farthest journey she is known to have made was over the hills to Bala, where she and a party of local Methodists would often go to receive the ministrations of the Rev. Thomas Charles on his

---

2 [John Hughes (1775–1854) of Pontrobert was emerging in this period as a young local leader among the Welsh Calvinistic Methodists in Montgomeryshire. He would become one of the most prominent leaders of that denomination in the first half of the nineteenth century. John Hughes was a prolific author of religious literature in a range of genres. He is best known for his hymn 'O! anfon Di yr Ysbryd Glân' ('O send the Holy Spirit'). He was a key figure in the preservation and publication of Ann's hymns and letters. – Ed.]

Communion Sundays. These journeys to Bala were both a spiritual stimulus and a social occasion, and meant a great deal to Ann.

Ann in her pre-Methodist days was a lively girl, fond of dancing and partying. After her conversion she adopted a much more sober way of life, continually on guard against what she regarded as worldly vanities and frivolous pleasures; but it is to this period of strict self-discipline that her hymn-writing belongs. It was not uncommon for devout people in those days to keep a record of their spiritual life in the form of a diary. Instead of that, Ann recorded her thoughts and experiences in verse, and so came the hymns. Her inborn love of music and rhythm, denied its previous outlet, now found fulfilment in giving utterance to her spiritual life.

Ann was not a practised poet with detailed knowledge of the rules and techniques of the art. Before she started writing hymns she had probably written no verse except perhaps an occasional *englyn*.[3] The versification of her hymns is often rough and irregular, not observing strict syllabic metre; but its movement is swift, vigorous, often exuberant, even at times breathless with excitement. The hymns sprang from her deepest thoughts and feelings, and sometimes took shape in moments when she was so seized by the power of her vision that she forgot her surroundings and the passage of time. Though several of them show high literary capacity in their

---

3 [*Englyn* (pl. *englynion*) refers here to an epigrammatical four-line stanza, one of the so-called 'strict metres' which characterise traditional Welsh syllabic verse, written in *cynghanedd* (lit. 'harmony'), a complex system of structured assonance and alliteration within each line of poetry. Ann's father belonged to a local circle of folk poets, and some *englynion* by him survived in oral tradition, together with one attributed to Ann herself, composed when she was about ten years of age. See E. Wyn James, 'Cushions, Copy-books and Computers: Ann Griffiths (1776–1805), Her Hymns and Letters and Their Transmission', *Bulletin of the John Rylands Library*, 90:2 (Autumn 2014), p. 172. – Ed.]

working out, they were not meant as literary compositions, but as crystallisations of intense vision in memorable words. It is characteristic that her earliest composition in this mode is said to have been the second verse of Hymn VI in this collection, '*O! f'enaid, gwêl addasrwydd / Y Person dwyfol hwn*' ('O my soul, behold the appropriateness of this divine Person'). She was on her way home from a Methodist meeting, so we are told, when she stopped for a while to meditate in solitude, and found this stanza taking shape in her mind. Later she built the rest of the hymn around it. And several stanzas are said to have been formulated by her directly after emerging from a trance-like state of abstraction. One such is the first verse of Hymn VIII, '*Mae bod yn fyw o fawr ryfeddod*' ('It is a matter of great wonder to be alive'), and another is the last verse of Hymn III, '*O! ddedwydd awr tragwyddol orffwys*' ('O blessed hour of eternal rest'). This last is said to have come to her after a rapture which she experienced while riding home from one of her visits to Bala.

There are no clear indications of date attached to any of the hymns, but in a few instances conclusions may be drawn. They must all be later than the date of Ann's joining the Methodists, which was some time in 1797. Ann's letters express many of the same ideas and experiences as the hymns, and one is often tempted to think that a particular hymn may have been written about the same time as a particular letter; but plausible guesses are not proofs. Let it simply be said that there is no evidence that Ann stopped writing hymns before the time of her death. Even so, her hymns must all have been produced within a short period of some eight years. It is an impressive achievement.

II

Nothing could be less deliberate or purposeful than the way in which Ann's hymns came to be written and published.

Homage to Ann Griffiths

She had no ambition to be known as a poetess, and cared little for the rules and traditions of the craft. She wrote primarily for her own benefit, to crystallise her more vivid ideas and experiences in a memorable form, though she let her verses be known to her family and through them to a wider circle in the Methodist community. Her chosen confidante was Ruth Evans. Ann would jot down her verses on scraps of paper; and Ruth, who could read although she could not write, would find them and commit them to memory. Or sometimes Ann would recite her newest composition to Ruth directly. Ruth urged her to publish her hymns and so ensure their preservation, but Ann said they were not worthy of publication, and in the outcome it was Ruth's powerful memory which transmitted them to us; for after her marriage to John Hughes she dictated all that she remembered of the hymns to her husband, who wrote them down in one of the two manuscript books in which he made copies of Ann's hymns and letters. These manuscript books, now in the National Library of Wales at Aberystwyth, are the nearest we can come to Ann herself. Confirmation of this is given by the one letter of Ann's which survives in her own hand, which is also by now in the National Library of Wales. At the end she has written out a verse of one of her hymns (the first verse of Hymn IV), and the text she gives is identical with that in John Hughes' manuscript.

For a hundred years after Ann's death the John Hughes manuscript kept its secret, while Ann's hymns were published and became well known in badly altered versions. At last in 1905 the reading of the Hughes manuscript and publication of its contents by O. M. Edwards made clear how far even the best of them had departed from what Ann wrote. They had been influenced by a desire to smooth out Ann's irregular metres, and to break up her long trailing sentences into more manageable units; also apparently to remove her more recondite biblical allusions and tone down her more daring expressions. And not only so, but the hymns as Ann conceived them had been broken up into their constituent verses, which were then recombined to form hymns which Ann herself never knew. For example, the hymn numbered 421 in the hymn-book of the Welsh Independents, *Y Caniedydd* (1961), beginning 'O! am fywyd o sancteiddio', can now be seen to be put together out of verse 4 of Hymn V in this collection, verse 2 of Hymn XIV, and the single-stanza Hymn XXX. In view of the proven popularity of this hymn it would be churlish to complain, but it is true to say that though Ann Griffiths wrote these verses, she did not write this hymn.

III

One feature of Ann's literary style which is often remarked upon is the richness and boldness of her imagery. The principal and almost the sole source from which she draws it is the Bible, and in that she does not differ from the general run of devout writers in the tradition to which she belongs. What is outstanding in her work is the richness of the texture into which she weaves this material. It is safe to say that the reader of Ann who is not familiar with the text of Scripture, not just its general drift but its actual words and phrases, will constantly fail to see her point.

It is fair to add that the hymns are not all alike in the profusion of imagery used, or the skill with which the threads are put together, or indeed the accuracy with which the sources are used. To illustrate this last point, in Hymns XVII and XXI we have two images from the Song of Solomon to which Ann has given a peculiar turn of her own. The observant reader will detect other instances where biblical ideas and phrases are used in an inaccurate form. Perhaps Ann misunderstood them, or misremembered them, or perhaps she felt free, as a poet, to mould them to her own purpose. How drastically she allows herself to blend images may be seen in Hymn XXVII, where the reader is identified with Ruth gleaning in the field of Boaz, and this field is at the foot of Mount Sinai, where the crucifixion of Christ is taking place. With patience this can be unplaited, but some modern readers will need more patience than Ann's contemporaries probably did, for this kind of extravagance is less fashionable now than it was. On the other hand Ann can write a perfectly clear plain statement when she will. Take for example Hymn XV, or Hymn XVIII, or Hymn XIX.

I have spoken of the extravagant way in which Ann sometimes combines images; but at her best she reveals a remarkable power of construction. See for example how Hymn IV is held together by a series of variations on the meaning of the word 'way'. First of all it is a 'way' of life, the way of the cross, counter to a corrupt human nature, but leading to heaven at last. But in verses 2 and 3 we are reminded that Christ is the Way, and all that is said of the Way in these two verses is really about him. Then in verse 4 we are led back to the eternal Covenant, made before time was, in which Christ was designated to fulfil this role. Thus a meditation on the single word 'way' leads Ann from the thought of the troubles of her daily life into the eternal counsels of God.

Or take Hymn II. Here a series of images shows us how one who is conscious of herself as the chief of sinners can find her way to acceptance and a royal welcome in the presence of God. Already in verse 1 she is on Mount Sinai where God is revealed in glory, but like Moses she has to hide in a cleft in a rock to catch a glimpse of the glory as God passes by. In verse 2 she is allowed into the Tabernacle where she is somehow brought face to face with the atoning sacrifice of Christ. In verse 3 she is in the throne-room at Susa, approaching her unapproachable husband and reading his acceptance in the sceptre pointing at her; but in verse 4 she is the bride in the great Song of Songs, moving in solemn procession to where her royal bridegroom sits with countenance unclouded. In the last four lines we are at Patmos in the presence of the Amen, the Faithful Witness, and our final glance once more is into the mystery of the eternal Covenant.

Hymn XXII, Ann's longest hymn, is her masterpiece, but its rich theological content is its chief glory. Its literary structure calls for less comment. It is a reasoned meditation on the Incarnation, the Atonement and the Passion, and the Incarnation again. Then in the last two verses Ann turns from the recital of God's wondrous acts in Christ to contemplate the blessedness of union with God which is to be hers hereafter.

IV

But let us turn to the theological content. In her hymns Ann reveals a great deal about how she saw the Christian Faith and how she responded to what she saw. Let us take both points in turn.

It goes without saying that a hymn-writer of Ann's place and time would have much to say about her experience of sin and salvation and her beliefs with regard to these things. The first thing to be said of Ann is that she shared the typical salvation-experience of the movement to which she belonged, and that her doctrinal expressions are true to the standard Calvinism of the time. We hear constantly of man's corrupt and helpless state, and of the saving work of Christ on the cross, where he bore God's wrath on our behalf, paid our debt, paid our ransom, defeated and despoiled the forces of evil, and so on. It is the usual story, the usual imagery; yet on closer inspection we already see signs of Ann's peculiar point of view. Though she glorifies the precious blood, she does not invite us to watch the bleeding. She does not, like Isaac Watts, show us how sorrow and love flow mingling down, or ask where else there was ever such love and sorrow. She does not, like Thomas Lewis of Talyllychau, dwell upon the furrows ploughed into that fair back, and the other details of the crucifixion. Her attention is turned not upon the sufferings, but upon who it was that suffered – God himself, true God, the Creator, without whose sustaining power the human agents of his passion could not even have carried out their appalling work.

And not only so, but behind the paradox of who he is and what he endures Ann's mind sees into the reason why he endures it. He is indeed God, but God the Son, who alike in his glorious eternal being and in his incarnate life is wholly devoted to honouring the Father. His resolve to take our nature upon him was part of the eternal Covenant wherein, before the world began, the heavenly Three decreed what they would jointly and severally do for the salvation of future sinners. This deeply concerns us, and is celebrated by paeans of praise and gratitude on the part of the redeemed. Christian hymnody echoes with them, and Ann's voice is in the chorus. But what especially strikes her is how the process of man's salvation redounds to the glory of God. Christ's death saves us precisely because in dying so he honoured God's law, and the wonder is that the transgressors of the law go free without any diminution of the respect due to the law. Not that these insights are peculiar to Ann. They were expressly stated in the *Confession of Faith* of the Welsh Calvinistic Methodist Connexion, only eighteen years after her death; e.g. 'the law was magnified, justice satisfied, the divine government honoured, and all God's attributes were glorified, in the life and death of Christ' (*Confession of Faith*, section 18). But she is outstanding in the prominence which she gives to this aspect of the truth.

The fact is that her whole vision of life and being is less

man-centred and more God-centred than most people's. And what does God mean to her? Supreme sovereign power? Yes, of course, but there is something deeper than that. It is noticeable how often in these hymns she speaks of his infinity and his perfection. He is infinite in his being and in his attributes, infinite in mercy and infinite in righteousness, perfect and changeless. The thought of him troubles Ann with a numinous awe (Hymn XX); and yet she has a hunger which no created thing can satisfy, which reaches out for the Incomprehensible (Hymn XIV). She longs to see him as he is, and also to honour him as he should be honoured, by a purity of life which she knows is beyond her. And Christ? She sees him as the breaker of the barriers, the doer of the impossible. His very being is a paradox: God and man in one Person, the Creator tortured by his creatures, the great Resurrection put to death and in his very death giving life to dead souls (Hymn XXII). He enables the divine righteousness to smile radiantly upon sinners without any diminution of its just claims; for he pays the debt of honour which we all owed to the law, and makes possible for us through grace that purity to which of ourselves we could never aspire. All this he does in his incarnate life as God-man; so the Incomprehensible can in him be seen and touched and held. In this life we know him in part, but hereafter we shall see him as he is, and here and hereafter alike we have in him a visible object of worship.

V

The right response to this tremendous vision is detachment from created things and unqualified devotion to God in Christ. In Ann's writings we see how far she attained to this, and how far she saw she had still to go. Finite things cannot satisfy her, now that the vision of the Incomprehensible has captured and enlarged her longings (Hymn XIV). They are mere idols, unfit in any way to vie with the true Object of her devotion. And yet, despite the power of the vision and the work of grace within her, corruption is still there, and she keeps straying from her Lord.

So far this is what any devout but self-critical Christian might say; but not every such Christian would echo the emphasis which Ann places upon what she calls the sins of thought. Sins of thought? What does that mean? From what Ann says in her letters we can see that it means two things. Firstly it means allowing anything other than God to occupy a high place in one's interests. And secondly it means allowing oneself to think, even of God, according to one's own ideas and fancies instead of keeping close to what has been revealed. Ann follows the ancient tradition of Christian teaching, that the human imagination is an undependable, irresponsible faculty, generating fancies which only veil reality from us. Her desire is to pierce through to a clarity of vision which would kill all imaginations (Hymn XIX) and bring her every thought into captivity to Christ (Hymn XV).

I have already mentioned those 'visitations' to which Ann was subject, those moments of intense realisation in which she would lose consciousness of her surroundings for a time, and from which occasionally a verse or a hymn might be born. Sometimes it was a moment of joy which made her shout and sing, and sometimes an intense meditation from which she would emerge in tears. But either way it was a moment of vision, when for the time being her aspiration to clear knowledge of the mysteries of God seemed to be fulfilled. Her friends were puzzled and alarmed by these experiences. They had not inherited any traditional wisdom about dealing with such phenomena. We know from one letter that Ann herself sometimes doubted whether these moments of revelation were what they seemed to be; though in another letter we see her accepting them as genuine and as foreshadowings of fuller disclosures yet to come, here or hereafter. In Hymn IX we see her marvelling at the grace by which one so corrupt as she feels herself to be is admitted to the holy mountain and given a vision of God's glory unveiled; and she looks forward with longing to a time of total detachment from worldly things and total union with Christ.

Ann follows that tradition, Puritan as well as Catholic, according to which Christ is the soul's Bridegroom and her union with him is to be a marriage union. It is worthwhile to reflect on the implications of this. Some people when they hear talk of union with God, think at once of a loss of individual personality, as a drop of water loses its individual existence when it falls into the sea. But a marriage is nothing unless there are two parties, each distinctly aware of the other and of himself or herself in relation to the other. Ann in these hymns gives us a clear picture of the heaven to which she looks forward. Christ is even here the supreme object of her loving contemplation and worship; hereafter she will see him as he is, the Invisible, the Incomprehensible, and will apprehend the secret of his twofold nature and of his victorious death. She will, in the Psalmist's words, 'kiss the Son' for ever, turning from him nevermore. For her union with him means more than the vision of his glorious being. It means being invested with his likeness; and in the enjoyment of that likeness she will lose the very possibility of falling away.

It has been said of the hymn-writer, David Charles of Carmarthen (a brother of Thomas Charles), that, so contagious was his sense of wonder at the mysteries of the Faith, those who heard him preach were apt to be left in the same state of astonishment as he was himself. Something similar might well be said of Ann's hymn-writing. Her hymns are full of expressions of wonder, and her frequent emphasis on the paradoxes of the Christian story has often been remarked on as a feature of her literary style. It is so, but it is also more. Ann is a good hand at an epigram, and we can hardly doubt that she enjoys surprising us sometimes, but it is not done as a display of skill. It is her way of bringing us into her own state of astonishment at the inherent wonders of the Faith. These wonders can be seen, and Ann sees them, on three distinct levels. First comes wonder in the sense of sheer surprise, and the Christian story is full of surprises which Ann delights to savour and to exhibit to us. But second, wonder may mean a mingling of awe and admiration, such as we feel on contemplating the divine wisdom, love and power. In Addison's phrase which Wesley borrowed, we are 'lost in wonder, love and praise'. And third, wonder may mean the recognition of a mystery, an incomprehensibility, such as we always find in the long run when we look into the being of God and his actions towards us. Ann is filled with wonder in all these three senses, even in this life; and heaven to her means living in the midst of a sea of wonders.

Ann's water imagery combines three biblical images, namely the pool of Bethesda, the life-giving river in Ezekiel's vision and the river of water of life in Revelation, and her own contribution is to make these waters broaden out into a sea which has no shore and no bottom, but in which the redeemed can freely swim. It is worth while pausing a moment to realise the implications of this. There are people who feel that heaven, as a place of total fulfilment, must be a place of inaction, and they do not find the prospect attractive. But Ann's heaven is a sea of wonders where she is free to explore for ever without ever coming to a limit. One is reminded of St Gregory of Nyssa, who teaches repeatedly that there is no limit to our growth in perfection or in the knowledge of God, and that the life even of the glorified is not a static condition of finished achievement but a perpetual reaching forward (*epektasis*) to explore the Inexhaustible. We may take it as certain that Ann knew nothing of St Gregory of Nyssa, but she shares his insight, and her picture of the glorified soul perpetually exploring the breadth and depth of the sea of divine wonders, and never finding a limit, is her way of expressing it.

Is Ann a mystic? That depends on how we use the word; and it is used in so many senses by different people that it might be wiser to refrain from using it at all in a brief account like this. What is important, after all, is not to attach this or that label to Ann but to see clearly what kind of person she was. But at least one can indicate what the characteristics are which incline some people to use the label in question. They are the penetrating vision with which Ann *sees* what so many Christians half-hesitantly *believe*, the depth of her insight into the sea of wonders, and the intensity of her aspiration to union with God in Christ. Let the reader think on these things, and then speak of Ann as he finds appropriate.

A NOTE OF INTRODUCTION TO 'ANN GRIFFITHS: A LITERARY SURVEY'[1]

ANN GRIFFITHS (1776–1805) is a classic of Welsh literature and of Welsh spirituality. A farmer's daughter, and later a farmer's wife, amid the hills of Montgomeryshire, child of a traditionally Church-going family, in the years 1796–97 she underwent a typical evangelical conversion, and for the rest of her life was a leading figure among the Calvinistic Methodists of her area. Her literary remains comprise some thirty hymns and eight letters. There are things here which can be of value to all who care for the things of the spirit, and some things of special interest perhaps to members of the Fellowship of St Alban and St Sergius.

Ann's background reading was confined to the Bible (which she knew very well indeed), seventeenth-century Puritan writers such as Richard Baxter and John Bunyan, and eighteenth-century Welsh evangelical writers. The only systematic theology which ever came her way was that of Calvin; those around her, in so far as they paid any attention to the Anglican Prayer Book and Articles, accepted unhesitatingly a Calvinist interpretation of them. What is interesting is that in these surroundings, against this background, she reveals such a distinctive vision and experience of the Christian Faith in which elements that

---

1 First published in *Sobornost: The Journal of the Fellowship of St Alban and St Sergius*, series 5: no. 5 (Summer 1967), as an introduction by H. A. Hodges to his translation of Saunders Lewis' lecture, 'Ann Griffiths: A Literary Survey'.

are characteristically Calvinist are mingled with others which remind us of the Fathers and the early spiritual and theological tradition of the Church.

Psychologically Ann was something of an ecstatic. The early Methodists were a noisy and exuberant people, always ready to break out into shouts and songs of praise; but Ann was outstanding even among them for her liability to be carried away. Sometimes, when at home, she would shut herself up in her own room and remain there until the excitement passed over, and people working about the farm could hear her shouting and singing in her jubilation. On the other hand she was also liable to go off into an abstraction, a state of forgetfulness of herself and her surroundings, and immediately after being thus carried away she would sometimes compose a hymn, apparently based on her thoughts and experiences during her rapture. These are the 'visitations' referred to in Mr Saunders Lewis' article, whose significance Ann was sometimes tempted to doubt, and which led the Rev. Thomas Charles to speak as he did. We need not linger over them. What matters to us is the content of the faith and experience to which her hymns and letters bear witness.

Ann's hymnody is at one and the same time doctrinal and experiential. Her mind is always fixed upon great central mysteries of the Faith; but her clear vision of the mysteries causes them to be not mere articles of belief, but personal experiences for her.

Of these central mysteries, the Trinity is referred to least often and least explicitly in Ann's writings. She knows that heaven means being within 'the dwelling places of the Three in One' and in 'the endless peace of the holy Three'; but what interests her much more about heaven is that it means being with Christ. If she meditates on the relations between the Persons,

A Note of Introduction to Ann Griffiths

it is in connection with the work of our salvation that she does so. 'Sweet it is to remember the covenant made yonder by Three in One.' That is the eternal Covenant, made before the world was, wherein the Son accepted his Father's commission to become incarnate and suffer for the salvation of yet-to-be-created man. Calvinist piety dwells upon this Covenant as the timeless source of our salvation and the unchangeable ground of our election. Ann is true to her tradition in this.

It is not here, however, that she shows her distinctive gift of vision and expression, but in her treatment of the mystery of the Incarnation.

To begin with, she is one of those favoured souls to whom the absolute reality of God and the nothingness of created things in comparison with God are immediately obvious. She lives in the consciousness of this ontological gap, this incommensurability between the objects of common experience and the only Object in which the human spirit could find repose. The gap is wider than it should have been because man is not merely a creature, but a creature in rebellion, and therefore in a lost and damnable condition. One sees in her letters how present a reality this damnable condition is to Ann.

But Christianity is a gospel of reconciliation. There is a Sacrifice for sin, a Mediator and a Covenant. Ann does not, like some of Christ's lovers, dwell imaginatively upon the details of his Passion; her mind goes at once beyond all that to the question, 'Who was on the cross?' For the work that Christ did in atonement for man's sin was a work which could not have been done by anyone else. And that is not all. Christ does not merely win for us salvation from hell and sin; he calls us to union with himself, to union with One who is both man and God; and so he is a Mediator in an ontological sense too. Not only the gap made by sin, but the gap inherent in our created status, is filled by Christ, and this not primarily because of what he has done, but because of who he is. He has brought Deity within our range and made it, in his own Person, an object of worship and love.

Hence Ann's devotion centres upon Christ, in the wonder of his Person, in the paradox of his human birth and suffering, in his office as Priest and King and Mediator of the Covenant, and finally in his capacity as Bridegroom. The Person of the Bridegroom is an object to be contemplated under all these many aspects with unceasing delight; but it is also a mystery through which the human soul in a manner penetrates into the Infinite.

It is sometimes asked whether, and in what sense, Ann is a mystic, and whether her mysticism, or any mysticism, is compatible with Calvinism. The question is a serious one for those who think that mysticism means the swallowing up of the individual soul in some sort of Ground of Being, as against a personal relationship with a Lord who is also a Beloved. Ann's expressions, however, leave no doubt about the nature of her experience. Though she thinks of the Godhead as a shoreless, bottomless sea, she does not lose herself in it, but swims in it, alert and self-possessed, wondering always at its inexhaustibility. She thinks of union with Christ not under the image of being a member of his Body, but as a marriage union, which entails the distinctness of the parties, as well as their possession of a common nature. And while she sometimes kisses the Son, as in the Psalm, and his arm goes round her, as in the Song of Songs, her usual relation to him is that of gazing and wondering and worshipping. As a recent writer has said, her joy in her Bridegroom is not a passive enjoyment of sensuous or emotional delight, but the most active kind of joy that there is, the joy of gazing, of that act which the Greeks called *theoria* (contemplation).

Christian contemplation involves ruthless criticism of one's

A Note of Introduction to Ann Griffiths

own thoughts and fancies. God is the object at which we aim, but it is hard to keep the mind on target. Ann Griffiths knew this too, and knew where one principal difficulty lies. In one of her letters we find her confessing that she has long been failing to do justice to the nature and work of the Holy Spirit. It is interesting to notice how she describes her mistake: she calls it 'a fanciful, misguided thought'. And she goes on to aspire to a fuller faith in the personal indwelling of the Spirit in her life, 'and that through revelation, not imagination, thinking to comprehend in what manner or by what means it happens, which is real idolatry'. Here is the authentic note of primitive Christian tradition with its distrust of the imagination and its determination not to go beyond what has been revealed, 'O to penetrate into the knowledge of the only true and living God to such a degree as would be death to imaginations of every kind.' In this life perhaps we cannot be wholly free from them, but riddance of imagination is part of Ann's idea of heaven. 'There I shall exalt the Name which God set forth to be a Propitiation, without imagination, veil, or covering, and with my soul fully in his likeness.'

There is much more to be said; but let Mr Saunders Lewis say it.

ANN GRIFFITHS:
A LITERARY SURVEY[1]

by Saunders Lewis
translated into English by H. A. Hodges

LET ME BEGIN with an appeal to the Board of the University of Wales Press. Ann Griffiths is one of the great classics of our literature. One cannot discuss the poetry of the nineteenth century without starting with Ann Griffiths. Today [in 1965] we have no standard text of her hymns or of her letters. This is a pitiful state of things. Some first-rate scholar should be invited to prepare within two years a reliable and definitive text of the hymns and letters, because the letters are classics too. The short memoir of her, published by John Hughes of Pontrobert in 1846, should be included in the volume.[2]

---

1   An address delivered in Welsh to the Honourable Society of Cymmrodorion, 5 August 1965, during the National Eisteddfod of Wales at Newtown, Montgomeryshire. The original Welsh lecture was first published in the *Transactions of the Honourable Society of Cymmrodorion for 1965*. The English translation first appeared in *Sobornost: The Journal of the Fellowship of St Alban and St Sergius*, series 5: no. 5 (Summer 1967), and was republished in *Homage to Ann Griffiths*, ed. James Coutts (Penarth: Church in Wales Publications, 1976).
2   [In 1998 the prestigious private press, Gwasg Gregynog, which is appropriately based only a stone's throw from Ann Griffiths' home, published a critical edition of her hymns and letters, together with the memoir of her by John Hughes of Pontrobert and his letters to Ann and to his future wife, Ruth Evans, while she was a maid at Dolwar Fach. The editor was E. Wyn James, and the volume included an introduction by A. M. Allchin. In

The best text we have at present is in the invaluable little volume published by O. M. Edwards in 'Cyfres y Fil'[3] in 1905, sixty years ago. Would that someone of like vision to O. M. Edwards had presided over the University of Wales Press. The classic textual criticism of O. M. Edwards' book is two articles by the late D. Morgan Lewis which appeared in the journal, *Y Llenor* ('The Littérateur'), in 1924. *Cofiant Ann Griffiths* ('A Memoir of Ann Griffiths') was published by Morris Davies of Bangor exactly one hundred years ago. This should be republished, because it is one of the best memoirs of the century, indispensable even today, casting much light upon its subject and containing much criticism which still remains valuable. Morris Davies' book is a minor classic in its way and its influence can be seen in the novel *Gwen Tomos* by Daniel Owen.[4]

I shall not go into details today regarding the problems relating to the text of Ann Griffiths because this is one of the popular meetings of the Cymmrodorion rather than one of their academic ones. You all know that one letter and one verse of hers are preserved in her own handwriting. We have copies of some of her letters made by John Hughes of Pontrobert, copies which have to be treated with caution. It was he also who preserved her hymns, copying them, according to Morris Davies, from what his wife, Ruth

---

republishing the Saunders Lewis lecture here, the quotations from the O. M. Edwards edition of 1905 have been replaced by those of the critical edition of 1998; however, it should be noted that the changes in those quotations relate almost entirely to matters of punctuation and orthography. – *Ed.*]

3   A series of books in which many Welsh classics were reprinted. – *Translator*. [Saunders Lewis' own copy of the O. M. Edwards volume, which includes marginal notes by Saunders Lewis, was gifted by him to A. M. Allchin and came to Gladstone's Library at the same time as A. M. Allchin's papers. – *Ed.*]

4   [Daniel Owen (1836–95) is regarded as the first major Welsh novelist. His last novel, *Gwen Tomos*, was published in 1894. It has been suggested that the Gwen Tomos of the novel was based in part on Ann Griffiths. – *Ed.*]

Hughes, remembered of them, but copying some of them from Ann's own letters, according to O. M. Edwards and Morgan Lewis. I am inclined to doubt this; but the problem cannot be settled without thorough study.

I must pause a little to consider the relation between Ann Griffiths and John Hughes. He was a year older than she when, at the age of twenty-five, he lodged at Dolwar in 1800. Here is what he says about this period:

> The writer of this memoir was running a school in the neighbourhood of Dolwar Fechan, and lodged at Dolwar Fechan for several months. ... During this period, he was many times for several hours together in conversation with Ann on matters of Scripture and experience, and this with such delight that hours went by unnoticed ...

Ann spoke of the same period in a letter to him: 'You knew more of my story in all its wretchedness than anyone else.'

O. M. Edwards published, along with the work of Ann Griffiths, parts of certain manuscript books written by John Hughes – another proof of O. M. Edwards' critical genius. In these books John Hughes gives us copies of his own unpoetic poetry, minutes of *seiat* meetings[5] at Mathafarn, minutes of Association meetings,[6] and copies of his own letters to his

---

5   The *seiat* (pl. *seiadau*) was the fundamental institution of Welsh Methodism. It was the local in-group, whose association with other similar cells built up the whole Body of the movement. Unlike a Church congregation, whether Anglican or Nonconformist, the *seiat* admitted to membership only those who had given evidence of being genuinely converted persons, in the evangelical sense of that phrase. They met to compare and discuss their day-to-day experiences in the spiritual life, under the direction of the leader of the *seiat*. There might of course be Bible-reading, prayer and hymn-singing; but the central function of the *seiat* was to be the training school of a spiritual elite. – *Translator*.

6   An Association meeting (*Cymdeithasfa* or *Sasiwn* in Welsh) was a conference of preachers, teachers and leaders in the Methodist movement, held in various places at monthly or quarterly or longer intervals. – *Translator*.

Ann Griffiths: A Literary Survey

future wife, Ruth Evans, who was a maid at Dolwar from 1801 onwards. He was in the habit of reading parts of Ann's letters to him in the *seiadau*, and the *seiat* minutes and the letters to Ruth Evans show a close connection with the hymns and letters of Ann Griffiths. In some cases it is probable that a letter from her gave the start to a discussion at a *seiat* which followed the same lines. But, on the other hand, there can be no doubt that his letters to Ann were the occasion of much of her poetry. A series of examples could be given in proof of this. Here is one instance. In a letter to Ruth Evans, John Hughes says:

> As man draws a little nearer to his idols, God draws away from him a little. O that it might become an honest wakeful cry: 'What have I to do any more with idols?'; and also: 'Forsake me not, O Lord!'

Without altering the words, which come from the Old Testament Book of Hosea, Ann turned this into verse:

> *Beth sy imi mwy a wnelwyf*
>   *Ag eilunod gwael y llawr? ...*
>   *O! am aros*
>   *Yn ei gariad ddyddiau f'oes.*

(What have I to do any more with the base idols of earth? ... O to abide in his love all the days of my life.)

Why this very close affinity between Ann Griffiths and John Hughes in the days of their youth and vigour? It is my firm though unfashionable opinion that they were never in the slightest degree enamoured of one another on the natural level. There was too great a social gulf between them. The testimony of John Morgan of Mold (*Cymru*, 30 (1906), pp. 29–36) is definite and valuable on this point. And after John

Hughes left Dolwar it is clear that he hesitated and doubted whether she would be ready even to receive a letter from him, because her first sentence in her first answering letter is this:

> Dear brother,
> I have had this opportunity to send you these few lines, in order to show my readiness to receive and answer your substantial letter.

Intellectual friendship, the discovery in one another of a passionate interest in the same manner of understanding religion, that is what explains those 'several hours together in conversation with Ann on matters of Scripture and experience'. They were absurdly different from one another in appearance and nature. He was notoriously ugly, awkward and clumsy and without breeding. She was handsome and good-looking and very much a lady. For him nothing existed but the eternal things. Religion and godliness were his whole life. Not so with Ann. She knew of spiritual experiences and 'visitations' which pertain to a very high level of contemplative prayer. For example:

> Dear sister, I am sometimes swallowed up so much into these things that I completely fail to stand in the way of my duty with regard to temporal things, ... although it is very good here 'through the lattice', and the Lord sometimes reveals 'through a glass, darkly', as much of his glory as my weak faculties can bear.

But her letters continually complain of her fickleness, 'the various things which were calling me to go after them', 'failing to abide – continually departing', so that she was sometimes driven to doubt 'the verity of the visitations'. Worse than this – to her who had so clear and penetrating a mind and such spiritual genius, even the most lofty experiences of communion in prayer bore marks of weakness and sin:

Pan fo'r enaid mwya' gwresog
  Yn tanllyd garu'n mwya' byw,
Y mae'r pryd hynny yn fyr o gyrraedd
  Perffaith sanctaidd gyfraith Duw.

(When the most ardent soul is most alive with burning love, even then it falls short of attaining to the perfect holy law of God.)

There is no hint of a sign that John Hughes knew anything of experiences like this. Much more could be said of the 'experiential' life of Ann.

What then did Ann Griffiths get from John Hughes of Pontrobert? My answer is: theology. Theology was his element, and to her theology came to be bread and wine. Before John Hughes came to Dolwar she had already been to Bala, she had listened to sermons, she had kneeled to receive Communion from Thomas Charles, but she never found anyone who could open up the fields of theology to her. John Hughes was the only theologian with whom 'hours went by unnoticed' while she listened to him and asked questions and discussed. That was what she got from John Hughes, and it was this, the deep things of theology, that turned Ann Thomas of Dolwar into Ann Griffiths, one of the greatest poets of Wales.

For John Hughes as for Ann Griffiths it is God, and not the salvation of man, that is the centre of religion. John Hughes says:

He is God. He is Jehovah; let all flesh be silent. Thanks that he is what he is.

And again:

> If we think we are loving the Lord under the aspect of his mercy only, without being able to love him under the aspect of his righteousness and his holiness, in that case we are loving ourselves, not loving God.

For John Hughes the greatest evil which follows from refusing to believe the gospel is not man's perdition or the penalty which man suffers for sin, but rather and much more the 'dishonour done to God': 'The way to give the greatest honour to God is to venture upon his mercy according to his plan.' That is the key to the theology of John Hughes; his debt to the Old Testament is clear; and that is what Ann Griffiths learned from him and made the central point of her poetry.

Let me now briefly follow up these ideas, and the characteristic vocabulary of John Hughes, in a quotation or two from her letters. We should do well to remember that the letters of Ann Griffiths – however strange their idiom may be to us in the second half of the twentieth century – contain some of the loftiest religious prose in Welsh. Here is an example:

> As regards the dishonour done to God by giving the first place to secondary things, this simply is my mind: if nature must be pressed into the grasp of death because it is too weak to bear the fiery rays of the sun of temptations, I sometimes think I will gladly see myself stripped of my natural life (if need be) rather than that glory should go under a cloud while nature gets its own way and its objects.

And again in another letter:

> I should heartily wish to give all the praise to God the Word alone for leading me and upholding me thus far, and that what remains of my life might be spent in continual communion

with God in his Son, because I can never glorify him more than, or so much as, by believing and accepting his Son. Heaven help me to do that! – not for my own pleasure alone, but out of reverence for him.

Two lines of a hymn will be enough to show the same idiom and the same spirit: '*O! am gael ei hanrhydeddu / Trwy dderbyn iechydwriaeth rad*' ('O to get to honour it [the law] by accepting free salvation'). That is to say, it is in order to honour God that man accepts his own salvation. To honour God, not to save man, is the first and principal object of the gospel of salvation.

It is for this, to render to God the honour which is due to him, that the Incarnation – '*Duw y duwiau wedi ymddangos / Yng nghnawd a natur dynol-ryw*' ('The God of gods has appeared in the flesh and nature of human kind') – was and is, and that is the first and main significance of Calvary – to reintegrate worship into sacrifice; to restore honour:

Fy enaid trist, wrth gofio'r frwydyr,
 Yn llamu o lawenydd sydd;
Gweld y ddeddf yn anrhydeddus
 A'i throseddwyr mawr yn rhydd;
Rhoi Awdwr bywyd i farwolaeth
 A chladdu'r Atgyfodiad mawr;
Dwyn i mewn dragwyddol heddwch
 Rhwng nef y nef a daear lawr.

(My sorrowful soul, on remembering the battle, leaps for joy; it sees the law held in honour and its greatest transgressors going free; the Author of life put to death and the great Resurrection buried; eternal peace brought in between the heaven of heaven and earth below.)

To show how essential this thought is to the whole life of Ann

Griffiths, here is part of her letter to Elizabeth Evans, which speaks of what she hopes from death:

> Dear sister, ... I can say that this is what cheers me more than anything else these days – not death in itself, but the great gain that is to be got through it: to be able to leave behind every inclination that goes counter to the will of God, to leave behind every ability to dishonour the law of God ...

This assurance of the sublime holiness and infinity of God is the key to all the poetry of Ann Griffiths:

Yn yr adnabyddiaeth yma
  Mae uchel drem yn dod i lawr,
Dyn yn fach, yn wael, yn ffiaidd,
  Duw'n oruchel ac yn fawr.

(In this knowledge lofty looks are brought low; man is little, wretched, loathsome, God is sublime and great.)

Reverence, honour, glory – to give these to God: 'I thought that there was need to pass beyond brethren and graces, and love the Giver above the gift.' And then, of necessity: 'Of them all, it is the sin of the mind which presses most heavily upon me. ... I have never had a greater longing to be pure.' There you have the way of purgation and a 'road of meditation'.[7]

---

7   *Heol myfyrdod*. *Myfyrdod* is thought, study, meditation. *Heol* is a way or road, or a street in a town. The phrase here is taken from a passage in one of Ann's letters, which in turn is based upon Canticles 3:1–4. ['Canticles', like the 'Song of Songs', is another name for the 'Song of Solomon'. – *Ed.*] The Bride goes by night through the city, seeking her Beloved '*trwy yr heolydd a'r ystrydoedd*' in the Welsh Bible; 'in the streets, and in the broad ways' in the Authorised Version (A.V.) and the Revised Version (R.V.). She meets the watchmen who patrol the city, but does not find the Beloved until she has passed beyond them. Ann in her letter mentions a text which has been a *heol myfyrdod* for her, a thought-road which has brought her to him at last. It is a

Ann Griffiths: A Literary Survey

What is Ann Griffiths' response to this theology? How does she react to the 'plan of salvation'? Let us look closely at her vocabulary. The word which comes most frequently in her poetry, the word which reveals her response, is *rhyfeddu* (to wonder), with the adjective *rhyfedd* (wonderful) and the noun *rhyfeddod* (a wonder). Examples are numerous. I will select a few:

Rhyfedd, rhyfedd gan angylion,
   Rhyfeddod fawr yng ngolwg ffydd.

(Wonderful, wonderful to angels, a great wonder in the eyes of faith.)

And again:

Rhyfeddaf fyth, fe drefnwyd pabell
   Im gael yn dawel gwrdd â Duw.

(I shall always wonder, a tabernacle has been set up for me to meet quietly with God.)

And again:

Ffordd a'i henw yn 'Rhyfeddol',
   Hen, a heb heneiddio, yw.

(A way whose name is Wonderful, it is old and yet it grows not old.)

---

text (in her interpretation of it) about passing beyond human help or advice and looking to God alone. Saunders Lewis here uses Ann's phrase for the line of thought which he has extracted from her writings and summarised here, the line of thought which bids us pass beyond all lower things and look to God alone, and goes on to the longing for purity and the purgative discipline. This is indeed a road that leads to the Beloved. – *Translator*.

And here is a final example, a cry which might have come from Rimbaud:

> *Mewn môr o ryfeddodau,*
>   *O! am gael treulio f'oes.*

(O to spend my life in a sea of wonders.)

You find the same word frequently in the letters:

> This is often my task at the throne of grace: wondering, giving thanks, and praying.

Sometimes in the letters we find *synnu* (to marvel) instead of *rhyfeddu* (to wonder):

> I am reverently ashamed, and rejoice marvelling, to think that he 'who humbleth himself to behold the things that are in heaven' has yet given himself as an object of love to a creature as wretched as I.

> To my mind it is a marvel who was on the cross. ... My mind is too overwhelmed to say anything more on the matter.

One way which Ann Griffiths has of expressing this dominant element of wonder and marvel in her worship has already attracted the keen attention of critics, namely her use of contradictions. The example which everyone remembers is '*Rhoi Awdwr bywyd i farwolaeth / A chladdu'r Atgyfodiad mawr*' ('The Author of life put to death and the great Resurrection buried'). There are many others through the length and breadth of the hymns, such as '*Efe yw'r Iawn fu rhwng y lladron*' ('He is the Satisfaction[8] that was between the thieves'); and there is

---

8   *Yr Iawn.* In current usage *yr Iawn* is the Welsh for the Atonement. But let us

the whole of that paradoxical hymn on the Way: '*Ffordd na chenfydd llygad barcut / Er ei bod fel hanner dydd*' ('A way no eye of kite[9] can discern though it is as noonday'), with its closing lines pointing to the Sacrament: '*Dyma'r gwin sy'n abal llonni, / Llonni calon Duw a dyn*' ('Here is the wine which is able to cheer, to cheer the heart of God and man').

Wondering, marvelling, running her fingers over the strings of the paradoxes of the Faith, we can easily see that this is poetry of the intellect. There is nothing more strange than the contrast between Ann Griffiths and Williams Pantycelyn.

---

look deeper. As an adjective, *iawn* means 'correct, right, just'. As an adverb it means 'very', like 'right' in old-fashioned English ('right glad' = 'very glad'). As a noun it means something done or given to make amends for an offence, a satisfaction; or something paid to make good a loss, a restitution or compensation. Thus in Exodus 22:12, if a man is robbed of something which is not his property, but of which he is for the time being in charge, he must pay the owner its equivalent: '*gwnaed iawn*' in the Welsh Bible; 'he shall make restitution' in the Authorised Version (A.V.). Christ is spoken of in Scripture as being himself a *Iawn*, in the sense of a propitiation or a propitiatory offering. Thus in 1 John 2:2, 4:10 and Romans 3:25 the A.V. speaks of Christ as 'the propitiation for our sins' (Greek *hilasmos, hilasterion*), where the Welsh Bible has *iawn* for 'propitiation', with *cymod* in the margin in some editions. *Cymod* means 'reconciliation'; it is the word used in the Welsh Bible for *katallage* in Romans 5:11 ('atonement' in the A.V.) and in 2 Corinthians 5:18 ('reconciliation' in the A.V.); *Dydd y Cymod* is the phrase for the Day of Atonement. But *iawn* is more properly the deed done, or the price paid, to bring about the reconciliation. In his action as Priest, Christ made a sacrifice, oblation and satisfaction (Welsh Prayer Book: *aberth, offrwm, ac iawn*) for the sins of the whole world. As Victim, he is himself the *Iawn*, by the offering of which the satisfaction is made. Ann is of course aware of all this, but in the line here quoted she reminds us that this *Iawn* is not only a salve for wounded honour, but a restitution for stolen property. The Father has not merely been insulted, he has been robbed. Man's perdition is a loss – by theft – of God's property. In the Person of the Crucified a full restitution is made to him – and that in the company of two thieves! – *Translator*.

9 Job 28:7: '*llwybr ... ni chanfu llygad barcud*' in the Welsh Bible, 'a path ... which eye of kite has not descried'. The Hebrew word '*ayyah* is translated 'vulture' by the Authorised Version in this passage, but 'kite' in Leviticus 11:14. The Revised Version has 'falcon' in both places. The Welsh in both places has *barcud*, which properly means a kite. *Barcut* is an alternative spelling of *barcud*. – *Translator*.

When it reaches its heights, Williams' poetry is feminine poetry in the finest sense of the word. The poetry of the woman from Dolwar is a masculine poetry, a poetry of mind and understanding. Perhaps I might define her religion by saying that it is an aesthetic religion. I am using the word carefully; a religion which looks outwards in appreciation and marvel and worship. And so, after *rhyfeddu* (to wonder) and *synnu* (to marvel), it is appropriate to find the words *edrych* (to look) and *syllu* (to gaze) describe her prayer:

> O! am gael ffydd i edrych
>   Gyda'r angylion fry
> I drefn yr iechydwriaeth ...

(O to have faith to look with the angels above into the plan of salvation ...)

Observe: to look into the plan; this implies a direct intellectual penetration. To look with the angels? How do the angels look into God's plan? Jacques Maritain in his chapter on Descartes has a section on angelic perception. I shall not follow him now, but when Ann Griffiths says *edrych i* (to look into) rather than *edrych ar* (to look upon), this implies a great deal of what he means. There is another virtue too which belongs to the angels' vision. The plan of salvation has nothing directly to do with them. It is an arrangement between God and man and the material creation. Hence, theirs is a selfless vision, a vision wholly appreciative, a vision full of wonder and worship and blessing and pure joy, without anything of self or any thought of self coming into it. And it is to worship the plan of salvation in this way, to look upon it together with the angels and worship it for its own sake, on account of its holiness and its divinity – it is for this that Ann Griffiths yearns.

Let us take the word *syllu* (to gaze): '*Tragwyddol syllu ar y*

Person / A gymerodd natur dyn' ('To gaze eternally upon the Person who took the nature of man'). And in another verse:

> Ni ddichon byd a'i holl deganau
>   Fodloni fy serchiadau yn awr,
> A enillwyd, a ehangwyd,
>   Yn nydd nerth fy Iesu mawr;
> *Ef*, nid llai, a eill eu llenwi
>   Er mai diamgyffred yw;
> O! am syllu ar ei Berson
>   Fel y mae Fe'n ddyn a Duw.

(The world and all its trinkets cannot now satisfy my affections, which were captured, which were widened in the day of my great Jesus' power; he, none less, can fulfil them, although he is incomprehensible; O to gaze upon his Person, as he is both man and God.)

The first couplet here could be part of a verse by Pantycelyn: '*Ni ddichon byd a'i holl deganau / Fodloni fy serchiadau yn awr*' ('The world and all its trinkets cannot now satisfy my affections'). But the next couplet is altogether peculiar to Ann Griffiths – the powerful intellectualising, the combination of passionate contemplation with intellectual adoration, and then the scriptural allusion, 'That ye ... may be able to *comprehend*[10] with all saints what is the breadth, and length, and depth, and height', and the whole ending in the pure aesthetic act, 'O to gaze upon his Person.' This young woman had a mind like Plato's. It is her idea of the holiness of God – '*O! am fywyd o sancteiddio / Sanctaidd enw pur fy Nuw*' ('O for a life of sanctifying the holy pure name of my God') – which causes *parch* (reverence) – 'I would fain love in the dust' – to be the essence of worship for her. Let us listen to her in a letter:

---

10 Ephesians 3:18. Welsh Bible, '*amgyffred*'; A.V. 'comprehend'; R.V. 'apprehend'. – *Translator*.

I never before knew so much reverence towards and love for the law, not in spite of the fact that it brings a curse, but because it brings a curse in every place outside of a Mediator. Thus it shows its beauty and perfection.[11]

Even in Calvin's own works, the stress is laid upon awe in face of the holiness of the law. But in Ann Griffiths it is love for its beauty. Beauty, perfection, objects to wonder at, to look at, to marvel at and gaze upon, to *see*. To see (*gweld*)?

> Gwela' *i'n sefyll*[12] *rhwng y myrtwydd*
> *Wrthrych teilwng o fy mryd;*
> *Er mai o ran, yr wy'n adnabod*
> *Ei fod uwchlaw gwrthrychau'r byd:*
> *Henffych fore*
> *Y caf ei weled fel y mae.*

(I *see* standing among the myrtles an object worthy of my whole mind, although it is in part I know that he is above all objects in the world; hail the morning when I shall *see* him as he is.)

In this short verse there are three quotations from the Bible. That, of course, is characteristic of Ann Griffiths' way of writing. Some critics have said that all she did was to string together sentences from Scripture and that there is not much of her own in her work. Exactly the same charge could be brought against Virgil. There are hardly three lines together in

---

11 [The text of Ann's letter Saunders Lewis used here was a later edited version which read '*ei harddwch a'i pherffeithnwydd*', 'its beauty and perfection'. The original text probably read '*ei phurdeb*', 'its purity'. – *Ed.*]

12 [There are two versions of this verse in the John Hughes manuscripts. Saunders Lewis here chose to use the version which opens with the more personal '*Gwela' i'n sefyll*', 'I see standing', rather than the version which opens '*Wele'n sefyll*', 'Behold standing'. This latter version is the one which is in most common current usage and may represent a revision by Ann herself of the other version. – *Ed.*]

all his works without a reminiscence of or a quotation from the work of earlier Greek or Latin poets. This is true of many poets of the first rank in Europe and China. In our own time Ezra Pound has taught this art to the poets of America. It is reflective poets, poets of the intellect, who have this gift. Reminiscence connects their present-day thought with a depth of tradition and with spiritual sources. To me this verse is a continual wonder. The first two lines, with the borrowing from the book of Zechariah, are so strangely lyrical: '*Gwela' i'n sefyll rhwng y myrtwydd / Wrthrych teilwng o fy mryd*' ('I see standing among the myrtles an object worthy of my whole mind'). And then in the next couplet there is the sudden drawing back, back to the unhappy ambiguous situation of man: '*Er mai o ran, yr wy'n adnabod / Ei fod uwchlaw gwrthrychau'r byd*' ('Although it is in part I know that he is above all objects in the world'). And after that, in conclusion, there is the jump forward to the dawn of the eternal vision: '*Henffych fore / Y caf ei weled fel y mae*' ('Hail the morning when I shall see him as he is').

Here is another verse on the same theme, with a music in it like organ music, and here *rhyfeddu* (to wonder) and *gweld y meddwl* (seeing one's mind) come together:

> *Rhyfeddu a wna' i â mawr ryfeddod*
>   *Pan ddêl i ben y ddedwydd awr*
> *Caf weld fy meddwl, sy yma'n gwibio*
>   *Ar ôl teganau gwael y llawr,*
> *Wedi ei dragwyddol setlo*
>   *Ar wrthrych mawr ei Berson Ef,*
> *A diysgog gydymffurfio*
>   *Â phur a sanctaidd ddeddfau'r nef.*

(I shall wonder with great wonder when the blessed hour is fulfilled for me to see my mind, which here darts after the base trinkets of earth, eternally settled upon the great object of his Person, and unshakeably conformed to the pure and holy laws of heaven.)

In that last couplet, purity of soul is part of her vision of the unity of all that is, and the frail fickle thought of man has been finally drawn into the unity of the eternal dance of the love which moves the stars.

Wondering, marvelling, looking, gazing, seeing – I should like to extend this series of aesthetic terms to include penetrating (*treiddio*): '*O am dreiddio i'r adnabyddiaeth*' ('O to penetrate into the knowledge'). And penetrating suggests sinking, swimming, and the sea. There is no mention of Ann Griffiths ever having seen the sea. But the sea is her symbol for Deity: '*Mewn môr o ryfeddodau, / O! am gael treulio f'oes*' ('O to spend my life in a sea of wonders'). And longing for the sea, the longing of one who was familiar only with the waters of brooks and rivers, is to be heard in these lines:

Cofiwch hyn mewn stad o wendid,
 Yn y dyfroedd at eich fferau sy,
Mai dirifedi yw'r cufyddau
 A fesurir i chwi fry. ...

O! ddedwydd awr tragwyddol orffwys
 Oddi wrth fy llafur yn fy rhan,
Ynghanol môr o ryfeddodau
 Heb weled terfyn byth, na glan. ...

(Remember ye this when in a state of weakness, amid the waters which are up to your ankles, that unnumbered are the cubits which are measured out for you above. ...

O blessed hour of eternal rest from my labour in my lot, in the midst of a sea of wonders with never a sight of a boundary or a shore. ...)

A sea of wonders, that is what God and life in God is to her: '*Nofio yn afon bur y bywyd, / Diderfyn heddwch sanctaidd Dri*' ('To swim in the pure river of life, the endless peace of the holy Three'). There is here a hint of a human soul sensing from afar what the consciousness of Deity is. No one was ever more reticent about her spiritual experiences than Ann Griffiths. Morris Davies has a very odd story of the agitation and alarm of Thomas Charles after he had been at Dolwar and talked with her.[13] But perhaps we shall understand what frightened Thomas Charles if we consider a couplet like this: 'Ymddifyrru *yn ei Berson / A'i addoli byth yn Dduw*' ('*Delighting in his Person and worshipping him for ever as God*'). There you have the whole aesthetic of the Faith.

In this lecture I have tried to come at the thought and poetry of Ann Griffiths through her vocabulary. Now, she has in the text published by O. M. Edwards one quite long hymn in seven verses, which contains almost the whole of this vocabulary and sums up all her themes and paradoxes. *Hymn* is its title in John Hughes' manuscript, but in my judgment it is one of the majestic songs in the religious poetry of Europe, and I shall make bold to ask you to listen to the whole of it, because Ann's words are better than any interpretation of them:

Rhyfedd, rhyfedd gan angylion,
   Rhyfeddod fawr yng ngolwg ffydd,
Gweld Rhoddwr bod, Cynhaliwr helaeth
   A Rheolwr pob peth sydd,
Yn y preseb mewn cadachau
   A heb le i roi ei ben i lawr,
Ac eto disglair lu'r gogoniant
   Yn ei addoli'n Arglwydd mawr.

---

13 The story is that Thomas Charles said one of three things would probably happen: she would meet with grievous trials, or she would die young, or she would backslide. She wept when he mentioned the third possibility. In fact it was the second which was realised. – *Translator.*

Pan fo Sinai i gyd yn mygu
    A sŵn yr utgorn uwcha' ei radd,
Caf fynd i wledda tros y terfyn
    Yng Nghrist y Gair heb gael fy lladd;
Mae ynddo'n trigo bob cyflawnder,
    Llond gwagle colledigaeth dyn;
Ar yr adwy rhwng y ddwyblaid
    Gwnaeth gymod trwy ei offrymu ei hun.

Efe yw'r Iawn fu rhwng y lladron,
    Efe ddioddefodd angau loes,
Efe a nerthodd freichiau ei ddienyddwyr
    I'w hoelio yno ar y groes;
Wrth dalu dyled pentewynion,
    Ac anrhydeddu deddf ei Dad,
Cyfiawnder, mae'n disgleirio'n danbaid
    Wrth faddau yn nhrefn y cymod rhad.

O! f'enaid, gwêl y fan gorweddodd
    Pen brenhinoedd, Awdwr hedd,
Y greadigaeth ynddo'n symud,
    Yntau'n farw yn y bedd;
Cân a bywyd colledigion,
    Rhyfeddod fwya' angylion nef;
Gweld Duw mewn cnawd a'i gydaddoli
    Mae'r côr, dan weiddi 'Iddo Ef!'

Diolch byth, a chanmil diolch,
    Diolch tra bo ynwy' i chwyth,
Am fod gwrthrych i'w addoli
    A thestun cân i bara byth;
Yn fy natur wedi ei demtio
    Fel y gwaela' o ddynol-ryw,
Yn ddyn bach, yn wan, yn ddinerth,
    Yn anfeidrol wir a bywiol Dduw.

Yn lle cario corff o lygredd,
 Cyd-dreiddio â'r côr yn danllyd fry
I ddiderfyn ryfeddodau
 Iechydwriaeth Calfari;
Byw i weld yr Anweledig,
 Fu farw ac sy'n awr yn fyw;
Tragwyddol anwahanol undeb
 A chymundeb â fy Nuw.

Yno caf ddyrchafu'r Enw
 A osododd Duw yn Iawn,
Heb ddychymyg, llen, na gorchudd,
 A'm henaid ar ei ddelw'n llawn;
Yng nghymdeithas y dirgelwch,
 Datguddiedig yn ei glwy',
Cusanu'r Mab i dragwyddoldeb
 Heb im gefnu arno mwy.

(Wonderful, wonderful to angels, a great wonder in the eyes of faith, to see the Giver of being, the abundant Sustainer and Ruler of everything that is, in the manger in swaddling clothes and with nowhere to lay his head, and yet the bright host of glory worshipping him as great Lord.

When Sinai is altogether in smoke, and the sound of the trumpet at its loudest, I can go to feast across the boundary in Christ the Word without being slain; in him all fullness dwells, enough to fill the gulf of man's perdition; in the gap between the two parties he made reconciliation through his self-offering.

He is the Satisfaction that was between the thieves, it was he who suffered the pains of death, it was he who gave to the arms of his executioners the power to nail him there to the cross; while paying the debt of brands plucked out of the burning, and honouring his Father's law, righteousness shines with fiery blaze as he pardons within the plan of the free reconciliation.

O my soul, behold the place where lay the chief of kings, the Author of peace, the creation moving in him, and he dead in the tomb; song and life of the lost, greatest wonder of the angels of heaven; the choir sees God in flesh and worships him together, crying out, 'Unto him!'

Thanks for ever, and a hundred thousand thanks, thanks while there is breath in me, because there is an object to worship and a subject for a song to last for ever; in my nature, tempted like the lowest of mankind, a babe, weak, powerless, infinite true and living God.

Instead of carrying a body of corruption, penetrating ardently with the choir above into the endless wonders of the salvation wrought on Calvary; living to see the Invisible, who was dead and now is alive; eternal inseparable union and communion with my God.

There I shall exalt the Name which God set forth to be a Propitiation, without imagination,[14] veil, or covering, and with my soul fully in his likeness; in the fellowship of the mystery revealed in his wounds, I shall kiss the Son to all eternity, and never turn from him any more.)

One must stop, though without finishing.

Before I stop, let me venture the suggestion that it would be no bad thing for us in Wales today to turn to meditate the work of Ann Griffiths.

In the religious debate which has been going on in the press and through the medium of the radio in Wales for the last year or more, I am in complete sympathy with the starting-point of Professor J. R. Jones,[15] namely that the crisis which is weighing upon Christians and ex-Christians today is not a crisis of guilt, but of doubt as to whether life has any meaning at all. There are many causes for this despair; there are two world wars, with the likelihood and near-certainty that there will be a third which will put an end to civilisation and perhaps to the human race. Concentration camps like

---

14 That is, 'without unruly fancies'. – *Translator*.
15 [J. R. Jones (1911–70) was Professor of Philosophy at the University College of Swansea. In 1964 he published a pamphlet, based on a television address, entitled Yr Argyfwng Gwacter Ystyr ('The Crisis of Meaninglessness'). – *Ed*.]

Belsen and Dachau remain with us as symbols of the value we attach to human beings.

Now, no philosopher or religious teacher from the beginning of history has ever been able to prove that the universe is rational. We all know that science today gives a dominating place to chance and accident in the evolution of life. It is an act of faith, not an act of reason, to believe in reason. For Ann Griffiths, as I have said more than once in this talk, the salvation and reconciliation of guilty man comes second in the Christian religion. As to what comes first she has not the slightest doubt:

Diolch byth. a chanmil diolch,
    Diolch tra bo ynwy' i chwyth,
Am fod gwrthrych i'w addoli ...

(Thanks for ever, and a hundred thousand thanks, thanks while there is breath in me, because there is an object to worship ...)

Ann is a poet putting off her shoes from off her feet, because the ground on which she stands at Llanfihangel-yng-Ngwynfa is holy ground. Where there is an object to worship, there cannot be a moment's doubt that life has eternal meaning, that meaning fills the universe, and that '*Y greadigaeth ynddo'n symud*' ('The creation [is] moving in him'). Afterwards, afterwards, in consequence of this, we shall grow to understand the desire of Ann Griffiths: 'I have never had a greater longing to be pure.'

The Hymns of Ann Griffiths

edited by E. Wyn James
translated by H. A. Hodges

I

1. O'm blaen mi wela' ddrws agored,
    A modd i hollol gario'r ma's
   Yng ngrym y rhoddion a dderbyniodd
    Yr Hwn gymerodd agwedd gwas;
   Mae'r tywysogaethau wedi eu hysbeilio,
    A'r awdurdodau, ganddo ynghyd,
   A'r carcharwr yn y carchar
    Trwy rinwedd ei ddioddefaint drud.

2. Fy enaid trist, wrth gofio'r frwydyr,
    Yn llamu o lawenydd sydd;
   Gweld y ddeddf yn anrhydeddus
    A'i throseddwyr mawr yn rhydd;
   Rhoi Awdwr bywyd i farwolaeth
    A chladdu'r Atgyfodiad mawr;
   Dwyn i mewn dragwyddol heddwch
    Rhwng nef y nef a daear lawr.

3. Pan esgynnodd 'r Hwn ddisgynnodd
    Gwedi gorffen yma'r gwaith,
   Y pyrth oedd yn dyrchafu eu pennau
    Dan ryfeddu yn eu hiaith;
   Dorau'n agor, côr yn bowio
    I Dduw mewn cnawd yr ochor draw;
   Y Tad yn siriol a'i gwahoddodd
    I eistedd ar ei ddeau law.

4. Digon mewn llifeiriant dyfroedd,
    Digon yn y fflamau tân,
   O! am bara i lynu wrtho,
    Fy enaid, byth yn ddiwahân:
   Ar ddryslyd lwybrau tir Arabia
    Y mae gelynion fwy na rhi';
   Rho gymdeithas dioddefiadau
    Gwerthfawr angau Calfari.

The Hymns of Ann Griffiths

I

1. There's an open door before me,
     Means of victory in store,
   Through the gifts he purchased for us
     Who a servant's form once wore.
   Principalities, dominations,
     He their overthrow procured,
   Spoiled them all, and jailed the jailer,
     Through the passion he endured.

2. When I think upon that battle,
     My sad soul leaps up with glee;
   See! the law is held in honour,
     Yet transgressors walk forth free;
   See! our Resurrection's buried,
     And our Life laid underground;
   See! our earth with highest heaven
     In eternal peace is bound.

3. When on high he reascended,
     All his work fulfilled below,
   Lofty gates their heads uplifted,
     All their wondering joy to show;
   Doors flew open, choirs sang welcome
     To the Incarnate in that land,
   And the Father, glad and radiant,
     Bade him sit at his right hand.

4. 'Tis enough 'mid flooding waters,
     'Tis enough 'mid flames of fire;
   Cling to him, my soul, for ever,
     Follow him, and never tire;
   On Arabia's desert pathways
     Foes unnumbered wait for me;
   Grant a share in his dear passion
     Who was slain on Calvary.

II

1. Dyma babell y cyfarfod,
    Dyma gymod yn y gwaed,
   Dyma noddfa i lofruddion,
    Dyma i gleifion feddyg rhad;
   Dyma fan yn ymyl Duwdod
    I bechadur wneud ei nyth,
   A chyfiawnder pur Jehofa
    Yn siriol wenu arno byth.

2. Pechadur aflan yw fy enw,
    O ba rai y penna'n fyw;
   Rhyfeddaf fyth, fe drefnwyd pabell
    Im gael yn dawel gwrdd â Duw:
   Yno y mae yn llond ei gyfraith
    I'r troseddwr yn rhoi gwledd;
   Duw a dyn yn gweiddi 'Digon!'
    Yn yr Iesu, 'r aberth hedd.

3. Myfi a anturiaf yno yn eon,
    Teyrnwialen aur sydd yn ei law,
   A hon a'i senter at bechadur,
    Llwyr dderbyniad pawb a ddaw;
   Af ymlaen dan weiddi 'Maddau!'
    Af a syrthiaf wrth ei draed,
   Am faddeuant, am fy ngolchi,
    Am fy nghannu yn ei waed.

4. O! am ddyfod o'r anialwch
    I fyny fel colofnau mwg
   Yn uniongyrchol at ei orsedd,
    Mae yno'n eistedd heb ei wg:
   Amen diddechrau a diddiwedd,
    Tyst ffyddlon yw, a'i air yn un;
   Amlygu y mae ogoniant Trindod
    Yn achubiaeth damniol ddyn.

II

1. Here within the tent of meeting
    Is the blood that can atone,
   Here the slayer's place of refuge,
    Here a healer's power made known;
   Here a place, hard by the Godhead,
    For the sinner's nest to lie,
   While the righteousness of heaven
    Smiles on him perpetually.

2. Sinner is my name and nature,
    Fouler none on earth can be;
   In the Presence here – O wonder! –
    God receives me tranquilly;
   See him there, his law fulfilling,
    For his foes a banquet laid,
   God and man 'Enough!' proclaiming
    Through the offering he has made.

3. Boldly I will venture forward;
    See the golden sceptre shine,
   Pointing straight towards the sinner;
    All may enter by that sign.
   On I'll press, beseeching pardon,
    On, till at his feet I fall,
   Cry for pardon, cry for washing
    In the blood which cleanses all.

4. O to come, like smoky pillars,
    From the desert to the throne
   Where with countenance unclouded
    Sits our royal Solomon.
   Faithful Witness, never changing,
    God's Amen ere time began,
   He displays the Triune glory
    In his saving work for man.

III

1. Bererin llesg gan rym y stormydd,
    Cwyd dy olwg, gwêl yn awr
  Yr Oen yn gweini'r swydd gyfryngol
    Mewn gwisgoedd llaesion hyd y llawr;
  Gwregys euraidd o ffyddlondeb,
    Wrth ei odrau clychau'n llawn
  O sŵn maddeuant i bechadur
    Ar gyfri' yr anfeidrol Iawn.

2. Cofiwch hyn mewn stad o wendid,
    Yn y dyfroedd at eich fferau sy,
  Mai dirifedi yw'r cufyddau
    A fesurir i chwi fry;
  Er bod yn blant yr atgyfodiad
    I nofio yn y dyfroedd hyn,
  Ni welir gwaelod byth nac ymyl
    I sylwedd mawr Bethesda lyn.

3. O! ddyfnderoedd iechydwriaeth,
    Dirgelwch mawr duwioldeb yw,
  Duw y duwiau wedi ymddangos
    Yng nghnawd a natur dynol-ryw;
  Dyma'r Person a ddioddefodd
    Yn ein lle ddigofaint llawn,
  Nes i Gyfiawnder weiddi, 'Gollwng
    Ef yn rhydd: mi gefais Iawn!'

4. O! ddedwydd awr tragwyddol orffwys
    Oddi wrth fy llafur yn fy rhan,
  Ynghanol môr o ryfeddodau
    Heb weled terfyn byth, na glan;
  Mynediad helaeth byth i bara
    I fewn trigfannau Tri yn Un;
  Dŵr i'w nofio heb fynd trwyddo,
    Dyn yn Dduw, a Duw yn ddyn.

III

1. Pilgrim, faint and tempest-beaten,
    Lift thy gaze, behold and know
   Christ the Lamb, our Mediator,
    Robed in vestments trailing low;
   Faithfulness his golden girdle;
    Bells upon his garments ring
   Free salvation for the sinner
    Through his priceless offering.

2. Think on this when to your ankles
    Scarce the healing waters rise –
   Numberless shall be the cubits
    Measured to you in the skies.
   Children of the resurrection,
    They alone can venture here;
   Yet they find no shore, no bottom
    To Bethesda's waters clear.

3. O the deeps of our salvation!
    Mystery of godliness!
   He, the God of gods, appearing
    In our fleshly human dress;
   He it is who bore God's anger,
    In our place atonement made,
   Until Justice cried, 'Release him,
    Now the debt is fully paid.'

4. Blessed hour of rest eternal,
    Home at last, all labours o'er;
   Sea of wonders never sounded,
    Sea where none can find a shore;
   Access free to dwell for ever
    Yonder with the One in Three;
   Deeps no foot of man can traverse –
    God and man in unity.

IV

1. Er mai cwbwl groes i natur
    Yw fy llwybyr yn y byd,
   Ei deithio a wnaf, a hynny'n dawel,
    Yng ngwerthfawr wedd dy wyneb-pryd;
   Wrth godi'r groes ei chyfri'n goron,
    Mewn gorthrymderau llawen fyw;
   Ffordd yn uniawn, er mor ddyrys,
    I ddinas gyfaneddol yw.

2. Ffordd a'i henw yn 'Rhyfeddol',
    Hen, a heb heneiddio, yw;
   Ffordd heb ddechrau, eto'n newydd,
    Ffordd yn gwneud y meirw'n fyw;
   Ffordd i ennill ei thrafaelwyr,
    Ffordd yn Briod, ffordd yn Ben,
   Ffordd gysegrwyd, af ar hyd-ddi
    I orffwys ynddi draw i'r llen.

3. Ffordd na chenfydd llygad barcut
    Er ei bod fel hanner dydd,
   Ffordd ddisathar anweledig
    I bawb ond perchenogion ffydd;
   Ffordd i gyfiawnhau'r annuwiol,
    Ffordd i godi'r meirw'n fyw,
   Ffordd gyfreithlon i droseddwyr
    I hedd a ffafor gyda Duw.

4. Ffordd a drefnwyd cyn bod amser
    I'w hamlygu wrth angen-rhaid
   Mewn addewid gynt yn Eden
    Pan gyhoeddwyd Had y Wraig;
   Dyma seiliau'r ail gyfamod,
    Dyma gyngor Tri yn Un,
   Dyma'r gwin sy'n abal llonni,
    Llonni calon Duw a dyn.

IV

1. Wholly counter to my nature
    Is the path ordained for me;
  Yet I'll tread it, yes, and calmly,
    While thy precious face I see;
  Count the cross a crown, and bear it,
    Cheerful live 'mid all life's woes –
  This the Way which, straight though tangled,
    To the heavenly city goes.

2. Old it is, yet never aging,
    And its name is Wonderful;
  Ne'er begun, yet new for ever,
    Making dead men rise up whole;
  Winning all who travel by it;
    Head and Husband 'tis to me;
  Sacred way, I'll pass along it
    Till in it my rest shall be.

3. Eye of kite could ne'er discern it,
    Though it shines with noontide blaze;
  None can tread it, none can see it,
    Save where faith its light displays;
  Breaking ne'er the law of justice,
    Godless souls it justifies.
  Leads them to God's peace and favour,
    Bids the dead to life arise.

4. Way made straight before creation,
    Kept to be revealed at need,
  When in days of old, in Eden,
    God proclaimed the woman's Seed;
  His new covenant's foundation,
    Once decreed ere time began,
  'Tis the wine whose ample virtue
    Glads the heart of God and man.

V

1. Mae'r dydd yn dod i'r had brenhinol
    Gael mordwyo tua'u gwlad
   O gaethiwed y priddfeini
    I deyrnasu gyda'u Tad;
   Eu ffydd tu draw a dry yn olwg,
    A'u gobaith eiddil yn fwynhad,
   Annherfynol fydd yr anthem,
    Dyrchafu rhinwedd gwerthfawr waed.

2. Mae fy nghalon am ymadael
    Â phob rhyw eilunod mwy,
   Am fod arni'n sgrifenedig
    Ddelw gwrthrych llawer mwy –
   Anfeidrol deilwng i'w addoli,
    Ei garu, a'i barchu, yn y byd;
   Bywyd myrdd o safn marwolaeth
    A gafwyd yn ei angau drud.

3. Arogli'n beraidd mae fy nardus
    Wrth wledda ar y cariad rhad;
   Sêl yn tanio yn erbyn pechod,
    Caru delw sancteiddhad;
   Torri ymaith law a llygad
    Ynghyd ag uchel drem i lawr;
   Neb yn deilwng o'i ddyrchafu
    Onid Iesu, 'r Brenin mawr.

4. O! am fywyd o sancteiddio
    Sanctaidd enw pur fy Nuw
   Ac ymostwng i'w ewyllys
    A'i lywodraeth tra fwyf byw;
   Byw dan addunedu a thalu,
    Byw dan ymnerthu yn y gras
   Sydd yng Nghrist yn drysoredig
    I orchfygu ar y maes.

V

1. Now the royal seed are summoned
    To their land beyond the sea,
  Freed from bondage in the brickworks,
    There to reign eternally.
  Yonder, faith is turned to vision,
    Hope enjoys its promised good;
  There they all, in endless anthem,
    Glorify the precious blood.

2. Gladly would I leave behind me
    All the idols I have known,
  Since I bear inscribed the likeness
    Of a more exalted One;
  Worthy of unending worship,
    Love, and reverence is he;
  By his precious death were myriads
    From the jaws of death set free.

3. Sweetly spreads my spikenard's fragrance
    While I feast on love unbought,
  Flame with zeal against all evil,
    Cherish every holy thought;
  Eye and right hand flinging from me,
    Lofty looks to earth bring down;
  Jesus over all exalting,
    Him alone with worship crown.

4. Let me only live to hallow
    God's pure name till life shall end,
  Bow before his will, and welcome
    All his providence may send,
  Vow, and pay my vows, receiving
    From the Lord's rich treasure-store
  Grace to strengthen and to crown me
    Victor in the conflict sore.

5. Addurna'm henaid ar dy ddelw,
    Gwna fi'n ddychryn yn dy law,
  I uffern, llygredd, annuwioldeb,
    Wrth edrych arnaf i gael braw;
  O! am gymdeithasu â'r Enw,
    Ennaint tywalltedig yw,
  Yn hallt i'r byd, gan bêr aroglau
    O hawddgar ddoniau eglwys Dduw.

5. Let me, clothed in thine own likeness,
    In thy hand a terror be,
  Hell, ungodliness, corruption
    Tremble at the sight of me.
  Seal me with thy Name, whose fragrance
    Is diffused in every place,
  Salting all the world, and sweetening
    With the beauteous gifts of grace.

VI

1. O! am gael ffydd i edrych
       Gyda'r angylion fry
   I drefn yr iechydwriaeth,
       Dirgelwch ynddi sy;
   Dwy natur mewn un Person
       Yn anwahanol mwy,
   Mewn purdeb heb gymysgu,
       Yn berffaith hollol trwy.

2. O! f'enaid, gwêl addasrwydd
       Y Person dwyfol hwn,
   Mentra arno'th fywyd
       A bwrw arno'th bwn;
   Mae'n ddyn i gydymdeimlo
       Â'th holl wendidau i gyd,
   Mae'n Dduw i gario'r orsedd
       Ar ddiafol, cnawd, a byd.

3. Rhyw hiraeth sy am ymadael
       Bob dydd â'r gwaedlyd faes,
   Nid â'r arch, nac Israel,
       Ond hunanymchwydd cas;
   Cael dod at fwrdd y Brenin,
       A'm gwadd i eiste'n uwch,
   A minnau, wan ac eiddil,
       Am garu yn y llwch.

4. Er cryfed ydyw'r stormydd
       Ac ymchwydd tonnau'r môr,
   Doethineb ydyw'r peilat,
       A'i enw'n gadarn Iôr;
   Er gwaethaf dilyw pechod
       A llygredd o bob rhyw,
   Dihangol yn y diwedd
       Am fod yr arch yn Dduw.

VI

1. O might I gain faith's insight,
      With angel-minds on high,
   Into heaven's secret counsels,
      Its saving mystery;
   Two natures in one Person
      Joined indivisibly,
   True, pure and unconfounded,
      Perfect in unity.

2. Behold him all-sufficient,
      My soul, thy need to fill;
   Take heart, and cast upon him
      The weight of every ill;
   True man, in all thy weakness
      He truly feels for thee;
   True God, o'er world, flesh, Satan
      He reigns victoriously.

3. Each day from the fierce conflict
      I long to turn aside –
   Not leave the ark, or Israel,
      But turn from human pride,
   And come to the King's table,
      Who bids me go up higher,
   When in the dust to love him
      Was all I durst desire.

4. Though strong may be the tempests
      And swellings of the sea,
   Yet Wisdom is the pilot –
      A mighty Lord is he;
   Though sin comes flooding round me,
      Its billows rising fast,
   The ark is God almighty,
      And all is safe at last.

VII

1. Pan fo'r enaid mwya' gwresog
     Yn tanllyd garu'n mwya' byw,
   Y mae'r pryd hynny yn fyr o gyrraedd
     Perffaith sanctaidd gyfraith Duw;
   O! am gael ei hanrhydeddu
     Trwy dderbyn iechydwriaeth rad,
   A'r cymundeb mwya' melys,
     Wedi ei drochi yn y gwaed.

2. Rhyfeddu a wna' i â mawr ryfeddod
     Pan ddêl i ben y ddedwydd awr
   Caf weld fy meddwl, sy yma'n gwibio
     Ar ôl teganau gwael y llawr,
   Wedi ei dragwyddol setlo
     Ar wrthrych mawr ei Berson Ef,
   A diysgog gydymffurfio
     Â phur a sanctaidd ddeddfau'r nef.

VII

1. Even when the soul most ardent
     Burns the most with living fire,
   It can ne'er to the perfection
     Of God's holy law aspire;
   O that I might pay it honour
     By accepting his free grace,
   And in that most sweet communion,
     Through the blood, might find a place.

2. I shall feel a mighty wonder
     When that blessed hour finds birth
   When my mind, that here goes wandering
     After the mean toys of earth,
   Finds its undistraught devotion
     To his Person henceforth given,
   And unshakably conforming
     To the holy laws of heaven.

VIII

1. Mae bod yn fyw o fawr ryfeddod
    O fewn ffwrneisiau sydd mor boeth,
   Ond mwy rhyfedd, wedi 'mhrofi,
    Y dof i'r canol fel aur coeth;
   Amser cannu, diwrnod nithio,
    Eto'n dawel, heb ddim braw;
   Y Gŵr a fydd i mi'n ymguddfa
    Y sydd â'r wyntyll yn ei law.

2. Blin yw 'mywyd gan elynion
    Am eu bod yn amal iawn;
   Fy amgylchu maent fel gwenyn
    O foreddydd hyd brynhawn;
   A'r rhai o'm tŷ fy hun yn benna'
    Yn blaenori uffernol gad;
   Trwy gymorth gras yr wyf am bara
    I ryfela hyd at waed.

VIII

1. Wonderful to come out living
     From the fiery furnace-blast,
   But yet more, that after testing
     I shall be fine gold at last;
   Time of cleansing! Time of winnowing!
     Yet 'tis calm, without dismay;
   He who soon shall be my refuge
     Holds the winnowing-fan today.

2. Weary is my life, by foemen
     Thick beset in savage throng,
   For like bees they come about me,
     Harass me the whole day long;
   They of mine own house and kindred
     Captain the infernal brood;
   But, through grace the strife sustaining,
     I'll contend even unto blood.

IX

1. Am fy mod i mor llygredig,
    Ac ymadael ynddwy' i'n llawn,
   Mae bod yn dy fynydd sanctaidd
    Imi'n fraint oruchel iawn;
   Lle mae'r llenni yn cael eu rhwygo,
    Mae difa'r gorchudd yno o hyd,
   A rhagoroldeb dy ogoniant
    Ar ddarfodedig bethau'r byd.

2. O! am bara i uchel yfed
    O ffrydiau'r iechydwriaeth fawr
   Nes fy nghwbwl ddisychedu
    Am ddarfodedig bethau'r llawr;
   Byw dan ddisgwyl am fy Arglwydd,
    Bod, pan ddêl, yn effro iawn
   I agoryd iddo'n ebrwydd
    A mwynhau ei ddelw'n llawn.

IX

1. Since I'm so corrupt by nature,
    Straying from thee constantly,
   'Tis for me a grace transcendent
    On thy holy mount to be;
   Here the veils are rent asunder,
    All concealment done away;
   Thou thine all-excelling glory
    Over all things dost display.

2. Let me drink for ever deeply
    Of salvation's mighty flood,
   Till I thirst no more for ever
    After any earthly good;
   Live expectant of his coming,
    Watchful every hour abide,
   Haste to open, and be fully
    With his likeness satisfied.

X

1. O! na bai fy mhen yn ddyfroedd
    Fel yr wylwn yn ddi-lai
   Am fod Seion, lu banerog,
    Yng ngwres y dydd yn llwfrhau;
   O! datguddia y colofnau
    A wnaed i'w chynnal yn y nos,
   Addewidion diamodol
    Duw ar gyfri' angau'r groes.

2. Cofia, Arglwydd, dy ddyweddi,
    Llama ati fel yr hydd,
   Ac na ad i'r Amaleciaid
    Arni'n hollol gario'r dydd;
   Mae'r llwynogod ynddi'n rhodio
    I ddifwyno'r egin grawn,
   S'ceina fwyfwy sy'n ymadael
    O foreddydd hyd brynhawn.

3. Deffro, Arglwydd, gwna rymuster,
    Cofia lw'r cyfamod hedd,
   Gwêl dy Enw mawr dan orchudd
    Ar y tystion yn y bedd;
   Gair o'th enau, dônt i fyny!
    Ti yw'r Atgyfodiad mawr,
   Ac argraffiadau yr Enw newydd
    Yn ddisglair arnynt fel y wawr.

4. Hwn yw'r ennaint tywalltedig,
    Ymddibynnol arno ei hun
   I ddwyn gelynion byth yn deilwng
    Wrthrychau cariad Tri yn Un;
   Mae edifeirwch wedi ei guddio,
    Am hyn er neb ni thry yn ôl
   Nes bod â'r llafur yn ddihangol
    I dragwyddoldeb yn ei gôl.

X

1. O that all my head were waters,
    Weeping ever, day and night,
   Since the bannered hosts of Zion
    Flinch and falter in the fight.
   O reveal the shining pillars
    Given of old her strength to be,
   Promises divine, unchanging,
    Won for us on Calvary.

2. Lord, thy fainting bride remember,
    As a hart leap to her side;
   Let not Amalek o'erthrow her
    Utterly in warlike pride;
   Prowling foxes wander through her,
    Spoil her clusters day by day;
   The Shekina of God's presence
    Slowly, slowly draws away.

3. Lord, awake! display thy valour,
    Thy great covenant maintain;
   See thy Name traduced and blackened
    Where thy witnesses lie slain;
   Thou who art the Resurrection,
    Speak the word, and they shalt rise,
   Thy new Name inscribed upon them,
    Radiant as the morning skies.

4. Thy new Name is precious ointment,
    Fragrant, powerful and free,
   Rendering foemen worthy objects
    Of the love of One in Three;
   For with God is no repentance;
    None shall e'er his work delay
   Till his sheaves lie in his bosom,
    Gathered in, and safe for aye.

XI

1. Yng nglyn wylofain bydd fy ymdaith
    Nes im weled dwyfol waed
 O'r Graig yn tarddu fel yr afon,
    Ynddo yn wynion myrdd a wnaed;
 Golau'r Maen i fynd ymlaen,
 Sef Iesu yn gyfiawnder glân.

2. Rwy'n hiraethu am yr amser
    Y caf ddatguddiad o fy mraint,
 Iesu Grist, gwir Bren y Bywyd,
    Hwn yw cyfiawnder pur y saint;
 Ei gleimio'n ail, a'm cadarn sail,
 Yn lle gwag obaith ffigys-ddail.

XII

Rhyfedda fyth, briodas-ferch,
I bwy yr wyt yn wrthrych serch;
O! cenwch, waredigol hil,
Rhagori y mae Fe ar ddeng mil.

XI

1. I shall tread the vale of weeping
    Till the blood divine is seen
   Pouring from the Rock, a river
    That has made ten thousand clean;
   If his light pierce the night
   I shall find my way aright.

2. I am longing for the moment
    That shall all my right disclose –
   Jesus, Tree of Life immortal,
    Source whence all our justice flows;
   Boldly there I'll repair,
   No more useless fig-leaves wear.

XII

O wonder always, happy bride,
To whom thou art in love allied;
Ye ransomed seed, his wonders tell,
Who o'er ten thousand doth excel.

XIII

1. Wele'n sefyll rhwng y myrtwydd
    Wrthrych teilwng o fy mryd;
   Er mai o ran, yr wy'n adnabod
    Ei fod uwchlaw gwrthrychau'r byd:
     Henffych fore
    Y caf ei weled fel y mae.

2. Rhosyn Saron yw ei enw,
    Gwyn a gwridog, teg o bryd;
   Ar ddeng mil y mae'n rhagori
    O wrthrychau penna'r byd:
     Ffrind pechadur,
    Dyma ei beilat ar y môr.

3. Beth sy imi mwy a wnelwyf
    Ag eilunod gwael y llawr?
   Tystio'r wyf nad yw eu cwmni
    I'w cystadlu â Iesu mawr:
     O! am aros
    Yn ei gariad ddyddiau f'oes.

XIII

1. There he stands among the myrtles,
    Worthiest object of my love;
   Yet in part I know his glory
      Towers all earthly things above;
        One glad morning
      I shall see him as he is.

2. He's the beauteous Rose of Sharon,
      White and ruddy, fair to see;
   Excellent above ten thousand
      Of the world's prime glories he.
        Friend of sinners,
      Here's their pilot on the deep.

3. What have I to do henceforward
      With vain idols of this earth?
   Nothing can I find among them
      To compete with his high worth.
        Be my dwelling
      In his love through all my days.

XIV

1. Ni ddichon byd a'i holl deganau
    Fodloni fy serchiadau yn awr,
   A enillwyd, a ehangwyd,
    Yn nydd nerth fy Iesu mawr;
   Ef, nid llai, a eill eu llenwi,
    Er mai diamgyffred yw;
   O! am syllu ar ei Berson,
    Fel y mae Fe'n ddyn a Duw.

2. O! na chawn i dreulio 'nyddiau
    Yn fywyd o ddyrchafu ei waed;
   Llechu'n dawel dan ei gysgod,
    Byw a marw wrth ei draed;
   Caru'r groes, a phara i'w chodi,
    Am mai croes fy Mhriod yw;
   Ymddifyrru yn ei Berson
    A'i addoli byth yn Dduw.

XIV

1. Earth cannot, with all its trinkets,
     Slake my longings at this hour;
   They were captured, they were widened,
     When my Jesus showed his power.
   None but he can now content me,
     He, the Incomprehensible;
   O to gaze upon his Person,
     God in man made visible.

2. Let my days be wholly given
     Jesus' blood to glorify,
   Calm to rest beneath his shadow,
     At his feet to live and die,
   Love the cross, and bear it daily,
     ('Tis the cross my Husband bore),
   Gaze with joy upon his Person,
     And unceasingly adore.

XV

Mewn môr o ryfeddodau,
  O! am gael treulio f'oes,
Ar dir pechadur aros
  A byw ar waed y groes,
A chael caethiwo'm meddwl
  Oll i ufudd-dod Crist,
A chydymffurfio â'i gyfraith,
  Bod drosto'n ffyddlon dyst.

XVI

Ni ddaeth i fwrdd cyfiawnder Duw
  Wrth gofio pechod
Ond cysgodau o'r sylwedd byw
  Oedd i ddyfod;
Y Jiwbili, pan ddaeth i ben,
  Y llen a rwygwyd,
A'r ddeddf yn Iesu ar y pren
  A ddigonwyd.

XV

Lapped in a sea of wonders
    O might I spend my days,
Upon the blood depending
    The while I tread earth's ways,
And find my thoughts made captive
    To Christ's authority,
And, with his law conforming,
    His faithful witness be.

XVI

God's table could provide no food,
    While sin was reigning,
But shadows of a future good,
    Our hope sustaining;
When came the day of Jubilee,
    The veil was riven;
The law, in Jesus on the tree,
    Saw justice given.

XVII

Nac edryched neb i gloffi
    Arnaf, am fy mod yn ddu;
Haul, a gwres ei belyderau,
    Yn tywynnu'n danbaid arnaf sy:
      Mae a'm cuddia
    Cysgod llenni Solomon.

XVIII

Pan gymerodd pechod aflan
    Feddiant ar y cyntaf ddau,
Duw y cariad aeth dan rwymau
    Yn ei hanfod i gasáu;
Eto'n caru ac yn achub
    Yr un gwrthrychau o'i ddwyfol lid
Mewn ffordd gyfiawn, heb gyfnewid,
    Ond perffaith fod yr un o hyd.

XVII

Let not any, for my blackness,
    Gaze upon me doubtingly;
'Tis the sun that, high in splendour,
    Shoots his fiery shafts at me;
        Yet I'm covered –
    Solomon's curtains give me shade.

XVIII

When the primal pair fell captive
    'Neath the law of sin and fate,
God, the God of love, by nature
    Found himself compelled to hate;
Yet though wrathful, still he loved them,
    Rescued them in their distress,
Nothing bated of his justice,
    Perfect in his changelessness.

XIX

1. O! am dreiddio i'r adnabyddiaeth
    O'r unig wir a'r bywiol Dduw
   I'r fath raddau a fo'n lladdfa
    I ddychmygion o bob rhyw;
   Credu'r gair sy'n dweud amdano,
    A'i natur ynddo, amlwg yw,
   Yn farwolaeth i bechadur
    Heb gael Iawn o drefniad Duw.

2. Yn yr adnabyddiaeth yma
    Mae uchel drem yn dod i lawr,
   Dyn yn fach, yn wael, yn ffiaidd,
    Duw'n oruchel ac yn fawr;
   Crist yn ei gyfryngol swyddau,
    Gwerthfawr anhepgorol yw;
   Yr enaid euog yn yr olwg
    A'i gogonedda megis Duw.

XIX

1. O to pierce into the knowledge
    Of the one, true, living Lord,
   Slaying all imaginations,
    Holding solely by the Word;
   To believe what there stands written,
    What from thence is clearly known:
   Sinners cannot live before him;
    He, he only, must atone.

2. Where this truth is seen and pondered,
    Lofty looks are overthrown;
   Man is little, weak and loathsome,
    God is great, and God alone;
   Christ, our precious Mediator,
    Can alone our state repair;
   Guilty souls, his work beholding,
    Worship God incarnate there.

XX

1. Mae'r Duw anfeidrol mewn trugaredd,
    Er mai Duw y cariad yw,
   Wrth ei gofio, imi'n ddychryn,
    Imi'n ddolur, imi'n friw;
   Ond ym mhabell y cyfarfod
    Mae Fe yno'n llawn o hedd,
   Yn Dduw cymodlon wedi eistedd,
    Heb ddim ond heddwch yn ei wedd.

2. Yno mae fy mwyd a 'niod,
    Fy noddfa a'm gorffwysfa wiw,
   Fy meddyginiaeth a fy nhrysor,
    Tŵr cadarn anffaeledig yw;
   Yno mae fy holl arfogaeth
    Yn wyneb fy ngelynion cas;
   Mae 'mywyd i yno yn guddiedig
    Pan wy' i yn ymladd ar y ma's.

3. Cael Duw'n Dad, a Thad yn noddfa,
    Noddfa'n graig, a'r graig yn dŵr,
   Mwy nis gallaf ei ddymuno
    Gyda mi mewn tân a dŵr;
   Ohono Ef mae fy nigonedd,
    Ynddo trwy fyddinoedd af;
   Hebddo, eiddil, gwan a dinerth,
    A cholli'r dydd yn wir a wnaf.

XX

1. God, though infinite in mercy,
    God of love although he be,
  When I think on him, affrights me,
    Troubles me, disquiets me;
  Yet within the tent of meeting
    Throned he sits as God of grace,
  Peace and reconciliation
    Gently radiant in his face.

2. There my food and drink are furnished,
    There my rest and refuge are,
  There my healing and my treasure,
    There my stronghold in the war;
  There I find my warlike harness,
    Arming me to face the foe;
  There my life is safely hidden
    When to conflict forth I go.

3. God my Father, God my Refuge,
    God my Stronghold, Rock and Tower –
  More I cannot ask when round me
    Fire and flood put forth their power;
  He my every want supplying,
    I'll repel an armed host;
  Lacking him, I'm weak and strengthless,
    And the day is truly lost.

XXI

Ei law aswy sy'n fy nghynnal
    Dan fy mhen yng ngwres y dydd,
A bendithion ei ddeheulaw
    Yn cofleidio'm henaid sydd;
Tynghedaf chwi, bwysïau natur,
    Sy'n prydferthu daear lawr,
Na chyffrôch, hyd oni fynno,
    Fy nghariad a'm gogoniant mawr.

XXI

His left hand, in heat of noonday,
    Lovingly my head upholds,
And his right hand, filled with blessings,
    Tenderly my soul enfolds.
I adjure you, nature's darlings,
    Beautiful in field and grove,
Stir not up, till he be willing,
    Him who is my glorious Love.

XXII

1. Rhyfedd, rhyfedd gan angylion,
    Rhyfeddod fawr yng ngolwg ffydd,
   Gweld Rhoddwr bod, Cynhaliwr helaeth
    A Rheolwr pob peth sydd,
   Yn y preseb mewn cadachau
    A heb le i roi ei ben i lawr,
   Ac eto disglair lu'r gogoniant
    Yn ei addoli'n Arglwydd mawr.

2. Pan fo Sinai i gyd yn mygu
    A sŵn yr utgorn uwcha' ei radd,
   Caf fynd i wledda tros y terfyn
    Yng Nghrist y Gair heb gael fy lladd;
   Mae ynddo'n trigo bob cyflawnder,
    Llond gwagle colledigaeth dyn;
   Ar yr adwy rhwng y ddwyblaid
    Gwnaeth gymod trwy ei offrymu ei hun.

3. Efe yw'r Iawn fu rhwng y lladron,
    Efe ddioddefodd angau loes,
   Efe a nerthodd freichiau ei ddienyddwyr
    I'w hoelio yno ar y groes;
   Wrth dalu dyled pentewynion,
    Ac anrhydeddu deddf ei Dad,
   Cyfiawnder, mae'n disgleirio'n danbaid
    Wrth faddau yn nhrefn y cymod rhad.

4. O! f'enaid, gwêl y fan gorweddodd
    Pen brenhinoedd, Awdwr hedd,
   Y greadigaeth ynddo'n symud,
    Yntau'n farw yn y bedd;
   Cân a bywyd colledigion,
    Rhyfeddod fwya' angylion nef;
   Gweld Duw mewn cnawd a'i gydaddoli
    Mae'r côr, dan weiddi 'Iddo Ef!'

XXII

1. Wondrous sight for men and angels!
    Wonders, wonders without end!
   He who made, preserves, sustains us,
    He our Ruler and our Friend,
   Here lies cradled in the manger,
    Finds no resting-place on earth,
   Yet the shining hosts of glory
    Throng to worship at his birth.

2. When thick cloud lies over Sinai,
    And the trumpet's note rings high,
   In Christ the Word I'll pass the barrier,
    Climb, and feast, nor fear to die;
   For in him all fullness dwelleth,
    Fullness to restore our loss;
   He stood forth and made atonement
    Through his offering on the cross.

3. He between a pair of robbers
    Hung, our Making-good to be;
   He gave power to nerve and muscle
    When they nailed him to the tree;
   He, his Father's law exalting,
    Paid our debt and quenched our flame;
   Righteousness, in fiery splendour,
    Freely pardons in his name.

4. See, my soul, where our Peace-maker,
    King of kings, was lowly laid,
   He, creation's life and movement,
    Of the grave a tenant made;
   Yet on souls fresh life bestowing –
    Angels view it with amaze;
   God in flesh with us adoring,
    Heaven's full chorus shouts his praise.

5. Diolch byth, a chanmil diolch,
    Diolch tra bo ynwy' i chwyth,
  Am fod gwrthrych i'w addoli
    A thestun cân i bara byth;
  Yn fy natur wedi ei demtio
    Fel y gwaela' o ddynol-ryw,
  Yn ddyn bach, yn wan, yn ddinerth,
    Yn anfeidrol wir a bywiol Dduw.

6. Yn lle cario corff o lygredd,
    Cyd-dreiddio â'r côr yn danllyd fry
  I ddiderfyn ryfeddodau
    Iechydwriaeth Calfari;
  Byw i weld yr Anweledig,
    Fu farw ac sy'n awr yn fyw;
  Tragwyddol anwahanol undeb
    A chymundeb â fy Nuw.

7. Yno caf ddyrchafu'r Enw
    A osododd Duw yn Iawn,
  Heb ddychymyg, llen, na gorchudd,
    A'm henaid ar ei ddelw'n llawn;
  Yng nghymdeithas y dirgelwch,
    Datguddiedig yn ei glwy',
  Cusanu'r Mab i dragwyddoldeb
    Heb im gefnu arno mwy.

5. Thanks for ever, thanks ten thousand,
      While I've breath, all thanks and praise
   To the God who all his wonders
      For my worship here displays;
   In my nature tried and tempted
      Like the meanest of our race,
   Man – a weak and helpless infant,
      God – of matchless power and grace.

6. Gone this body of corruption,
      'Mid the fiery hosts on high,
   Gazing deep into the wonders
      Wrought of old on Calvary;
   God, the Invisible, beholding –
      Him who lives, yet once was slain;
   Clasped in close eternal union
      And communion I'll remain.

7. There, new-fashioned in his likeness,
      Veils and fancies done away,
   To the Name by God exalted
      Highest homage I shall pay.
   There, communing in the secret
      Seen in those deep wounds he bore,
   I shall kiss the Son for ever,
      Turning from him nevermore.

XXIII

1. Os rhaid wynebu'r afon donnog,
    Mae Un i dorri grym y dŵr,
   Iesu, f'Archoffeiriad ffyddlon,
    A chanddo sicir afael siŵr;
   Yn ei gôl caf weiddi 'Concwest!'
    Ar angau, uffern, byd, a bedd,
   Tragwyddol fod heb fodd i bechu,
    Yn ogoneddus yn ei wedd.

2. Melys gofio y cyfamod
    Draw a wnaed gan Dri yn Un,
   Tragwyddol syllu ar y Person
    A gymerodd natur dyn;
   Wrth gyflawni yr amodau,
    Trist iawn hyd angau ei enaid oedd;
   Dyma gân y saith ugeinmil
    Tu draw i'r llen â llawen floedd.

3. Byw heb wres na haul yn taro,
    Byw heb allu marw mwy,
   Pob rhyw alar wedi darfod,
    Dim ond canu am farwol glwy';
   Nofio yn afon bur y bywyd,
    Diderfyn heddwch sanctaidd Dri,
   Dan d'w'niadau digymylau
    Gwerthfawr angau Calfari.

XXIII

1. Must I face the stormy river?
    There is One to still the wave;
  Jesus, my High Priest, is with me,
    Strong to hold me, strong to save;
  In his bosom I'll cry conquest,
    (Death, and world, and hell defied),
  Lacking now all means of sinning,
    In his likeness glorified.

2. Sweet to think upon the cov'nant
    Made on high ere time began,
  Gazing ever on the Person
    Who assumed the form of man;
  Unto death his soul was troubled,
    All the agreement to fulfil;
  Now the ransomed seven-score-thousand
    Shout and sing on Zion's hill.

3. There no fiery sun at noonday
    Smites; there death itself is slain;
  Freed from sorrow, there the blessed
    Sing of One in mortal pain;
  There they swim in life's pure river
    Flowing from the holy Three,
  'Neath those peaceful rays unclouded
    Streaming down from Calvary.

XXIV

1. Gwna fi fel pren planedig, O! fy Nuw,
   Yn ir ar lan afonydd dyfroedd byw,
   Yn gwreiddio ar led, a'i ddail heb wywo mwy,
   Ond ffrwytho dan gawodydd dwyfol glwy'.

2. Gwlad dda, heb wae, gwlad wedi ei rhoi dan sêl,
   Llifeirio mae, a'i ffrwyth o laeth a mêl;
   Grawnsypiau gwiw i'r anial dir sy'n dod;
   Gwlad nefol yw, uwchlaw mynegi ei chlod.

3. Jehofa yw, yn un â'i Enw pur,
   Cyflawnwr gwiw ei addewidion gwir;
   Mae'n codi ei law, cenhedloedd ddaw i maes,
   Nodedig braw' o'i rydd anfeidrol ras.

4. Cenhadon hedd, mewn efengylaidd iaith,
   Sy'n galw i'r wledd dros fôr yr India faith;
   Caiff Hotentots, Goraniaid dua' eu lliw,
   Farbaraidd lu, eu dwyn i deulu Duw.

XXIV

1. God, make me like a tree well-planted grow
   In fertile ground where living waters flow,
   Wide-rooting, ever green, and fruiting free
   'Neath showers from that dire wound on Calvary.

2. God's promised land is good; it knows no woe;
   In all its borders milk and honey flow;
   Fine clusters thence are brought on desert ways;
   A heavenly land, and none can speak its praise.

3. Jehovah he, and true to his great Name;
   His promises are true, his word the same;
   He lifts his hand, forth comes a new-born race,
   To all a proof of his free boundless grace.

4. Heralds of peace, in evangelic tongue,
   Call to the feast far Indian seas among;
   Hottentots, black Koranians drawn we see
   (Barbaric hosts) into God's family.

XXV

A raid i'm sêl, oedd farwor tanllyd
    Unwaith dros dy ogoniant gwiw,
A charedigrwydd fy ieuenctid,
    Fynd yn oerach at fy Nuw?
Breswylydd mawr yr uchelderau,
    Yn awr datguddia'th wyneb llon,
A diddyfna fy enaid bellach
    Oddi ar fronnau'r greadigaeth hon.

XXVI

Mae sŵn y clychau'n chwarae
    Wrth odrau Iesu mawr
Ac arogl y pomgranadau
    I'w clywed ar y llawr;
Maddeuant i bechadur
    Yn effeithio i fwynhad,
Er mwyn yr aberth difai
    A lwyr fodlonai'r Tad.

XXV

Must my zeal, that for thy glory
    Like a fiery coal once glowed,
And my youthful loving ardour,
    Now wax colder towards my God?
Thou whose dwelling is high heaven,
    Now thy matchless beauty show;
From the breasts of this creation
    Wean my soul for ever now.

XXVI

The bells are sweetly ringing
    Great Jesus' robes around;
The odour of pomegranates
    Suffuses all the ground;
Forgiveness for the sinner,
    And peace and joy supplied
Through him whose faultless offering
    The Father satisfied.

XXVII

Cofia ddilyn y medelwyr,
    Ymhlith 'r ysgubau treulia dy oes;
Pan fo Mynydd Sinai'n danllyd,
    Gwlych dy damaid wrth y groes;
Gwêl ddirgelwch mawr duwioldeb,
    Cafwyd allor wrth dy droed,
Duw a dyndod arno yn diodde',
    Llef am ole' i ganu ei glod.

XXVIII

Y mae dyfroedd iechydwriaeth
    A'u rhinweddau mewn parhad,
Y mae ynddynt feddyginiaeth
    Anffaeledig ac yn rhad;
Deuwch, gleifion codwm Eden,
    I ddefnyddio'r dyfroedd hyn;
Ni bydd diwedd byth ar rinwedd
    Sylwedd mawr Bethesda lyn.

XXVII

Follow on behind the reapers,
    'Mid the sheaves thy dwelling make;
When Mount Sinai burns and trembles,
    At the cross thy morsel take;
See thy God, in his deep counsels,
    At thy feet an altar raise;
God-in-man is suffering on it;
    Cry for light to sing his praise.

XXVIII

Still the streams of our salvation,
    Filled with living virtue, flow,
Free unfailing gifts of healing
    Ever ready to bestow;
Sufferers from the fall in Eden,
    Use these waters for your cure;
Never-ending are the virtues
    Of Bethesda's substance pure.

XXIX

Mi gerdda'n ara' ddyddiau f'oes
Dan gysgod haeddiant gwaed y groes,
    A'r yrfa redaf yr un wedd,
Ac wrth ei rhedeg sefyll wnaf,
Gweld iechydwriaeth lawn a gaf
    Wrth fynd i orffwys yn y bedd.

XXX

Dyma Frawd a anwyd inni
    Erbyn c'ledi a phob clwy';
Ffyddlon ydyw, llawn tosturi,
    Fe haeddai gael ei foli'n fwy:
Rhyddhawr caethion, Meddyg cleifion;
    Ffordd i Seion union yw;
Ffynnon loyw, Bywyd meirw;
    Arch i gadw dyn yw Duw.

XXIX

I'll walk on softly day by day,
The cross o'ershadowing all my way,
    And as I walk, my course I'll run,
And as I run I'll stand and see
The full salvation that shall be
    When I'm no more beneath the sun.

XXX

Lo, to us is born a Brother,
    Born for hard and troublous days,
Faithful, full of consolation,
    Worthy of yet higher praise.
Freedom sealing, sickness healing.
    Way to Zion straight and free,
Fount clear-flowing, life bestowing,
    God our saving ark is he.

The Letters of Ann Griffiths

translated by H. A. Hodges

LETTER I

Ann Thomas to John Hughes

28 November 1800

Dear brother,

I have had this opportunity to send you these few lines, in order to show my readiness to receive and answer your substantial letter, as I fully believe that it was in the field of Boaz that you gleaned the ears of corn, so full and so charged with blessing, which you sent me, bidding me rub them and feed on them; and I think they had so much effect on my mind as to make me sigh for the Rock, for you could not have sent anything more pertinent to my condition, as was your intention, because you knew more of my story in all its wretchedness than anyone else.

I am glad, glad, to hear of your perseverance in meditation on your condition and in the Word, and I wish you prosperity in all.

As for us at Pontrobert, in bodily health as usual; spiritually, the *seiat* as a body is much more alert, and the ministry generally full of unction.

I have not much to say at present about any persons in particular, but I should be glad to relate how it is with me. I have had some very smart trials, and strong winds, so that I almost lost my breath on the slopes; but I considered myself to have been pulled up the hill by the following two chains: 'And a Man shall be as an hiding place,' &c.; 'Come, my people, – and hide thyself,' &c. It was quiet and warm for a time.

I have had another trial concerning spending time in the Church of God, deciding my religion to be based on false motives from the start, and thinking of giving up. I was lifted up thus: 'Seeing then that we have a great high priest,' &c. But at present, very cloudy and doubtful regarding my matter, with the question beating upon my mind whether a true work has been begun in me or not. But in the face of everything, I say this: 'Though he slay me,' &c.

We have had precious privileges in these past days, the ordinance twice, with a sweet savour at the breaking of the bread.

Dear brother, I was glad to hear the point about the circumstances of God's Church being made manifest to those who profess faith, because I think this is not altogether strange to me in these turbulent days of the winnowing of Zion. All awakened Christians are specially bound in this matter to grieve over the sight of 'the stones of the sanctuary in the top of every street', such as fornication, theft and the like. I desire of you also to take the bride of the Lamb to the throne of grace. Sigh much for her restoration. Commend her to her Bridegroom, for 'God will not cast away his people which he foreknew', because the covenant is a covenant by oath, although she is a whore.

Two scriptures have been particularly on my mind, one was mentioned above, and the other is this: 'The cup is in the hand of the Lord, and the wine is red; it is full mixed, and it is poured out of the same; and all the wicked of the earth shall drink the dregs thereof.' Light dawned upon my mind; for if one of the cups that are spoken of is poured out, the children will only be purged, because they are in a Father's hand. But let us pray much for help to suffer the treatment, be it bitter as it may, to bring us to our place.

I will close now; and this from your fellow-pilgrim on the journey to eternity.

ANN THOMAS, Dolwar

LETTER II

Ann Thomas to John Hughes

17 February 1801

Dear brother in the Lord,

I have had an opportunity to send you these lines, to let you know that I have received your letters kindly, hoping that the weighty things contained in them will find a place in my mind.

I am glad to hear of how things are with you also in relation to your condition. Precious is 'a friend that sticketh close', as you said.

A word gripped my mind, which it would perhaps be profitable for me to mention, on the matter: 'Simon, son of Jonas, lovest thou me more than these?' I thought that there was need to pass beyond brethren and graces, and love the Giver above the gift.

Another word gripped my mind: 'Buy the truth, and sell it not.' It came to my mind that I was content to give all that I possessed, be it good or bad, for the Son in a marriage union. I think that every idle word, and all levity of spirit, and all behaviour which appears contrary to gospel holiness, is a total denial that we know Jesus Christ. But in the face of our great wretchedness, how precious it is to think of that word: 'The Lord turned, and looked upon Peter.'

I am cheered by the thought that a sinner is free to speak so much of Jesus Christ before the throne of grace, with heaven smiling and hell trembling. Let us magnify our privilege that we have known something of the effects of the eternal covenant decreed above. O to remain under the drops of the sanctuary until the evening, and to acknowledge that they have been purchased by blood. This would make sinners drop to the dust. O to be at the feet of our good God while we are in the world.

Now, I will send you some account of how things are with the *seiat* at Pontrobert. In general quite bedewed and quite awake as regards the greater part of the church at present. I think she [the church] is no stranger to the wine which is being distributed among the disciples here on their journey.

If I should tell how it is with me, I should wish to speak well of God for remembering me in the face of many doubts. I have never seen so much cause to cry out for the Rock in all weathers; and whether I die or live, this is my cry: 'O to be found in him, not having mine own righteousness, which is of the law.'

I have heard a simile of a shopkeeper who went to Chester to buy two hundred pounds' worth of goods; he received a bill of parcels; that hung in the shop, noting the names and quantity of the goods; and a man came in and asked for a crown's worth of one of them; he replied, 'I haven't got a pennyworth of it.' Though many may make a grand show in the profession of religion, yet in the face of temptation you ask, 'Where is their faith?' A shout arose: 'Little children, cry out for the wagon to come home; it is heavily laden, namely ministers of the Word.'

I will close now; and this from one who desires to wish the prosperity of those who journey to Zion.

ANN THOMAS, Dolwar

LETTER III

Ann Thomas to John Hughes

Dear brother,

I have had this opportunity to write to you, hoping you are well, and to let you know I have received your valuable letter. I would wish that you would not neglect to send profitable things, and not pay attention to our own neglectfulness, because you know the cause, a lack of having hardly anything of value to send.

Dear brother, I should have been glad to see you many times when in distress of mind and gnawed by doubts of the verity of the visitations, and the partial revelation of a Mediator, in view of a damnable, lost condition. And despite trying many roads, failing to achieve my purpose. But on the road of meditation I had a lesson from the advice given to Moses by his father-in-law, to appoint sixty elders to judge the people in cases which were commonplace and evident, but to bring the great and obscure cases to him. I thought it necessary for my perplexing condition to pass beyond 'the watchmen that go about the city', and everyone, to God alone. It is a comfort to me to think of this: when my condition is at its darkest to me and my brethren, it is clear daylight in the court of the High Priest. Thanks forever for this!

I have found much pleasure in meditating on the Shunammite woman setting aside a room on the wall for the man of God to rest in when he passed by, placing in it a bed, a table, a stool, and a candlestick. Perhaps that woman, in her longing for the prophet, often paced the room, and found cheer in expectation of the man. But be that as it may, it comforts the heart of a believer, in the absence of the visible countenance of his Lord, that the furniture is still there in some senses. For one thing, it is a sign that he has not been given up. For another thing, it is too hot a lodging for a devil. 'When the enemy shall come in like a strong river, the Spirit of the

Lord shall chase him out.' He cannot so much as raise his head in the temple of God without trembling, nor look upon anything within it, except his own footprints, without being terrified. Therefore let us cry much for the Holy Spirit to make his home in our condition.

Dear brother, things are quite dark at present for the church at Pontrobert, under fire from the world, and backsliders. I found great pleasure one evening in view of these things in thinking what the Holy Spirit says of her [the church]. Two scriptures were on my mind: 'Glorious things are spoken of thee, O city of God'; 'The Lord thy God in the midst of thee is mighty.'

This at present from your sister,

ANN THOMAS, Dolwar

LETTER IV

Ann Thomas to John Hughes

Dear brother,

I have been very glad many times to send to tell you how things are with me. I have received much pleasure and blessing from reading your letters, which is a very strong encouragement for me to beg you earnestly not to withhold your hand.

Dear brother, the warfare is as hot now as ever, enemies within, enemies without. But of them all, it is the sin of the mind which presses most heavily upon me.

I find particular pleasure today in thinking of that word: 'And to Jesus, the Mediator of the new covenant, and to the blood of sprinkling.' Something new from loving the doctrine of purification. That word is on my mind: 'And the blood of Jesus Christ his Son cleanseth us from all sin.' I have never had a greater longing to be pure. That word is on my mind: 'The house, when it was in building, was built of stones that had been fully dressed.' I sometimes think I have no need ever to change my garment, but a longing to be clean in my garment.

I should be well pleased to abide more in the sanctuary, as you mentioned so extensively and valuably. I often expect to encounter some troublesome weather, though I do not know what. That word is on my mind tonight: 'By this shall the iniquity of Jacob be purged,' &c. O for help to abide with God, whatever may come my way! And thanks forever that the furnace and the fountain are so close to one another!

There is nothing else in particular on my mind at present, but remember me often, and send to me soon.

I am, your unworthy sister who loves your prosperity in body and spirit,

ANN THOMAS, Dolwar

LETTER V

Ann Thomas to John Hughes

Dear brother in the Lord,

I am writing to you at present because it is the course of my mind, in the face of all kinds of weather, to tell you how it is with me, dear brother.

Dear brother, the most particular thing that is on my mind is the great obligation I am under to be grateful to the Lord for upholding me in the face of the winds and the flood waters. I can say that my thoughts have never been seized by the same degree of fear as in these days; but in the face of everything I think to hang quietly upon that precious promise: 'When thou passest through the waters, I will be with thee.' I think it is enough to support me in the place where two seas meet. Thanks forever for a God who fulfils his promises!

Dear brother, the most pressing thing that is on my mind is the sinfulness of letting any visible thing take precedence in my mind. I am reverently ashamed, and rejoice marvelling, to think that he 'who humbleth himself to behold the things that are in heaven' has yet given himself as an object of love to a creature as wretched as I.

As regards the dishonour done to God by giving the first place to secondary things, this simply is my mind: if nature must be pressed into the grasp of death because it is too weak to bear the fiery rays of the sun of temptations, I sometimes think I will gladly see myself stripped of my natural life (if need be) rather than that glory should go under a cloud while nature gets its own way and its objects.

That word is on my mind tonight: 'Go forth, O ye daughters of Zion, and behold king Solomon with the crown wherewith his mother crowned him in the day of his espousals, and in the day of the gladness of his heart.' I think there is a high and peculiar calling for all who are subjects of the covenant to leave their own 'cieled houses' to see their King 'wearing the crown of thorns, and the purple robe'.

No wonder the sun hid its rays when its Creator was pierced by nails. To my mind it is a marvel who was on the cross: he whose eyes are as a flame of fire piercing through heaven and earth at the same moment unable to see his creatures, the work of his hands. My mind is too overwhelmed to say anything more on the matter. But on looking at the majesty of the Person, it is no wonder that that word has been set down: 'The Lord will be well pleased for his righteousness' sake; he will magnify the law, and make it honourable.'

Dear brother, it is no wonder that that word has been set down: 'Kiss the Son, lest he be angry.'

Dear brother, there is nothing particular on my mind to enlarge upon at present. But this I will say in conclusion: I desire that the remaining part of my life should be a communion so close that it might never again belong to me to say, 'I will go and return.' I should think, if only this could be, I should be calm to meet providence in its frown and its crosses.

I desire a special place in your prayers. Remember to send soon. I am longing for a letter.

I am, your loving sister,

ANN THOMAS, Dolwar

LETTER VI

Ann Thomas to John Hughes

[April 1802]

Dear brother and father in the Lord,

I received your letter yesterday, and I was very glad to have it, hoping that the valuable things which are in it will be of blessing to me. I was very glad of the scripture which you remarked upon in my brother's letter.

But to proceed to tell you something of how things are with me at present. I have been finding it very stormy for a long time now. Finding very many disappointments in myself continually. But I must say this, that all trials, all winds of whatever sort, work together thus, namely to bring me to see more of my wretched condition by nature, and more of the Lord in his goodness and unchangeableness towards me.

I have lately been particularly far gone in spiritual whoredom from the Lord, while yet holding up in the face of the ministry like one keeping house well and remaining in the fellowship. But despite all my skill the Lord of his goodness broke through in these words: 'If I be a Father, where is mine honour? if I be a Master, where is my fear?' Thanks to God always for the pills of heaven to send the sickness on its way!

My stomach was so weak that I could not feed on free mercy, in view of the path I was following – 'having forsaken God, the fountain of all real consolations, and hewn out for myself broken cisterns'. This word lifted me a little onto my feet again: 'The Lord is my shepherd; I shall not want.' I going astray, he a Shepherd; I powerless to return, he an almighty Lord. O Rock of our salvation, wholly self-dependent in the matter of saving a sinner! Dear brother, I should wish to be for ever under the treatment, be it as bitter as it may.

Another word was a particular blessing to me lately when I tried to tell the Lord about the various things which were calling me to go after them. This is the word: 'Look unto me, all the ends of the earth, that ye may be saved: for I am God, and there is none else.' As if God were saying, 'I know of every call that is upon you, and how various they are; but I also am calling. World is but world, flesh is but flesh, devil is but devil. It is I who am God, and there is none else.'

I am under obligation to be grateful for the Word in its invincible authority. I should heartily wish to give all the praise to God the Word alone for leading me and upholding me thus far, and that what remains of my life might be spent in continual communion with God in his Son, because I can never glorify him more than, or so much as, by believing and accepting his Son. Heaven help me to do that! – not for my own pleasure alone, but out of reverence for him.

Dear brother, there is not much else on my mind to expand upon, but remember often Zion throughout the world, and in particular your old 'mother' at Pontrobert, for the shadows of the evening are almost covering her, and grey hairs are spreading over her, and in a small measure she knows this. This word is much on my mind, and on the minds of others too, at the sight of her weak, disorderly, dejected appearance: 'Is this Naomi?' Wrestle much with the Lord in prayer for her sake, as a body of witnesses for God in the world, because his great Name is in some measure being concealed by her in our backslidings.

Dear brother, I am very glad to hear how things are in relation to your new work. Two scriptures have been on my mind on the matter, one: 'Thus shall it be done unto the man whom the king delighteth to honour'; and the other: 'Surely the Lord's anointed is before me – but God seeth not as man seeth', that is why it was necessary to send for David.

I will close now, with a request that you send to me speedily.

I am, your unworthy sister who is running swiftly to the world that lasts for ever,

ANN THOMAS, Dolwar

LETTER VII

Ann Thomas to John Hughes

Dear brother,

I have had an opportunity to send these few lines to you, to let you know that I received your letter kindly, and to greet you in obedience to the exhortation which it contained; but not only that, but I am glad to be able to send to you regarding how it is with me at present.

Dear brother, I have never conversed personally or in a letter with such a low view of my religion as this time. I feel ashamed as I say this, because my view has been for so long so different to this word which first broke through to me: 'Behold, I have set before thee an open door, and no man can shut it: for thou hast a little strength.' Thanks to God for ever for taking his precious Word in his hand to discipline me! I reverently believe that it is so, and from that time until tonight I believe that the blows of the hammer are to some degree at the one 'root of bitterness' of self-esteem and pride which troubles me. Yet, more of my damnable condition has been revealed to me of late than ever, and more of the glory of the wise design to justify the ungodly, and of 'God in Christ, reconciling the world unto himself, not imputing their trespasses unto them'.

This is often my task at the throne of grace: wondering, giving thanks, and praying. Wondering that the Word should have found a way free to treat the condition of such a damnable, corrupt and guileful wretch as I, without slaying me. Thanks for the lawfulness of the way, and because it glorifies its Author more than because it rewards its travellers. I pray for the privilege of spending the remainder of my days as a life of dealing with God in his Son.

I would be very glad to be prevented from ever venturing to offer to God's holy law less than that which has satisfied it; not only because it will not accept anything else, but out of reverence for it. I never before knew so much reverence towards and love for the law, not in spite of the fact that it brings a curse, but because it brings a curse in every place outside of a Mediator. Thus it shows its purity.

Dear brother, I was glad to read the letter you sent to my brother, and the one to my dear friend, Sara Griffiths, and their valuable exhortations in relation to reading the Word. I too think, whatever we may have in hand apart from the Word, that we are 'spending our money for that which is not bread, and our labour for that which satisfieth not'; because the stomach of the new nature cannot tolerate anything else, and all climates bring sickness except the breezes of the sanctuary alone.

These words are of great value in my estimation – 'Thy neck is like the tower of David; wherein there hang a thousand shields' – in the face of being naked without armour, and without strength in ourselves to meet our enemies. If I may only turn to the tower, I shall find armour and strength to run through faith in him, for 'it pleased the Father that in him should all fulness dwell'. Another word is on my mind: 'A garden inclosed is my sister, my spouse.'

Dear brother, I am under great obligation, if I could, to speak well of God, and to be grateful to him for a degree of communion in 'the fellowship of the mystery'. But this is my grief: failing to abide – continually departing. I see my loss is great; but the dishonour and disrespect to God is greater. O for this: help to abide. This word has been much on my mind: 'Meditate upon these things, and in these things abide.'

Dear brother, there is nothing else in particular on my mind, but to desire you to send me your thoughts on this word: 'In all points tempted like as we are, yet without sin.'

Two other scriptures are on my mind in relation to Zion being in such a low state these days:

1. 'How is the gold become dim, the most fine gold!'
2. 'How is the princess amongst the provinces become a tributary!'

There are some woeful signs that grey hairs have been spreading in great measure over Zion in these days and that the shadows of the evening almost cover her. All awakened souls are under obligation to wrestle much with the Lord, that he may send his winds upon his withered garden, 'that the spices thereof may be spread abroad', so that hell and all its subjects may lose their breath through the strength of the perfume.

Now to conclude. I desire you to remember me before the throne of grace. I desire you to send to me at the first opportunity.

And this from your unworthy sister who is swiftly travelling through a world of time to the world which lasts forever,

ANN THOMAS, Dolwar

LETTER VIII

Ann Thomas to Elizabeth Evans

Dearest sister in the Lord,

In accordance with your wish I have written these few lines to you, and I am very glad to have an opportunity to make known to you how things are with me.

Dear sister, the most particular thing that is on my mind at present as a matter has to do with grieving the Holy Spirit. That word came into my mind: 'Know ye not that your bodies are temples of the Holy Spirit which dwelleth in you?' And on penetrating a little into the wonders of the Person, and that he dwells or resides in the believer, I think simply that I have never been possessed to the same degree by reverential fears lest I should grieve him; and along with that I was brought to see one cause, and the chief cause, why this great sin has made such a slight impression upon the mind, on account of my low, blasphemous thoughts about so great a Person.

This is how my thoughts ran about the Persons of the Trinity. (I hear my mind being seized by shame, yet under a constraint to speak because of the harmfulness of it.) I thought of the Person of the Father and the Son as coequal; but as for the Person of the Holy Spirit, I regarded him as a functionary subordinate to them. O what a fanciful, misguided thought about a divine Person who is all-present, all-knowing, and all-powerful to continue and complete the good work which he has begun in accordance with the free covenant and the counsel of the Three in One regarding those who are the objects of the primal love. O for the privilege of being of their number.

Dear sister, I feel a degree of thirst to increase in the belief in the personal indwelling of the Holy Spirit in my condition; and that through revelation, not imagination, thinking to comprehend in what manner or by what means it happens, which is real idolatry.

Dear sister, when I look a little at the inherent sinfulness of grieving the Holy Spirit, and on the other hand look into the depths of the great fall and see myself wholly divested of all power to do anything but grieve him, I am indeed in somewhat of a strait. But this word is on my mind: 'Watch and pray'; as if the Lord were saying, 'Although the commandment is so harsh, and thou art so powerless to accomplish one thing in a thousand there, on that ground, in respect of thy mind, come forth, try the throne, for the fervent prayer of the righteous availeth much. My grace is sufficient for thee: my strength is made perfect in weakness.' Thanks forever for a God who is full of his promises!

Dear sister, I should like to say much about the efficacy of secret prayer, but you know more than I can say about it; but I am fully convinced that it much surpasses a host of armed men for facing enemies. I know from experience of finding myself surrounded by enemies and having nothing to do but that: 'And I give myself unto prayer'; and that answering the purpose by causing them to fall backwards. O for the privilege of being under the detailed supervision of the Holy Spirit. I think quite simply that a supervision less detailed than the one in that word will never fit my condition: 'I will water it every moment.' Thanks forever for a Bible which fits a condition that has sunk so deep!

Dear sister, it is such a great privilege that one's condition can be found reflected in God's Word. O to hold it up to the holy mirror to the end of making use of a Mediator.

One thing in particular on my mind last night with regard to finding one's condition in the Word. R. J. spoke very valuably as regards matter, and there was I so dry, so distant as regards my experience. Neither law nor gospel had any effect at all on me, and that brought a degree of fear into my mind, failing to think I could find my condition in the Word, because law and gospel were seemingly useless. That word came into my mind: 'Go thy way forth by the footsteps of the flock'; and I failing to see the footsteps of the flock in that situation. But that word came into my mind with light and warmth: 'Awake, O north wind; and come, thou south.' Thanks forever for the rock of the Word to set foot on to start, and the impossibility of starting without that!

Dear sister, I see more need than ever to spend that which remains of my life in giving myself up daily and continually, body and soul, into the care of him who 'is able to keep that which is committed unto him against that day'. Not to give myself once, but to live constantly giving myself, right up until and in the moment when I put off this tabernacle.

Dear sister, the thought of putting it off is particularly sweet sometimes. I can say that this is what cheers me more than anything else these days – not death in itself, but the great gain that is to be got through it: to be able to leave behind every inclination that goes counter to the will of God, to leave behind every ability to dishonour the law of God, every weakness being swallowed up by strength, to become fully conformed to the law which is already on one's heart, and to enjoy God's likeness for ever.

Dear sister, I am sometimes swallowed up so much into these things that I completely fail to stand in the way of my duty with regard to temporal things, but look for the time when I may find release and 'be with Christ; which is far better', although it is very good here 'through the lattice', and the Lord sometimes reveals 'through a glass, darkly', as much of his glory as my weak faculties can bear.

Dear sister, I am glad to say this in conclusion. (I should like to say it with thankfulness.) In spite of all my corruption, and the device of hell, the world and its objects, through God's goodness alone I have not changed the object of my love until tonight; but rather I desire from my heart to 'rest in his love and to be glad in him always with singing', although I cannot attain to that in the slightest degree on this side of death except by violence.

Dear beloved sister, I particularly desire you to send to me with speed; do not refuse me; I shall not be able to help taking it unkindly if you do. Ruth wishes to be remembered kindly to you. I have nothing in particular to send to you by way of news except this, that there is a certain spirit abroad of 'hoping all things' to see signs of the restoration of Rachel Pugh.

And this from your dear sister, swiftly journeying through a world of time to the great world which lasts forever,

ANN THOMAS

Wholly counter to my nature is the path ordained for me;
Yet I'll tread it, yes, and calmly, while thy precious face I see;
Count the cross a crown, and bear it, cheerful live 'mid all life's woes –
This the Way which, straight though tangled, to the heavenly city goes.

Notes on the Hymns of Ann Griffiths

NOTES ON THE HYMNS OF ANN GRIFFITHS

Editorial Note:
It would appear that H. A. Hodges and A. M. Allchin originally intended to include literal prose translations of Ann Griffiths' hymns into English in their proposed edition of her work. When Ann's hymns were published in the volume *Homage to Ann Griffiths* in 1976, they were accompanied not by those prose translations but by metrical English versions of the hymns by H. A. Hodges. However, the prose translations have survived in typescript, and since metrical versions, however good, can never be as close to the original as literal prose translations – as indicated by the caveat in *Homage to Ann Griffiths*, 'Please note that the English hymns are not an exact translation of the Welsh text' – it was decided to include those prose translations here at the beginning of the notes on each hymn.

HYMN I

1. Before me I see an open door, and a way of wholly winning the day in the strength of the gifts which he received who took the form of a servant; the principalities have been despoiled, and the powers, all of them, by him, and the jailer is in the jail through the virtue of his costly suffering.

2. My sorrowful soul, on remembering the battle, leaps for joy; it sees the law held in honour and its great transgressors going free; the Author of life put to death and the great Resurrection buried;

eternal peace brought in between the heaven of heaven and earth below.

3. When he ascended who had descended, after finishing the work here, the gates were lifting up their heads, wondering in their language; doors opening, a choir bowing to God in flesh on yonder side; the Father joyfully invited him to sit on his right hand.

4. Enough in the flood of waters, enough in the flames of fire, O to cling continually to him, my soul, for ever inseparable: on the tangled paths of the land of Arabia are enemies beyond number; grant the fellowship of the sufferings of the precious death on Calvary.

Verse 1. The thought of this stanza is based on Ephesians 4:8, '*Pan ddyrchafodd i'r uchelder, efe a gaethiwodd gaethiwed, ac a roddes roddion i ddynion*' ('When he ascended up on high, he led captivity captive, and gave gifts unto men'). But behind this is Psalm 68:18, '*Dyrchefaist i'r uchelder, caethgludaist gaethiwed: derbyniaist roddion i ddynion*' ('Thou hast ascended on high, thou hast led captivity captive: thou hast received gifts for men'). Ann, though thinking within the New Testament framework, follows the text in the Psalm, 'received gifts' instead of 'gave gifts'. That is, Christ after his spoliation of the principalities and powers (Colossians 2:15) entered heaven in triumph and received gifts – evidently from the Father – which he distributed to men. These are the gifts of grace which he now showers upon us, and upon which Ann depends for victory in her own warfare. 'The jailer is in the jail' is her interpretation of 'he led captivity captive'. Thomas Charles (in *Geiriadur Ysgrythyrol*, his Scriptural Dictionary, under '*caethglud*') mentions the existence of this interpretation, without saying whose it is.

Verse 2. Morris Davies in his memoir of Ann Griffiths (1865) reports that John Williams of Pantycelyn, the son of the great hymn-writer, when he first heard this verse, jumped to his feet and said, 'If I ever meet the woman who composed that verse, I shall feel honoured to take off my hat to her.'

Verse 2, line 6. On 'the great Resurrection', see the note on Hymn X, verse 3, line 6.

Verse 3, line 4: '*dan ryfeddu*' ('wondering'). This is the original reading in the John Hughes manuscript, but it was altered to '*dan orfoleddu*' ('exulting') by the same hand.

HYMN II

1. Here is the tent of meeting, here is atonement in the blood; here is a refuge for the blood-guilty, here for the sick is a free physician; here is a place hard by the Godhead for a sinner to make his nest, and the pure righteousness of Jehovah brightly smiling upon him for ever.

2. Foul sinner is my name, the chiefest of the kind alive; I shall always wonder, a tabernacle has been set up for me to meet quietly with God; there he is, in the fulness of his law, giving a banquet for the transgressor; God and man crying 'Enough!' in Jesus the peace-offering.

3. As for me, I will venture thither boldly, it is a golden sceptre he has in his hand, and this pointing straight at the sinner, full acceptance for all who come; I shall go forward crying 'Forgive!', I shall go and fall at his feet, for forgiveness, for washing me, for cleansing me in his blood.

4. O to come up out of the wilderness like pillars of smoke, straight to his throne, where he sits without his frown; an Amen without beginning and without end, a faithful Witness he is, whose word is unchanging; he manifests the glory of the Trinity in the salvation of lost man.

This is one of the best constructed of Ann's hymns. In it a striking sequence of images develops the concept of reconciliation between God and man. In the first verse we have the Tent of Meeting, associated with other such images as a city of refuge and the soul's nesting place in the cleft of the rock. In the second verse we have the Tabernacle again as a place not merely to meet with God but to be feasted by him by virtue of the peace-offering of Christ. In the third verse it has changed into the throne-room at Susa, and Ahasuerus is on his throne holding out the golden sceptre in token of grace and acceptance. In the fourth and final verse Ahasuerus has changed into Solomon, the messianic Bridegroom, and we are in the bridal procession coming up out of the wilderness to meet him. Christ appears in the first verse as the cleft rock in which the sinner can make his nest. In verse 2 he is the Presence in the Tabernacle, the Peace-Offering, the Fulfiller of the law, the Giver of the feast. In the third verse the nuptial idea is hinted at (Esther, to whom the sceptre is pointed, is the wife of Ahasuerus), and in verse 4 we see the Bride approaching her royal Bridegroom – a well-prepared and satisfying climax.

Some readers may detect eucharistic overtones in the hymn, especially in verse 2. It is impossible to say whether Ann intended this. The first two verses are strongly reminiscent of a passage in a letter written by John Hughes to Ruth Evans on 4 March 1803:

> Wonderful always! there is no need for a sinner to live far away from God. 'Behold, there is a place by me, and thou shalt stand upon a rock' [Exodus 33:21; Welsh Bible: '*Wele fan yn fy ymyl, lle y cei sefyll ar graig*']. A place by God for a sinner to look upon his glory without being slain. And not only this, but a pure God brightly smiling upon him as well; yes, and the law which he has transgressed smiling upon him, and the sinner smiling upon the law. Wonderful always! the law and the transgressor, as it were shaking hands and kissing each other. How did this come about? Not without shedding of blood; and not the blood of bulls and goats and calves, but of Jesus Christ his Son. There

Notes on the Hymns of Ann Griffiths

is for the law and for the guilty one enough [*digon*] in this wonderful Person.

For the possibility that John may be under Ann's influence here, see our Additional Note on Letter VI.

Verse 1. One of the ways of creating emphasis which came naturally to Ann was the use of repetition: either using the same word again and again, or expressing the same idea many times over in slightly differing forms. In this verse, '*dyma*' ('here') is repeated five times at the beginning of five successive lines to introduce five symbols representing different aspects of the Atonement. In verse 3, the note of urgency of Ann's approach to the Throne is reflected in the repeated words '*af*' and '*am*' in lines 5–8, lines which have a somewhat breathless feel about them.

Verse 1, line 6: '*wneud ei nyth*' ('to make his nest'). Why a nest? When God showed Moses a place beside him ('*fan yn fy ymyl*') where he might stand on a rock, the place was said to be in a cleft of the rock ('*o fewn agen yn y graig*'): see Exodus 33:21, 22. But in Canticles 2:14 the phrase 'in the clefts of the rock' ('*yn holltau y graig*') describes the dwelling-place of the dove (i.e. the Bride), and a dove's dwelling-place is a nest.

Verse 2, lines 5–8. Our meeting with God in the Tabernacle (Exodus 40) takes the form of an encounter with Christ crucified. He is the rock on which we stand, in the cleft of which we make our nest, and he is also the form in which God shows his glory to us. The realising vision of the Crucified plays a central part in evangelical piety. Frequently in the language of Methodist hymns and poems the moment of conversion is linked with an experience of 'seeing' Christ on the cross. What is meant is not that the soul resolves its difficulties by creating for itself, by imaginative construction, a mental picture of the event; but that God himself by an act of grace imprints on the soul a vivid realisation of the event and of its saving significance, not merely for sinners in general, but for me. In the background is the biblical image of the Son of Man lifted up as Moses lifted up the serpent in the wilderness, when a single glance was enough to give life to the dying. And then, of course, the Lord's Supper falls into place as an occasion specially created by Christ's own ordinance for us to find the saving vision and the accompanying assurance, or to have it continually renewed in us. Furthermore, the appropriate kind of devotion for use at the Supper will naturally consist in meditations on the Passion and on the doctrine of our redemption. It was on the cross that God in the Person of Christ fulfilled his law, and it is the broken body and the shed blood which are the feast he gives us.

Verse 2, line 7. Does Ann think of God and man as two distinct parties who agree in finding full satisfaction in Christ? Or does 'God and man' mean Christ himself, who cried out 'Enough' when he cried 'It is finished' on the cross?

Verse 2, line 8: '*yn yr Iesu, 'r aberth hedd*' ('in Jesus the peace-offering'). The peace-offering was a form of sacrifice in which the worshipper ate part of what had been offered; and the purpose of the offering was often (though not always) thanksgiving. Of course Christ fulfils the purposes of all the Old Testament sacrifices, and especially the sacrifices for sin. By so doing he creates peace or reconciliation between God and man; and in calling him a peace-offering Ann need not perhaps have meant more than this. If however she has in mind the peace-offering properly so called, then that connects with the reference to a feast in line 6 of this verse and strengthens the suggestion of an eucharistic background to this hymn.

Verse 3, lines 1–4. The imagery here is from the Book of Esther 4:11, 5:1–2.

Verse 4, lines 1–4: see Canticles 3:6–11. Commentators have discussed who it is that comes up out of the wilderness – Solomon or the Bride. Ann takes it to be the Bride, as in Canticles 8:5. And apparently she takes the chariot ('*cerbyd*') of Canticles 3:9 to be really a throne, or to be equivalent to a throne when Solomon is seated in it. We come up out of the wilderness and he is there seated in majesty to receive us, '*heb ei wg*' ('without his frown'). 'His frown'; has he a frown then? Certainly he has; he wears it when he says 'Depart from me, ye cursed' (Matthew 25:41). But not now, for this is a nuptial occasion, he is greeting his Bride. The last verse of this passage in the Canticle is quoted and elaborated by Ann in Letter V. We may add that the day of Christ's espousals, 'the day of the gladness of his heart', when he wears the nuptial crown (Canticles 3:11), is Good Friday, when he 'fulfilled the terms' (Hymn XXIII, verse 2) and won his Bride. So it could be held that his throne is the cross, and that we here enjoy the same encounter with the Crucified as in the second verse of this hymn. True, he is now glorified, but the glorification does not blot out the Passion, it absorbs it into itself. Christ is eternally on the cross, though not everlastingly in agony on it. Perhaps the type of crucifix which shows him robed and crowned as Priest and King is a fair expression of Ann's thought here.

HYMN III

1. Pilgrim, weak from the might of the storms, lift thy gaze, see now the Lamb serving in his mediatorial office in garments trailing to the ground; a golden girdle of faithfulness, on his garment's hem bells full of the sound of pardon for a sinner on account of the infinite Satisfaction.

2. Remember ye this when in a state of weakness, amid the waters which are up to your ankles, that unnumbered are the cubits which are measured out for you above; although being children of

the resurrection to swim in these waters, a bottom or an edge will never be seen to the great substance of Bethesda pool.

3. O the depths of salvation! It is the great mystery of godliness – the God of gods has appeared in the flesh and nature of human kind; here is the Person who suffered in our stead the fullness of wrath, until Righteousness cried out, 'Let him go free! I have received a Ransom.'

4. O blessed hour of eternal rest from my labour in my lot, in the midst of a sea of wonders with never a sight of a boundary or a shore; abundant freedom of entrance, ever to continue, into the dwelling places of the Three in One; water to swim in, not to be passed through, man as God and God as man.

This hymn begins with Christ as our High Priest and Mediator, but goes on at once to the mystery of his Person as the unfathomable central mystery of the Faith.

Verse 2. Ezekiel 47 describes the prophet's vision of a river issuing from under the threshold of the Temple and flowing towards the Dead Sea. It is the river of life, the river of grace which God pours out for his people. At first it is a shallow brook, ankle deep, easily forded; but ultimately it becomes 'waters to swim in, a river that could not be passed over'. Ann clearly thinks this stage is not reached in this life but in the next. We have to be children of the resurrection (Luke 20:36), i.e. glorified in heaven, to swim in these deep waters; but glorified and powerful swimmers as we then are, we never find a bottom or a farther side to it. Ann seems to regard this river as an outflow from the pool of Bethesda (John 5:1–9). Why is it bottomless and boundless? Ezekiel does not say so. The phrase 'waters to swim in, a river that could not be passed over' (which Ann paraphrases in verse 4, line 7) means only that the river is too deep to ford. It is Ann who makes it widen out into a sea. Of course she had to, if she was going to use the river as a symbol of the mystery of Christ. It could not be less than boundless and bottomless.

Verse 3, lines 1–4: 1 Timothy 3:16, '*mawr yw dirgelwch duwioldeb; Duw a ymddangosodd yn y cnawd*' ('great is the mystery of godliness: God was manifest in the flesh').

Verse 3, lines 7–8: Job 33:24, '*Yna efe a drugarha wrtho, ac a ddywed, Gollwng ef, rhag disgyn ohono i'r clawdd: myfi a gefais iawn*' ('Then he is gracious unto him, and saith, Deliver him from going down to the pit: I have found a ransom'). The phrase '*myfi a gefais iawn*' could equally well be rendered, 'I have received satisfaction'; but the context forbids it here. God does not receive satisfaction from man's penitence; he himself 'finds' (i.e. contrives and provides) a ransom, which he makes available for the penitent – a very different thing.

Verse 4, lines 1–2: '*orffwys oddi wrth fy llafur*' ('rest from my labour'): see Revelation 14:13, '*fel y gorffwysont oddi wrth eu llafur*' ('that they may rest from their labours'). '*Yn fy rhan*' ('in my lot'): see Daniel 12:13, '*canys gorffwysi, a sefi yn dy ran yn niwedd y dyddiau*' ('for thou shalt rest, and stand in thy lot at the end of the days').

Verse 4, lines 5–6: see 2 Peter 1:11, '*Canys felly yn helaeth y trefnir i chwi fynediad i mewn i dragwyddol deyrnas ein Harglwydd a'n Hachubwr Iesu Grist*' ('For so an entrance shall be ministered unto you abundantly into the everlasting kingdom of our Lord and Saviour Jesus Christ').

HYMN IV

1. Wholly counter to nature though my path is in the world, I shall tread it, and that quietly, in the precious sight of thy countenance; taking up the cross and counting it a crown, living joyfully in tribulations; it is a way leading straight, although so tangled, to a city of habitation.

2. A way whose name is Wonderful, it is old and yet it grows not

old; a way without a beginning, yet new, a way that makes the dead alive; a way to win those who travel on it, a way that is a Husband, a way that is a Head, a consecrated way – I shall go along it to rest in it beyond the veil.

3. A way no eye of kite can discern though it is as noonday; a way untrodden, invisible to all but the possessors of faith; a way to justify the ungodly, a way to raise up the dead alive, a lawful way for transgressors to peace and favour with God.

4. A way that was planned before time was, to be revealed at need in a promise long ago in Eden, when the Seed of Woman was proclaimed; here are the foundations of the second covenant, here is the counsel of the Three in One, here is the wine which is able to cheer, to cheer the heart of God and man.

This great hymn on Christ the Way is kept moving by a perpetual play on different meanings of the word 'way', as a road or path, as a means or method of achieving something, or simply as a title of Christ. From the first verse to the beginning of the last, the whole hymn is a rhapsody on the idea of the Way. At first the word is introduced in a perfectly ordinary sense: cheerfulness in suffering is a direct way to a city of habitation, i.e. to heaven. 'Way' here means a route or mode of access. But immediately following that, the Way is named Wonderful, and is clearly identified with Christ; and from then on we have a brilliant dialectical display, sentences which could refer to a road or path alternating with sentences which can only refer to Christ, with an occasional one which is ambiguous and could refer to either, and the word 'way' varying from 'route' or 'path' to 'means' and 'method', while occasionally becoming little more than a title for Christ.

Verse 1, lines 1–2. John Hughes in his report of a *seiat* at Mathafarn in 1800 remarks that God's law is wholly counter to our nature: '*bod ei gyfraith yn hollol groes i'n natur*'.

Verse 4, lines 7–8: see Judges 9:13, '*A'r winwydden a ddywedodd wrthynt hwy, A ymadawaf fi â'm melyswin, yr hwn sydd yn llawenhau Duw a dyn, a myned i lywodraethu ar y prennau eraill?*' ('And the vine said unto them, Should I leave my wine, which cheereth God and man, and go to be promoted over the trees?'). Christ is the Vine whose wine cheers the heart of God and man. Wine is a drink which God and man will share when Christ drinks it new with us in the Father's kingdom (Matthew 26:29).

HYMN V

1. The day is coming for the royal seed to get to sail for their country from the captivity of the bricks to reign with their Father; yonder their faith will turn to sight, and their feeble hope to enjoyment; endless will be the anthem, exalting the virtue of the precious blood.

2. My heart would fain depart from every kind of idol henceforth, because inscribed upon it is the likeness of a far greater object – infinitely worthy to be worshipped, loved, and reverenced in the world; the life of myriads was snatched from the jaws of death in his precious death.

3. My spikenard sends forth a sweet smell while I feast on the free love; zeal flaming against sin, loving the image of holiness; cutting away hand and eye, and bringing down lofty looks; none worthy to be exalted save Jesus the great King.

4. O for a life of sanctifying the holy pure name of my God and submitting to his will and his governance as long as I live, to live vowing and fulfilling vows, to live growing strong in the grace that is treasured up in Christ, so as to conquer in the field.

5. Adorn my soul in thy likeness, make me a terror in thy hand, that hell, corruption, ungodliness at the sight of me may feel fear; O to have fellowship with the Name: it is an ointment poured forth, salt to the world, with sweet odours from the lovely gifts of the church of God.

The theme which holds together the somewhat varied imagery of this hymn is total dedication to God in Christ.

Verse 1, lines 5–6. These seem to echo a line which occurs twice in almost the same form in hymns by John Thomas (1730–1804?), who was first a Methodist preacher and then an Independent minister: '*Pan droer fy ffydd yn olwg, / A'm gobaith yn fwynhad*' ('When my faith is turned into sight, and my hope into enjoyment'), and again, '*Fy ffydd a droir yn olwg, / A'm gobaith yn fwynhad*' ('My faith shall be turned into sight, and my hope into enjoyment').

Verse 5, lines 6–8: Canticles 1:3, '*Oherwydd arogl dy ennaint daionus, ennaint tywalltedig yw dy enw*' ('Because of the savour of thy good ointments thy name is as ointment poured forth'). It has been felt that this image of sweet ointment clashes with the mention of salt in line 7. But the word 'sweet' has a wider meaning in the Welsh of this period. Thomas Charles (in his Scriptural Dictionary under '*halen*') says that the element of salt in the Jewish sacrifices typified the sweetness ('*pereidd-dra*') of Christ's Sacrifice, and in expounding 'Ye are the salt of the earth' (Matthew 5:13) he says that Christians are as salt to sweeten ('*pereiddio*') the world; and cf. Williams Pantycelyn, '*Gwna fi fel halen peraidd iawn*' ('Make me like very sweet salt').

HYMN VI

1. O to have faith to look with the angels above into the plan of salvation, there is a mystery in it: two natures in one Person, inseparable henceforth, in purity, unmixed, perfect through and through.

2. O my soul, behold the appropriateness of this divine Person, venture thy life upon him and cast upon him thy burden; he is man to sympathise with all thy weaknesses together, he is God to win the throne over devil, flesh, and world.

3. I have a longing to depart every day from the bloodied field –

not from the ark or Israel, but hateful self-conceit; to get to come to the King's table, and to be invited to sit higher, while I, weak and feeble, would fain love in the dust.

4. However strong be the storms and the swelling of the sea's waves, Wisdom is the pilot, and his name is mighty Lord; in spite of the deluge of sin and corruption of every kind, safe at the last because the ark is God.

Verse 1, line 1. On the significance of the phrase '*edrych i*' ('to look into') as against '*edrych ar*' ('to look at or upon'), see the lecture by Saunders Lewis, 'Ann Griffiths: A Literary Survey', in this volume.

Verse 1, lines 5–6: cf. Article 2 of the Thirty–Nine Articles, 'two whole and perfect Natures ... were joined together in one Person, never to be divided'. Cf. also Great-heart's words to Christiana, *The Pilgrim's Progress*, Part II: 'He has two natures in one person – plain to be distinguished, impossible to be divided.'

Verse 1, line 8: cf. the words of the *Quicungue Vult* ('The Athanasian Creed'): 'perfect God and perfect man'.

Verse 2, lines 5–6: '*cydymdeimlo*' ('to sympathise'): cf. Hebrews 4:15. In Hebrews 4:15, the Welsh Bible has '*cyd-ddioddef*' ('to suffer together'), not '*cydymdeimlo*', but the meaning is basically the same.

Verse 2, lines 7–8: '*i gario'r orsedd*' ('to win the throne'). Christ in one sense is eternally on the throne and never left it. In another sense he left it at his Incarnation and won it on a fresh title by his life and death. Ann here sees his deity manifested in the victoriousness of his humanity.

Verse 4, line 8: '*yr arch yn Dduw*' ('the ark is God'). There is a long tradition, reaching back into the New Testament itself, of regarding Noah as a type of Christ. (See Jean Daniélou, *Sacramentum Futuri* (Paris, 1950), 55*ff*.) In this tradition the ark is taken to typify the Church. In one passage of St Augustine certain physical features of the ark typify certain biographical facts about Christ (see Daniélou, 92n.), but nowhere in this tradition is the ark itself made a type of Christ.

There are however two relevant passages in St John of the Cross, both in his commentary on the Spiritual Canticle. In the second redaction of this work, in the preliminary exposition of stanzas 14 and 15, we hear of the soul's 'flight' to the 'divine ark of the bosom of God'. We are reminded that Noah's ark contained many stalls for different animals and plenteous stocks of food; similarly Christ says that in his Father's house are many mansions, in which, says St John of the Cross, the soul finds every abundance of sustenance and delight. Later, in the exposition of stanza 34, '*La blanca palomica / Al arca con el ramo se ha tornado*' ('The little white dove has returned to the ark with the branch'), we are told that the dove (i.e. the soul) left the ark of God's omnipotence when it was created, and flies back to the ark of its Creator's bosom. Thus under several aspects St John bids us regard God as the ark. But it is hard to think how any knowledge of his writings could have reached Ann.

[In his notes, H. A. Hodges adds, 'It is not clear how Ann arrived at the equation "ark" = "Christ". Traditionally the ark is the Church, which is the Body of Christ, but the conclusion that the ark is Christ was not drawn. Perhaps what was in Ann's mind was the simple thought that, as Noah and his family were saved by being in the ark, we are saved by being in Christ. This simple play upon the word "in" could well have suggested itself to Ann independently.' However, Thomas Charles (in his Scriptural Dictionary under '*Arch Noah*') treats the ark as a type of Christ. In this he is perhaps following the Puritan, Morgan Llwyd, in his allegorical volume, *Llyfr y Tri Aderyn* ('The Book of the Three Birds'), published in 1653. – *Ed.*]

HYMN VII

1. When the most ardent soul is most alive with burning love, even then it falls short of attaining to the perfect holy law of God; O to get to honour it by accepting free salvation, and the most sweet fellowship, plunged in the blood.

2. I shall wonder with great wonder when the blessed hour is fulfilled for me to see my mind, which here darts after the base trinkets of earth, eternally settled upon the great object of his Person, and unshakeably conformed to the pure and holy laws of heaven.

Verse 1, lines 5–6. The thought of showing honour to God's law occurs frequently in Ann's writings. These two lines are reminiscent of what she says in Letter VII. She shows reverence for the law by not trying to satisfy it with works, but by acknowledging that nothing can satisfy it but the free atonement made by Christ. To acknowledge this, by accepting the atonement in all simplicity as a free gift, is by implication to acknowledge the sublime perfection of the law.

Verse 1, lines 7–8: '*a'r cymundeb mwya' melys*' ('and the most sweet fellowship'). '*Cymundeb*' can be translated 'communion'. However, this can hardly be the sacrament of Holy Communion, because then line 8 would be meaningless. It must be the communion of saints. There may be a clue in 1 John 1:7, '*y mae i ni gymdeithas â'n gilydd, a gwaed Iesu Grist ei Fab ef, sydd yn ein glanhau ni oddi wrth bob pechod*' ('we have fellowship one with another, and the blood of Jesus Christ his Son cleanseth us from all sin'). This is the fellowship of what Charles Wesley calls the 'blood-besprinkled bands'.

Verse 2 is admirably clear and simple.

HYMN VIII

1. It is a matter of great wonder to be alive within furnaces which are so hot, but more wonderful that, after being tried, I shall come into the midst like fine gold; a time of cleansing, a day of winnowing, yet quiet, without any fear; the Man who will be to me a refuge is the one who has the winnowing fan in his hand.

2. Arduous is my life because of enemies, for they are very numerous; they compass me about like bees from morning until evening; and they of my own household are foremost in leading the hellish host; through the help of grace I shall continue to do battle unto blood.

Verse 1, line 2: '*ffwrneisiau*' ('furnaces'), namely 'in a gold refinery'.

Verse 1, line 4: Job 23:10, '*wedi iddo fy mhrofi, myfi a ddeuaf allan fel aur*' ('when he hath tried me, I shall come forth as gold'). But Ann says '*y dof i'r canol*' ('I shall come into the midst'). Why 'into the midst'? The midst of what? D. Morgan Lewis (in the journal, *Y Llenor*, in 1924) suggests that Ann had come across a description of what happens in refining gold, how the ore is put into the furnace, the dross is burnt away, and the pure metal, liquefied, runs together to form a globule in the middle.

Verse 1, lines 6–7. The text 'a man shall be as an hiding place' (Isaiah 32:2) and the phrase 'it was quiet' occur together in Letter I, whose date is November 1800. That might be an indication of the approximate date of this stanza.

Verse 2, line 5: '*a'r rhai o'm tŷ fy hun*' ('and they of my own household'). Cf. Matthew 10:36, '*A gelynion dyn fydd tylwyth ei dŷ ei hun*' ('And a man's foes shall be they of his own household').

HYMN IX

1. Because I am so corrupt, and full of departing, to be in thy holy mountain is to me a very sublime privilege; where the veils are rent, the covering is continually destroyed there, and thy glory is supreme over the passing things of the world.

2. O to continue to drink deep of the streams of the great salvation until my thirst for the passing things of earth is wholly quenched; to live watching for my Lord, to be, when he comes, wide awake to open to him quickly and enjoy his likeness to the full.

Verse 1, line 2: '*ymadael*' ('departure', i.e. falling away). Cf. Ann's use of the word in Letter VII.

Verse 1, lines 3–6: cf. Isaiah 25:7, '*Ac efe a ddifa yn y mynydd hwn y gorchudd sydd yn gorchuddio yr holl bobloedd, a'r llen yr hon a daenwyd ar yr holl genhedloedd*' ('And he will destroy in this mountain the face of the covering cast over all people, and the vail that is spread over all nations').

Verse 2, lines 5–8. This is based on Canticles 5:2–6. The Beloved comes to the Bride's chamber in the night and asks to be let in: she is asleep, and when she rouses herself to open the door he has given up and gone away. Ann wants to be wide awake so as to let him in at once and to enjoy – what? When the Beloved visits the Bride at night and is admitted to her chamber, what do we expect will follow? Some kind of love-passage between them, of course. Now see what Ann says in line 8. The satisfaction of her loving desire for Christ consists in her being invested with his likeness. She has it already in a degree, of course; as she says in Hymn V, the likeness of an object greater than all the world's idols is inscribed upon her; but only in a degree. She looks forward to enjoying it to the full when he visits her. Cf. also Psalm 17:15, '*digonir fi, pan ddihunwyf â'th ddelw di*' ('I shall be satisfied, when I awake, with thy likeness').

It is not possible for her to possess his likeness to the full without a transforming action of grace within her. In some Catholic writers it is clear that the soul is expected to be conscious of the divine presence and action within herself, and it is here, in this intimate metaphysical penetration of the creature by the Creator, that the union of the two is consummated. Ann knows of course that such a divine action in the soul must take place, but she does not here speak of being conscious of it, only of its effect in conforming her to Christ's likeness. This has been cited as a sign of her Calvinist soberness and level-headedness. But we must not underestimate how high she flies. To enjoy Christ's likeness to the full is nothing less than the 'deification' of which we hear both from the eastern Christian tradition and from St John of the Cross.

For a more discursive treatment of Canticles 5:2–6, leading up to the same concept of Christ's likeness, cf. Elfed's hymn, '*O! Iesu, maddau fod y drws ynghau*' ('O Jesus, forgive the door being shut'). Elfed (H. Elvet Lewis; 1860–1953) spins out his penitence through four verses. But he has also been thinking of Revelation 3:20, where the familiar image of a banquet for a feast of love is used: 'if any man hear my voice, and open the door, I will come in to him, and sup with him, and he with me'. Elfed closes his hymn with the line: '*Cael dod yn debyg i ti fydd y wledd!*' ('To become like thee will be the feast!'). If anyone is to be quoted as an instance of soberness and level-headedness, it should be Elfed, who never raises his voice, not the exuberant Ann. Even when their sequence of thought is the same, there is a whole world of difference in intensity between them.

HYMN X

1. O that my head were waters, that I might weep without ceasing because Zion, an army with banners, is losing heart in the heat of the day; O reveal the pillars that were made to support her in the night, the unconditional promises of God on account of the death on the cross.

2. Remember, Lord, thy bride, leap to her like the hart, and let not the Amalekites wholly win the day against her; the foxes are going about in her to spoil the tender shoots, the Shekinah withdraws increasingly from morning until evening.

3. Awake, Lord, act mightily, remember the oath of the covenant of peace, see thy great Name lying covered upon the witnesses in the grave; a word from thy mouth, they will arise – thou art the great Resurrection – with the new Name inscribed brightly upon them like the dawn.

4. This is the ointment poured forth, dependent upon itself to bring enemies for ever to be worthy objects of the love of the Three in One; repentance has been hid, therefore he will not turn back for any until he has the fruits of his husbandry safe to all eternity in his bosom.

There is almost certainly a relation of literary dependence between this hymn, Ann's Letter VI, and the letter from John Hughes to Ruth Evans, dated 4 March 1803. For a suggestion as to what the relation may have been, see our Additional Note on Letter VI.

Verse 1, lines 1–2: Jeremiah 9:1, '*O! na bai fy mhen yn ddyfroedd ... fel yr wylwn ddydd a nos*' ('Oh that my head were waters ... that I might weep day and night'). Ann echoes the words with which the prophet begins a similar lament to her own.

Verse 1, line 3: '*lu banerog*' ('an army with banners'). A description of the Bride, see Canticles 6:4, 10.

Verse 2, lines 1–6. This is based on a scene in the Song of Solomon. Line 2: Canticles 2:8, '*Dyma lais fy anwylyd! wele ef yn dyfod, yn neidio ar y mynyddoedd, ac yn llamu ar y bryniau*' ('The voice of my beloved! behold, he cometh leaping upon the mountains, skipping upon the hills'). Lines 5–6: Canticles 2:15, '*Deliwch i ni y llwynogod, y llwynogod bychain, y rhai a ddifwynant y gwinllannoedd: canys y mae i'n gwinllannoedd egin grawnwin*' ('Take us the foxes, the little foxes, that spoil the vines: for our vines have tender grapes').

Verse 2, lines 7–8. The Shekinah is edging gradually away. The best commentary on this is a passage in the letter from John Hughes to Ruth Evans, dated 4 March 1803, where he is developing the text in Hosea 7:9, 'gray hairs are here and there upon him [namely Ephraim], yet he knoweth not'. Spiritual decline, he says, is slow and gradual, like the greying of a man's hair:

> not getting into total disarray all at once, but the qualms becoming somewhat fewer from time to time, and the consolations becoming somewhat fewer and feebler, after the manner of the Shekinah departing from the Temple, until one is so poor as to lose the feeling of one's poverty: 'He knoweth not.' As man draws a little nearer to his idols, God draws away from him a little.

Verse 3 has behind it Revelation 11:3–12. God's two witnesses bear their testimony and are slain and suffered to lie unburied (not 'in the grave' as Ann says here). God's Name, Christ's new Name, was inscribed upon them, so Ann infers, as it is upon all victorious Christians (Revelation 3:12), and their death brings discredit upon the Name. But after a time the witnesses return to life, and a voice from heaven says to them, 'Come up hither' ('*Deuwch i fyny yma*'), and they ascend up to heaven in a cloud.

Verse 3, line 6 echoes the first line of a hymn by Ellis Wynne (1671–1734): '*Myfi yw'r Atgyfodiad mawr*' ('I am the great Resurrection').

Verse 4, lines 1–2: '*Hwn*' ('This'), namely Christ's Name, which is '*ennaint tywalltedig*' ('as ointment poured forth'), Canticles 1:3. '*Ymddibynnol arno ei hun*' ('dependent upon itself'); the Name has in itself the power to convert sinners. A similar phrase occurs in Letter VI, where it is God himself, described as the 'Rock of our salvation', who is 'wholly self-dependent in the matter of saving a sinner'.

Verse 4, line 5: Hosea 13:14, '*O law y bedd yr achubaf hwynt; oddi wrth angau y gwaredaf hwynt: byddaf angau i ti, O angau; byddaf dranc i ti, y bedd: cuddir edifeirwch o'm golwg*' ('I will ransom them from the power of the grave; I will redeem them from death: O death, I will be thy plagues; O grave, I will be thy destruction: repentance shall be hid from mine eyes'). In other words, 'I shall not change my mind.'

Verse 4, line 6: Jeremiah 32:40, '*A mi a wnaf â hwynt gyfamod tragwyddol, na throaf oddi wrthynt, heb wneuthur lles iddynt*' ('And I will make an everlasting covenant with them, that I will not turn away from them, to do them good').

HYMN XI

1. My journey will be in the vale of weeping until I see divine blood flowing from the Rock like the river, in it myriads have been made white; light of the Stone whereby to go forward, namely Jesus, a holy righteousness.

2. I am longing for the time when I shall have a revelation of my right, Jesus Christ, the true Tree of Life – he is the pure righteousness of the saints; to claim him as my second, and my strong foundation, in place of the vain hope of fig leaves.

This is a pilgrim's hymn.

Verse 1, lines 1–4. The vale of Baca (the vale of weeping) is on the pilgrims' way (Psalm 84:6). Ann's journey is through a vale of weeping whenever she loses the realising vision of the Crucified. Christ on the cross is the rock from which flows both water and blood; in historical fact only a few drops, but in Christian iconography a great and cleansing stream. The rock from which Moses drew water in the desert, and the Temple rock from which Ezekiel saw the river flowing, are of course types of Christ, and when he is called simply the Rock, as here, it is legitimate to remember these types.

Verse 1, line 5: '*golau'r Maen*' ('light of the Stone'). Christ is often spoken of in the Bible as a rock ('*craig*'), and several times as a stone ('*carreg*', and occasionally '*maen*'). The principal places where '*maen*' occurs are Isaiah 28:16 (the foundation stone laid in Zion), Psalm 118:22 (the stone which the builders rejected) and Zechariah 4:7 (the headstone of the Temple). The first of these has some links with the thought of this hymn. It is a foundation stone, '*sylfaen*', cf. verse 2, line 5 '*a'm cadarn sail*' ('and my strong foundation'); and the 'he that believeth shall not make haste' at the end of Isaiah 28:16 might apply to the pilgrims, who in the assurance of their faith go forward quietly and steadily. But this is not all we need here, for how could this stone be a source of light?

In the description of the heavenly Jerusalem we read in Revelation 21:11, '*a'i golau hi oedd debyg i faen o'r gwerthfawrocaf, megis maen iasbis, yn loyw fel grisial*' ('and her light was like unto a stone most precious, even like a jasper stone, clear as crystal'). But later, in Revelation 21:23, the glory of God illuminates the city, and 'the Lamb is the light thereof' ('*a'i goleuni hi ydyw'r Oen*'). There are several colours of jasper, and one of them is white like crystal. So the light of the Stone is the crystal-clear light of Christ which is the light of heaven. Ann can see it sometimes even *in via*. Walter Hilton similarly speaks of the light of Christ which shines from Jerusalem for the pilgrim, and he instructs us how to distinguish it from false lights (*Ladder of Perfection*, II, 25, 26).

Verse 2, line 2: '*fy mraint*' ('my right'); see Revelation 22:14, '*fel y byddo iddynt fraint ym mhren y bywyd*' ('that they may have right to the tree of life'). The word translated '*braint*', 'right', is *exousia*. But in the Welsh New Testament of 1567 the verse is rendered '*mal y gallo y cyfiawnder hwy vod ymhren y bowyd*' ('that their righteousness may be in the tree of life'). If Ann knew of that rendering, it would help to explain the fourth line of this verse.

Verse 2, line 5: '*a'm cadarn sail*' ('and my strong foundation'). The phrase is from 2 Timothy 2:19, where according to Thomas Charles (in his Scriptural Dictionary under '*sail*') it means the decree of election. But Ann here is applying it to Christ himself. Cf. Williams Pantycelyn in one of his hymns on Christ: '*Dyma sylfaen gadarn gref*' ('Here is a strong firm foundation').

We began by saying that this is a pilgrim's hymn. It is interesting to observe that the verse, Revelation 22:14, is inscribed in gold lettering over the gate of the Celestial City in *The Pilgrim's Progress*, Part I.

HYMN XII

Wonder always, O bride, to whom thou art an object of love; O sing, ye redeemed race, he excells over ten thousand.

It has been suggested that this may have been composed for Ruth Evans on the occasion of her marriage. Also that Ann may be addressing these words to herself. Neither suggestion is needed. These lines could quite well be addressed to any Christian soul, or to the collective 'Bride' meeting at Pontrobert, the '*gwaredigol hil*' ('redeemed race') of line 3.

HYMN XIII

1. Behold standing among the myrtles an object worthy of my whole mind, although it is in part I know that he is above all objects in the world; hail the morning when I shall see him as he is.

2. Rose of Sharon is his name, white and ruddy, fair of form; he excells over ten thousand of the chiefest objects in the world; friend of sinner, here is his pilot on the sea.

3. What have I to do any more with the base idols of earth? I testify that their company cannot compete with great Jesus; O to abide in his love all the days of my life.

This is one of Ann's best known and best loved hymns.

Verse 1, line 1. The opening line with its reference to the myrtles has a pleasant pastoral flavour, but what bearing has it on the rest of the hymn? What does Ann make of the vision in Zechariah 1:7–17 from which the myrtles come?

In the Zechariah passage, the Authorised Version has 'myrtle trees', but there is nothing in the Hebrew corresponding to the word 'tree' and the myrtle is in fact a shrub rather than a tree. The Welsh has simply '*y myrtwydd*'. The shrub meant is the *myrtus communis* or common myrtle, an evergreen with dark fragrant leaves, bearing white flowers and white berries which later turn blue-black. It favours low-lying moist ground, and rises to a height of three or four feet, or more if the ground is very moist. According to Thomas Charles (in his Scriptural Dictionary under '*myrtwydd*') these low growing bushes signify God's people in their poverty and abasement, among whom Christ stands armed and mounted as their defender. To Ann, it seems, they are the many attractive objects in this world, over which Christ towers as the chiefest among ten thousand.

However, the numerous members of the *myrtus* family are mostly inhabitants of the tropics. In Europe the name 'myrtle' has been applied to plants of the genus *myrica*, chiefly to the plant variously called in English 'sweet gale', 'Dutch myrtle' and 'bog myrtle', which resembles the true myrtle at least in being fragrant. But further, a plant of the heath family, variously called in English 'bilberry', 'blaeberry' or 'whortleberry', has for centuries been known as *myrtillus*, French: *myrtille* (whence the English word 'myrtle'), and now has the official botanical name *vaccinium myrtillus*. In popular usage, the word 'myrtle' is very widely used for the bilberry, and though Ann may have known what she was talking about in this verse, it is likely that large numbers of those who have sung her hymn will have taken it to picture Christ standing on a hillside covered with bilberries, such as can frequently be seen in Wales. The bilberry has none of the symbolic values of the true myrtle: it is not fragrant, it is not evergreen, and it is not tall enough for a man to need to be on horseback in order to appear above it. In short, this interpretation robs Ann's line of most of its point.

Verse 1, line 2: '*wrthrych teilwng o fy mryd*' ('an object worthy of my whole mind). *Bryd* ('mind') is not the same as *meddwl* ('thought'); it includes the affective and volitional side of the personality as well. That is why we have rendered it 'my whole mind' although the word 'whole' is not in the original Welsh. Christ is an object which merits Ann's total attachment.

Verse 3, lines 1–2: Hosea 14:8, '*Ephraim a ddywed, Beth sydd i mi mwyach a wnelwyf ag eilunod?*' ('Ephraim shall say, What have I to do any more with idols?').

HYMN XIV

1. The world and all its trinkets cannot now satisfy my affections, which were captured, which were widened, in the day of my great Jesus' power; he, none less, can fulfil them, although he is incomprehensible; O to gaze upon his Person, as he is both man and God.

2. O that I might spend my days as a life of exalting his blood;

sheltering quietly under his shadow, living and dying at his feet; loving the cross, and continuing to take it up, because it is my Husband's cross; delighting in his Person and worshipping him for ever as God.

Verse 1, lines 1–4. The thought here is worthy of note. We hear often enough that Christ meets all our needs and desires; but Ann says that he actually widens them. We do not know the full extent of our needs and longings until we are shown their fulfilment in him.

Verse 1, lines 5–8. Although he is beyond comprehension, he can fulfil our desires because, being incarnate, he can be contemplated by us. Here is the metaphysical passion which in Ann is mated so inseparably with the evangelical faith. Christ Incarnate is not merely the necessary and sufficient answer to the question posed by our sin, he is also the necessary and sufficient answer to the question posed by our finitude.

Verse 2. In lines 1–6 Ann speaks of Christ's work for us and our participation in his Passion; but again in lines 7–8 she looks beyond his work to his Person, and finds there her ultimate delight.

Verse 2, line 5: '*caru'r groes*' ('loving the cross'). One might have expected *cario* ('to carry'); but the unexpected *caru* ('to love') is a master stroke, and the next line spells out its meaning.

HYMN XV

O to spend my life in a sea of wonders, staying on sinner's ground and living on the blood of the cross, and to bring my every thought captive to the obedience of Christ, and to conform to his law, to be for him a faithful witness.

Line 3 is undecipherable in the John Hughes manuscript. The most likely reading is '*Ar dir bechadur aros*' ('Staying on sinner's ground').

HYMN XVI

To the table of God's righteousness, when sin was remembered, came nought but shadows of the living substance which was to come; when the Jubilee was fully come, the veil was rent, and the law in Jesus on the tree was satisfied.

Line 1: '*bwrdd cyfiawnder Duw*' ('the table of God's righteousness') = the sacrificial altar.

HYMN XVII

Let none look to stumble over me because I am black; it is the sun, and the heat of its rays, that is shining ardently upon me; there is that which covers me, the shade of the curtains of Solomon.

See Canticles 1:5–6: '*Du ydwyf fi, ond hawddgar, merched Jerwsalem, fel pebyll Cedar, fel llenni Solomon. Nac edrychwch arnaf, am fy mod yn ddu, ac am i'r haul edrych arnaf*' ('I am black, but comely, O ye daughters of Jerusalem, as the tents of Kedar, as the curtains of Solomon. Look not upon me, because I am black, because the sun hath looked upon me'). Note that in the Canticle the curtains of Solomon are an object of comparison to illustrate the Bride's beauty. Ann makes them a cover for her tanned complexion. The Bride's beauty is not her own, it is Solomon's beauty which covers her own unsightliness.

HYMN XVIII

When foul sin took possession of the first pair, the God of Love was constrained by his nature to hate; yet loving and saving those same objects of his divine wrath, in a just way, without changing, but perfectly being the same for ever.

This hymn is outstanding because it conveys Ann's deepest insight into the Atonement. She deduces it from what in

Letter VIII she calls 'the primal love'. God is love; and yet there is that in his nature which in certain circumstances compels him to hate. He hates sin, and when men sin they incur his wrath and the consequent threat of destruction. But since God is love, and he does not change, he takes steps to avoid this, to lay aside his wrath and save men from destruction. And since his wrath was an assertion of his justice, his design for laying aside his wrath must also be one which asserts and manifests his justice. He saves men 'in a just way, without changing, but perfectly being the same for ever'. This is Ann's deepest insight. It goes behind even the eternal Covenant; for the Covenant is God's just design for saving men, but this verse tells us why God willed to save them, and why it had to be done in a just way. Ann has not, however, tried to go behind the given duality of God's love and his justice. It is noteworthy that here, in uttering her deepest vision, Ann gives up her rich language of images and her wealth of biblical references, and speaks plain Welsh, as clearly and simply as one could wish.

HYMN XIX

1. O to penetrate into the knowledge of the only true and living God to such a degree as would be death to imaginations of every kind; believing the word which speaks of him and about his nature, it is manifest that it is death to a sinner without a Satisfaction of God's planning.

2. In this knowledge lofty looks are brought low; man is little, wretched, loathsome, God is sublime and great; Christ in his mediatorial offices is precious, indispensable; the guilty soul, beholding, glorifies him as God.

This hymn might almost be a commentary on the preceding one. It brings out other aspects of the knowledge of God to which Ann aspires, its content and its effects on the soul. It has the same clarity of vision and simplicity of statement.

Verse 1: Note the distrust of imagination, which is characteristic of the ancient Christian spiritual tradition. It appears again in the last verse of Hymn XXII. We must not be misled by the favourable sense which has been placed upon 'imagination' since the romantic period. In the modern interpretation, imagination is the capacity for insight and creativity, in contrast with conventional ideas and attitudes. To be unimaginative is to be a dull dog. But in the tradition of Christian spirituality, imagination is thought of as the wayward aspect of the mind. It generates fantasies which reflect our own foolish and sinful thoughts and desires, even when it professes to be giving us a picture of some objective reality. It prevents the mind from seeing clearly and it inflames the passions. Our aim should be to become free from it and attain to the calm clarity of intellectual apprehension. It is interesting to see this tradition still alive in Ann.

HYMN XX

1. The God infinite in mercy, although he is the God of love, when I think of him, is to me a terror, to me a pain, to me a wound; but in the tent of meeting he is there full of peace, seated as a reconciled God, with nothing but peace in his countenance.

2. There is my food and my drink, my refuge and my fair resting place, my healing and my treasure, a strong unfailing tower is he; there is all my armament in face of my hateful enemies, my life is hidden there while I am fighting on the battlefield.

3. To have God as a Father, and a Father as a refuge, a refuge that is a rock, and that rock a tower, more I cannot desire to have with me amid fire and water; of him is my sufficiency, in him I shall go through troops; without him I am feeble, weak and powerless, and shall truly lose the day.

Verse 3: It has been suggested that the series of titles for God in this verse, namely Father, refuge, rock and tower, is an anticlimax: for to call God Father is to state the fullest and noblest truth about him, and any succeeding epithet must represent a descent from that height. However, what Ann is doing here is spelling out just a few of the things that God as Father means to her. Williams Pantycelyn did not disdain a similar descending movement, if such it is:

> *Ti yw 'Nhad, a Thi yw 'Mhriod,*
>   *Ti yw f'Arglwydd, Ti yw 'Nuw,*
> *F'unig Dŵr, a'm hunig Noddfa,*
>   *Wyt i farw neu i fyw.*

(Thou art my Father, and thou art my Husband, thou art my Lord, thou art my God, my only Tower, and my only Refuge, whether in death or in life.)

Pantycelyn has another striking parallel to this stanza:

> *Gyda Thi mi af drwy'r fyddin,*
>   *Gyda Thi mi af drwy'r tân;*
> *'D ofnaf ymchwydd llif Iorddonen*
>   *Ond i Ti fynd yn y blaen:*
> *Ti yw f'amddiffynfa gadarn,*
>   *Ti yw 'Mrenin, Ti yw 'Nhad;*
> *Ti dy Hunan oll yn unig*
>   *Yw fy iechydwriaeth rad.*

(With thee I shall go through the troop, with thee I shall go through the fire; I fear not the swelling of Jordan's flood if only thou wilt go before: thou art my strong defence, thou art my King, thou art my Father; thou thyself, all and only, art my free salvation.)

In these two verses by Williams Pantycelyn we may

reasonably see the inspiration and the model for this verse by Ann.

Verse 3, line 6: Psalm 18:29, '*Oblegid ynot ti y rhedais trwy fyddin*' ('For by thee I have run through a troop').

HYMN XXI

His left hand upholds me under my head in the heat of the day, and the blessings of his right hand embrace my soul; I charge you, O posies of nature, that beautify the earth below, that ye stir not up, until he wills, my love and my great glory.

Lines 1–4 are based on Canticles 2:6, '*Ei law aswy sydd dan fy mhen, a'i ddeheulaw sydd yn fy nghofleidio*' ('His left hand is under my head, and his right hand doth embrace me'). The heat of the day, in the picture language of the Song of Solomon, means noontide, siesta time, when the shepherd gives rest to his flock (Canticles 1:7); as applied by Ann it means the heat of the spiritual combat (cf. Hymn X, verse 1). The soul lives a hidden life, resting upon Christ, even when engaged in outward combat (cf. Hymn XX, verse 2).

Lines 5–8 are based on Canticles 2:7, '*Merched Jerusalem, tynghedaf chwi trwy iyrchod ac ewigod y maes, na chyffrôch, ac na ddeffrôch fy nghariad, hyd oni fynno ei hun*' ('I charge you, O ye daughters of Jerusalem, by the roes, and by the hinds of the field, that ye stir not up, nor awake my love, till he please').

Line 5: '*bwysïau natur*' ('posies of nature'). The word '*pwysi*' / '*posi*' ('posy') seems to have been more widely used in Welsh about this period than it ever was in English. A poem by 'Taliesin o Eifion' (Thomas Jones, 1820–76) refers to hymn-tunes as '*pwysiau Seion*' ('posies of Zion'); and cf. Pantycelyn: '*Fe ddarfu blas, fe ddarfu chwant / At holl bosïau'r byd*' ('Gone is the taste, gone the desire, for all the world's posies'). What or whom is Ann addressing in this way? Posies of nature, beautifying the earth, can hardly be a description of the daughters of Jerusalem. Nor is it very appropriate to the roes and hinds of the field; and why should Ann appeal to them anyhow? Perhaps Ann is thinking of those worldly pleasures and attractions which she elsewhere calls '*teganau*', toys, playthings, trinkets, things pleasant in their way but liable to distract the dedicated soul. Perhaps she fears that, if these things engross her attention, the Beloved will be aroused by her own restlessness and inconstancy, and will get up and go away. He is free to leave her whenever he will, of course, but she does not wish to drive him away by any wandering thoughts of her own.

HYMN XXII

1. Wonderful, wonderful to angels, a great wonder in the eyes of faith, to see the Giver of being, the abundant Sustainer and Ruler of everything that is, in the manger in swaddling clothes and with nowhere to lay his head, and yet the bright host of glory worshipping him as great Lord.

2. When Sinai is altogether in smoke, and the sound of the trumpet at its loudest, I can go to feast across the boundary in Christ the Word without being slain; in him all fullness dwells, enough to fill the gulf of man's perdition; in the gap between the two parties he made reconciliation through his self-offering.

3. He is the Satisfaction that was between the thieves, it was he who suffered the pains of death, it was he who gave to the arms of his executioners the power to nail him there to the cross; while paying the debt of brands plucked out of the burning, and honouring his Father's law, righteousness shines with fiery blaze as he pardons within the plan of the free reconciliation.

4. O my soul, behold the place where lay the chief of kings, the Author of peace, the creation moving in him, and he dead in the tomb; song and life of the lost, greatest wonder of the angels

of heaven; the choir sees God in flesh and worships him together, crying out, 'Unto him!'

5. Thanks for ever, and a hundred thousand thanks, thanks while there is breath in me, because there is an object to worship and a subject for a song to last for ever; in my nature, tempted like the lowest of mankind, a babe, weak, powerless, infinite true and living God.

6. Instead of carrying a body of corruption, penetrating ardently with the choir above into the endless wonders of the salvation wrought on Calvary; living to see the Invisible, who was dead and now is alive; eternal inseparable union and communion with my God.

7. There I shall exalt the Name which God set forth to be a Propitation, without imagination, veil, or covering, and with my soul fully in his likeness; in the fellowship of the mystery revealed in his wounds, I shall kiss the Son to all eternity, and never turn from him any more.

This is the longest and most splendid of Ann's hymns. If hymns like '*Dyma babell y cyfarfod*' (Hymn II) rank as great sonatas, this is a symphony. Nowhere else does she take so wide-ranging a combination of themes, or work out so lovingly the counterpoint of the paradoxes. It is throughout an affirmation of faith that God has become man, that God has taken human nature upon himself, that he has penetrated into the depths of man's existence, working reconciliation and peace. Besides the gulf that there is between sinful man and the righteous God, Ann sees another gulf which is that between the finite and the infinite, between the creature and the Creator. The creature cannot be at rest without the vision of the Creator, the Absolute Beauty and Goodness, which because he is a creature, and finite, he cannot see. But God has made himself visible in Christ, in whom Ann finds an object to worship, an object worthy to engage her whole mind. The Incarnation here appears in a new light, and the mystery of the Person of Christ acquires a new dimension. Christ, simply by being who and what he is, has filled the metaphysical breach as well as the moral one. Apart from Christ, no man shall see God and live; but in Christ the Word, Ann can climb the thundering mountain without being killed, and banquet in the presence of God.

Verse 1, line 8. The John Hughes manuscript has '*yn ei addoli'n Arglwydd mawr*' ('worshipping him as great Lord'); and this was changed in John Hughes' own hand to '*yn ei addoli ef yn awr*' ('worshipping him now'). This latter may seem to be a weaker reading, but it does emphasise that it is precisely now, in the moment of Christ's abasement, that the angels worship him.

Verse 2, line 1: Exodus 19:18, '*A mynydd Sinai oedd i gyd yn mygu*' ('And mount Sinai was altogether on a smoke').

Verse 2, line 3: '*tros y terfyn*' ('across the boundary'). Exodus 19:12, '*A gosod derfyn i'r bobl o amgylch, gan ddywedyd, Gwyliwch arnoch, rhag myned i fyny i'r mynydd, neu gyffwrdd â'i gwr ef: pwy bynnag a gyffyrddo â'r mynydd a leddir yn farw*' ('And thou shalt set bounds unto the people round about, saying, Take heed to yourselves, that ye go not up into the mount, or touch the border of it: whosoever toucheth the mount shall be surely put to death').

Verse 2, line 4: '*heb gael fy lladd*' ('without being slain'). John Hughes in his letter to Ruth Evans, dated 4 March 1803 (the passage quoted in our note on Hymn II), speaks of a place for the sinner to look upon God's glory without being slain ('*heb ei ladd*'). Ann here uses the phrase in a different connection, and with a further reference to Exodus 24:9–11, where the elders of Israel go up the mountain and eat and drink in God's presence in safety.

Notes on the Hymns of Ann Griffiths

Verse 2, line 7: '*ar yr adwy*' ('in the gap'). Cf. Ezekiel 13:5, '*Ni safasoch yn yr adwyau, ac ni chaeasoch y cae i dŷ Israel, i sefyll yn y rhyfel ar ddydd yr Arglwydd*' ('Ye have not gone up into the gaps, neither made up the hedge for the house of Israel to stand in the battle in the day of the Lord'). Also Ezekiel 22:30, '*Ceisiais hefyd ŵr ohonynt i gau y cae, ac i sefyll ar yr adwy o'm blaen dros y wlad, rhag ei dinistrio; ac nis cefais*' ('And I sought for a man among them, that should make up the hedge, and stand in the gap before me for the land, that I should not destroy it: but I found none').

Verse 3, line 1. *Iawn* means a propitiation or a propitiatory offering. Christ is spoken of as a *iawn* or propitiation in 1 John 2:2, 4:10 and Romans 3:25. But *iawn* also means a payment in restitution for damage or loss sustained, and Christ is a *iawn* in that sense too. God sustained loss in the fall of man; he was robbed of what was rightfully his, namely man's love and allegiance. In his incarnate life and death Christ gave himself in full restitution for the loss, and the crowning act of the restitution was made while he hung between two robbers. [See also H. A. Hodges' note on *iawn* in his translation of Saunders Lewis' lecture, 'Ann Griffiths: A Literary Survey', in this volume. – *Ed.*]

Verse 3, lines 7–8. John Hughes, in his letter to Ruth Evans dated 4 March 1803, writes, 'For his [i.e. God's] righteousness and all his attributes shine out in the most glorious manner in his plan ['*trefn*'] of being merciful to sinners in Christ.'

Verse 4. In the lines which see the Creator in the grave, there is an astounding likeness to the hymnography of the Eastern Church, and even to its iconography, which prefers to depict the resurrection by means of the scene of the harrowing of hell.

Verse 5, lines 7–8. Cf. John Hughes, in a record of a *seiat* meeting at Bwlch Aeddan, Guilsfield: 'A baby ['*yn ddyn bach*';

literally 'a little man'] too helpless to hold himself up and walk, although in respect of his deity he was upholding the worlds. ... Christ, when under the greatest contempt in the world, was filling heaven with his glory.'

Verse 7, line 7: '*heb ddychymyg*' ('without imagination'). See the note on Hymn XIX.

HYMN XXIII

1. If I must face the rushing river, there is One to break the force of the water, Jesus, my faithful High Priest, and he has a safe sure grasp; in his bosom I shall cry 'Conquest!' over death, hell, world, and grave, and be eternally without the means of sinning, glorious in his likeness.

2. Sweet it is to remember the covenant made yonder by Three in One, to gaze eternally upon the Person who took the nature of man; as he fulfilled the terms, his soul was exceedingly sorrowful unto death; here is the song of the seven-score-thousand beyond the veil with a joyful shout.

3. To live without stroke of heat or sun, to live unable to die any more, every kind of sorrow at an end, nought but singing of the death-wound; to swim in the pure river of life, the endless peace of the holy Three, under the cloudless rays of the precious death on Calvary.

Verse 3: On swimming in the river of life, see the notes on Hymn III.

HYMN XXIV

1. Make me, O my God, like a tree planted and growing luxuriously on the bank of rivers of living waters, rooting widely, and its leaves never withering henceforth, but fruiting under showers from the divine wound.

2. A good land, without woe, a land put under seal, it flows with

its fruit of milk and honey; fine grape-clusters come to the desert country; it is a heavenly land, whose praise is above telling.

3. Jehovah is he, at one with his pure Name, fitting fulfiller of his true promises; he lifts his hand, nations come forth, a notable proof of his free and infinite grace.

4. Messengers of peace, in the language of the gospel, are calling to the banquet across the sea of extensive India; Hottentots, Korana of blackest hue, a barbaric host, will be brought into the family of God.

The connection of thought between these four stanzas is not immediately obvious. It is tempting to ask whether several originally independent units got associated as they are here in the John Hughes manuscript simply because they are Ann's only compositions in this metre. Morris Davies, following earlier printed editions, treats the first and second stanzas as separate hymns; but that is not a very satisfactory arrangement either. Perhaps after all we can find a connection between the verses as follows. *Verse 1*: Ann prays to become as a fruitful tree rooted in the soil of paradise. *Verse 2*: Fruits of paradise come to us even here in our desert habitation; and possession of that land has been promised to us. *Verse 3*: God can and does fulfil his promises; he is the Creator of nations and – *Verse 4* – is now sending his gospel abroad among them. This is more of a loose meditation than the working out of a single theme, but that need not surprise us in Ann.

This is the only hymn which Ann wrote in this metre, and the style has other features which are uncharacteristic of her. It has been suggested that she wrote it under the influence of Edward Jones (1761–1836) of Maes-y-plwm, who was a poet in the literary tradition in a sense in which Ann was not. He used this metre, for example, in his well-known hymn, '*Cyfamod hedd, cyfamod cadarn Duw*' ('The covenant of peace, the strong covenant of God'). He cultivated a formalised poetic diction which is in general very uncharacteristic of Ann's work, but of which there are traces in this hymn. It is possible that Ann experimented with his style, but decided that it was not for her.

Verse 1. The picture of the tree here owes something to Psalm 1:3 and something to Jeremiah 17:8.

Verse 4, lines 3–4. [When H. A. Hodges wrote his original note on this verse he followed the suggestion that '*Coraniaid*' ('Coranians') referred to a legendary people mentioned in medieval Welsh literature. They were a race with magical powers who tyrannised Britain and were said to have come from Arabia, and were thus, says Hodges, 'a race of dark-skinned mysterious strangers from the neighbourhood of the Indian Ocean'. However, it has now been shown that the 'Hottentots' and 'Coranians' in Ann's verse are actually references to the Khoekhoe and the Korana (or Griqua), some of the native peoples of southern Africa. The London Missionary Society began missionary work in the Cape area in 1799. Ann Griffiths' mentor, Thomas Charles of Bala, who was a keen supporter of the London Missionary Society, met three converted Khoekhoe ('Hottentots') in London in December 1803, and subsequently published a booklet in Welsh in 1804 on the Society's mission to southern Africa. This, therefore, is the context in which one must place Ann's verse. John Davies (1772–1855), who was a member of the same Methodist *seiat* as Ann Griffiths, sailed for Tahiti in May 1800 to be a missionary there under the auspices of the London Missionary Society, and it is probably correct to assume that it was he who was primarily in Ann's mind when she refers to missionaries calling to the gospel banquet across the Indian Ocean. – *Ed.*]

HYMN XXV

Must my zeal, that was once coals of fire for thy fair glory, and the kindness of my youth, grow colder towards my God? O thou great dweller of the high places, now reveal thy glad countenance, and wean my soul henceforth from the breasts of this creation.

Line 1: '*marwor tanllyd*' ('coals of fire'). Cf. Habakkuk 3:5, '*aeth marwor tanllyd allan wrth ei draed ef*' ('burning coals went forth at his feet'). For a live coal ('*marworyn*') on God's altar, cf. Isaiah 6:6. Ann applies this phrase to her own early zeal. It was a spark of divine fire; perhaps of altar-fire. [See also Song of Solomon 8:6. – *Ed.*]

Line 3: '*a charedigrwydd fy ieuenctid*' ('and the kindness of my youth'). The John Hughes manuscript has '*dy ieuenctid*' ('thy youth'), which are the actual words in Jeremiah 2:2, where God is speaking to Israel. Here, where Ann is applying the words to herself, '*dy*' ('thy') must be changed to '*fy*' ('my'), and the manuscript reading is an oversight, giving the wording in Jeremiah rather than the amended wording. However, J. R. Jones in an article in the journal, *Taliesin*, in July 1967 suggested that the manuscript reading is correct, and that the person addressed in lines 1–4 is not Christ but some boyfriend whom Ann had once had and had subsequently lost. The existence of such a boyfriend was first suggested by Rhiannon Davies Jones in her novel, *Fy Hen Lyfr Cownt* (1961), and J. R. Jones thinks that the present stanza is evidence in support of her otherwise unsupported suggestion. It was for this young man's 'kindness' and 'fair glory' that Ann's zeal once glowed like fiery coals, and now that she has transferred her affections to Christ, the memory of the ancient flame intrudes and cools her love for God. So in the last four lines of the stanza she prays God to wean her from this creaturely attachment.

One may doubt whether the Ann whom we know would

use biblical language like this in reference to a sweetheart of her unregenerate days. Nor is it wholly convincing to allege a Freudian slip which escaped Ann's critical awareness; for it would hardly have escaped Ruth, who would have demanded clarification. Our own view, that the manuscript reading is due to Ruth and/or John Hughes substituting the actual words of the text in Jeremiah for the modification of them which the context requires, is simple and natural and sufficient as it stands. The hypothesis of Ann's lost sweetheart is too great a weight to rest upon a single letter in John's manuscript.

HYMN XXVI

The sound of the bells playing at the garment's hem of great Jesus, and the scent of the pomegranates, are to be perceived on earth; pardon for a sinner, bringing about enjoyment, for the sake of the faultless sacrifice which fully satisfied the Father.

This hymn draws on the description of the high priest's garments in Exodus 28 (cf. Hymn III, verse 1).

HYMN XXVII

Remember to follow the reapers, pass thy life amid the sheaves; when Mount Sinai is fiery, dip thy morsel at the cross; see the great mystery of godliness, an altar has appeared at thy foot, God and humanity suffering on it; cry for light to sing his praise.

In this stanza we are identified with Ruth, whom Boaz has told to follow behind his reapers and 'dip her morsel' (i.e. have her lunch) with his servants (Ruth 2:14). Cf. the reference to the field of Boaz in the first paragraph of Letter I. The field is the Scriptures, and we are to glean among them; and if Mount Sinai is fiery (i.e. if we are alarmed by the demands of the divine law), we are to find rest and refreshment at the cross.

At the giving of the law at Sinai, God is on the mountain top, girt about with fire and thunder. At the foot of the mountain, Moses builds an altar on which he offers sacrifices; he reads the book of the covenant to the people and sprinkles them with the sacrificial blood (Exodus 24). This is the 'blood of the covenant' to which Christ alluded in his words at the institution of the eucharist. Charles Wesley is fond of referring to the incident; the aspect of it which interests him is the sprinkling of the people, as an image of absolution and justification. Ann mentions the sprinkling in Letter IV.

The reference to Sinai here, however, is not historical, but symbolic; and the covenant sacrifices at the foot of the mountain, which foreshadowed the crucifixion of Christ, are replaced by the crucifixion itself, the 'altar' being now the actual cross. That is how both Sinai and Calvary, not as historical events but as symbols of spiritual realities, can appear in the field of Boaz. Here the altar, which is the cross, is '*wrth dy droed*' ('at thy [i.e. the reader's] foot').

Line 5: 'great is the mystery of godliness' (1 Timothy 3:16), i.e. Ann's favourite mystery of the Incarnation.

HYMN XXVIII

The waters of salvation and their virtues abide, in them is healing infallible and free; come, ye who are sick from the fall in Eden, to make use of these waters; there will never be an end to the virtue of the great substance of Bethesda pool.

Line 8: 'Bethesda pool': cf. Hymn III, verse 2.

HYMN XXIX

I shall walk slowly all the days of my life under the shadow of the merit of the blood of the cross; and I shall run the course in the same way; and as I run it I shall stand, and see the full salvation I will receive as I go to rest in the grave.

Lines 1–2. The background is Isaiah 38:15. Modern commentators and even translators differ widely on this passage. The Welsh version, which is Ann's source, reads: '*mi a gerddaf yn araf* ['I shall walk slowly'] *fy holl flynyddoedd yn chwerwedd fy enaid.*' The Authorised Version reads: 'I shall go softly all my years in the bitterness of my soul.' On the face of it this means that although Hezekiah has recovered from his serious illness, it has made a lasting impression on him; he will conduct himself in a subdued and chastened manner henceforth, as one who has been taught a lesson; cf. what is said of Ahab in 1 Kings 21:27. Thomas Charles however (in his Scriptural Dictionary under '*araf*') argues that the word translated 'go softly' or 'walk slowly' here means to walk as in a procession; it is used in Psalm 42:4, obviously referring to a joyful procession. The meaning according to Thomas Charles is, 'I shall walk with joy all my life, because I have been delivered from the bitterness of my soul.' [Although the first volume of Charles' Scriptural Dictionary was not published until after Ann's death, it began appearing in parts from around June 1802 onward, and the first five parts (as far as the word '*dannedd*') had appeared before Ann's death. – Ed.] This meaning is more appropriate as an image of the Christian, still full of the memory of his mortal danger and how he was delivered from it, stepping out among his fellow-worshippers in solemn rejoicing 'under the shadow of the merit of the blood of the cross' – a sobering shadow if also a protective one.

Line 4: 'I shall stand'; cf. Exodus 14:13, '*sefwch, ac edrychwch ar iachawdwriaeth yr Arglwydd*' ('stand still, and see the salvation of the Lord'). Also 2 Chronicles 20:17, '*sefwch yn llonydd, a gwelwch ymwared yr Arglwydd tuag atoch*' ('stand ye still, and see the salvation of the Lord with you'). It does not rest with God's people to destroy their enemies; God destroys them while his people look on. The destruction is completed, according to Ann's theology of the last things, at the moment of death; but she can stand still and watch it beginning even while running her course.

HYMN XXX

Lo a Brother has been born to us, for adversity and all injury; faithful is he, full of compassion, he would deserve yet greater praise: liberator of captives, physician of the sick, a straight way to Zion is he; a clear fount, life of the dead, an ark to save man is God.

This hymn is outstanding for the use in it of *cynghanedd*, the complex system of structured assonance and alliteration found in traditional Welsh poetry. In each of the first two couplets we have an instance of *cynghanedd sain*, namely a series of three words, where the first rhymes with the second and the second alliterates with the third: *inni – c'ledi – clwy'* and *tosturi – foli – fwy*. The repeated internal rhyming in the last four lines is obvious to any reader. Ann never did anything like this elsewhere (except in the one stanza in the traditional *englyn* metre which she is said to have composed when she was around ten years of age). One asks oneself, if she was able to write like this, why did she not do so more often? Did she regard it as a form of worldly frivolity from which she must abstain? Or should we take the *cynghanedd* in this stanza as evidence that she is not its author? The authorship is uncertain, and the verse does not occur in the John Hughes manuscripts, although he does include it in the edition of her hymns he published in 1847. On the other hand, this verse has all the vigour which we associate with Ann's writing, and some of her characteristic ideas. Note the conception of Christ as the straight road to Zion, and above all the conception of Christ as the ark. See the note on Hymn VI, verse 4.

Lines 1–2: cf. Proverbs 17:17, '*a brawd a anwyd erbyn caledi*' ('and a brother is born for adversity'). The thought is expanded in a verse by Dafydd William (1721–94) of Llandeilo Fach:

Hosanna, Haleliwia,
  Fe anwyd Brawd i ni;
Fe dalodd ein holl ddyled
  Ar fynydd Calfari;
Hosanna, Haleliwia,
  Brawd ffyddlon diwahân;
Brawd erbyn dydd o g'ledi,
  Brawd yw mewn dŵr a thân.

(Hosanna, Hallelujah, a Brother is born to us; he paid our whole debt on Mount Calvary; Hosanna, Hallelujah, a Brother faithful, inseparable; a Brother for a day of adversity, he is a Brother amid water and fire.)

Line 4: '*haeddai gael ei foli'n fwy*' ('he would deserve yet greater praise'). Greater than what? Greater than whose? The idea of Jesus Christ meriting greater glory (than Moses) in consequence of being faithful – cf. line 3 here: '*ffyddlon ydyw*' ('faithful is he') – occurs in Hebrews 3:2, 3, '*Yr hwn sydd ffyddlon i'r hwn a'i hordeiniodd ef, megis ag y bu Moses yn ei holl dŷ ef. Canys fe a gyfrifwyd hwn yn haeddu mwy gogoniant na Moses*' ('Who was faithful to him that appointed him, as also Moses was faithful in all his house. For this man was counted worthy of more glory than Moses'). This however seems too remote to be a direct source for Ann, though the words may have had a resonance at the back of her mind. Moses has no place in her explicit thought here; and whereas in Hebrews Moses was faithful in God's house (i.e. a faithful servant of

God), and Jesus is similarly faithful to God who appointed him, in Ann's verse the words '*ffyddlon ydyw*', taken in their full context, clearly mean that he is a faithful friend to us; cf. the lines by Dafydd Jones (1711–77) of Caeo: '*Dyma Gyfaill haeddai'i garu / A'i glodfori'n fwy nag un*' ('Here is a Friend who would deserve to be loved and to be praised more than any'). But Ann does not say 'more than any'. The plain meaning of her words is that Jesus deserves higher praise than simply to be called faithful and full of consolation – which is a feebler utterance than we should have expected of her. Perhaps the words of Dafydd Jones of Caeo and of Hebrews were both somewhere at the back of her mind, but what she succeeded in saying is less forceful than either. It is an undeniable weakness in an otherwise memorable stanza.

Notes on the
Letters of Ann Griffiths

NOTES ON THE LETTERS OF ANN GRIFFITHS

THE LETTERS BY Ann Griffiths which have survived were all written when she was 'Ann Thomas', i.e. before her marriage to Thomas Griffiths in October 1804. Seven of the eight letters were addressed to John Hughes. He made copies of the seven in one of his manuscript books, and those copies are the nearest we have to the originals, which are no longer extant. The original of the eighth letter, to Elizabeth Evans, has survived.

Ann's letters were written with no thought of publication and no effort at literary style. Their content is straightforward and their manner unaffected. They are the work of someone writing out her thoughts; yet there is no waste of words and no looseness of thought. Ann knows what she wants to say and says it in the plainest way she can. There are several fine passages where the sheer power of what Ann is saying is reflected in the words through which she says it. There is no element of mere gossip or news-telling in the letters. They are, and were clearly meant to be, part of an exchange of ideas and experiences which was continually going on within the Methodist community. Evidently these people showed their correspondence to one another, and so a common mind and experience must have been to some extent created and maintained. Ann's letters show us something of what she gained from these exchanges and what she contributed to them

Ann's letters do not at once yield up their secret. All without exception deal almost exclusively with the inner life of their writer. In the hymns Ann's gaze is fixed on the mysteries of Christ; she herself appears almost incidentally. In the letters it is her own condition which she seeks to lay bare and understand. Nevertheless we find in them ample evidence that the power of vision which is revealed in the hymns did not wholly desert her when she put pen to paper in prose. Hurried and unstudied as they seem to be, they still have a noble simplicity, a kind of urgent longing which tells us much about the composer of the hymns.

LETTER I

'**I have had this opportunity ...**' This opening section illustrates several aspects of the complex relationship between Ann and John Hughes. She assures him of her willingness to correspond with him, which suggests that he had expressed a doubt of it; though at the same time it appears that he had taken the initiative by writing her a 'substantial letter'. She recognizes that he has a unique understanding of her past history and present state, and that his intention in writing was to say something helpful, and she evidently thinks he has succeeded very well. But she writes as an independent soul with her own judgment about her. However much she may appreciate John's help towards her spiritual progress, she does not hesitate to express an interest in his; at this stage, at any rate, the relation is a reciprocal one. For the reference to Boaz, see Hymn XXVII.

'**pulled up the hill by the following two chains**'. Perhaps an image derived from a quarry which has little trucks for the quarried stone, moving on rails and drawn by chains or cables.

'**I have had another trial ...**' Ann has been wondering whether perhaps her spiritual life has made (in some unexplained way) a false start, and whether her present religious life and experience are the genuine thing. Such doubts are normal in sensitive souls accustomed to self-examination; so too is the capacity to recover balance. We cannot tell what precisely Ann thought had been wrong. The relevance of the text from Hebrews 4:14, 'Seeing then that we have a great high priest', to Ann's form of discouragement will be seen if we go on to the words which follow those quoted in the letter: 'let us hold fast our profession', and a little later, 'Let us therefore come boldly unto the throne of grace.' Perhaps she was also conscious of Exodus 28:38, where Aaron as high priest is given the function of bearing 'the iniquity of the holy things which the children of Israel shall hallow in all their holy gifts', i.e. the high priest atones for the inherent imperfections of our religious life and observances. (Cf. Walter Marshall, *The Gospel-Mystery of Sanctification*, XIII, 5.)

'the ordinance': i.e. the Lord's Supper.

'the stones of the sanctuary …' (Lamentations 4:1).

'God will not cast away his people …' The original Welsh letter reads, '*ni wrthyd Duw ei bobl, y rhai a adnabu Fe o'r blaen*', a loose quotation from Romans 11:2: '*Ni wrthododd Duw ei bobl, yr hwn a adnabu efe o'r blaen*' ('God hath not cast away his people which he foreknew').

'The cup is in the hand of the Lord …' (Psalm 75:8). Ann's quotation in the original Welsh letter is a loose version of the Welsh text of the Psalm, but nothing hangs on the differences. The Psalm is about God as the Judge of human society, who will demote the wicked and exalt the righteous.

'the children will only be purged': here at the beginning is the theme of purgation or purification, which runs all through this correspondence.

LETTER II

'Simon, son of Jonas, lovest thou me more than these?' (John 21:15). The natural interpretation of these words in their context is that Christ asks Peter, 'Do you love me more than the other apostles do?' Something like this claim had been implicit in Peter's words, 'Though all should deny thee, yet will not I deny thee', and he had not made good his claim when crisis struck. But Ann takes the words to mean, 'Do you love me more than you love these things?', namely the various gifts of nature and grace.

'Buy the truth, and sell it not' (Proverbs 23:23). The previous verses warn against excess in eating and drinking; it is better to be prudent in one's enjoyment of good things. But Ann would surrender the good things of life as well as the bad ones for the sake of the spiritual marriage.

'every idle word ...': i.e. not only wrong speech and action, but levity of spirit. We know from Letter IV how concerned Ann is about the inward discipline, the control of wayward thoughts. Two comments suggest themselves here. (1) A kind of perfectionism is natural and normal in souls which have been touched by love of the divine Perfection, or by the longing for spiritual union with that Perfection. Such souls come to see and feel vividly the contrast between their inherent perversity and corruption (what Ann calls her 'damnable, lost condition', Letter III) and the graces which are nevertheless bestowed upon them. It is a part of Christian wisdom to know how to take this paradox. Ann took it hard; for all her grounding in evangelical theology, she was puzzled by the *simul justus et peccator* ('at the same time righteous and a sinner') when she experienced it in herself, though the full assurance of hope always prevailed over the doubt. (2) One can always ask the perfectionist where he draws the line between what is acceptable and what is not. The answer cannot be expected to be the same for all souls at all periods and in all states of life. Accepting Ann's own expressions in this paragraph, we wonder what she regards as idle speech or levity of spirit, and what behaviour she thinks of as appearing contrary to gospel holiness. Similarly in Letter IV we wonder just what preoccupations or trains of thought she regards as sinful. We cannot know; but certainly the discipline of early Methodism was austere, and Ann was one who would take in deadly earnest what less sensitive souls might take more lightly, and this will have been a factor in the continual tension which is reflected in these letters. She says here that every idle word, etc., is a total denial that we have known Christ. Total denial? In Catholic language this seems to exclude the possibility of venial sins or even mere frailties; they are all mortal sins. Ann must have been merciless in self-judgment; she could not have kept on an even keel if her religion had not been firmly based on the doctrine of free grace and the repudiation of personal merit.

'a simile'. This should probably be understood as a story which Ann heard told by a preacher during a sermon. The point of the story would be against those Church-people, outwardly devout but inwardly unawakened, of whom Ann's own family had once been an instance. The 'shout' will have been uttered by the preacher himself, turning to the congregation and saying, 'Little children, cry out for the goods-wagon of Methodist preachers, true ministers of the Word, to come home to us with a full load.'

LETTER III

'the advice given to Moses'. In Exodus 18 the people must take their disputes to the ordinary judges to whom Moses has delegated his judicial functions, but in obscure cases they are to bypass these and go to Moses himself. Ann interprets this anagogically to mean that in her own perplexity of mind she must go beyond the Methodist leaders and counsellors, who do not understand her, to God himself. She links this with a passage in Canticles 3:1–4. The Bride seeks her Beloved by night in the streets and in the broad ways, '*trwy yr heolydd a'r* *ystrydoedd*'. She meets the watchmen who patrol the city, but does not find the Beloved until she has passed beyond them. Ann's advisers have been as unhelpful as the watchmen were to the Bride, but the text about Moses, in Ann's interpretation of it, encouraging her to appeal from them to the high court, is a road (*heol*) which has brought her to the Beloved himself. [See also H. A. Hodges' note on *heol* in his translation of Saunders Lewis' lecture, 'Ann Griffiths: A Literary Survey', in this volume. – *Ed.*]

'the Shunammite woman'. In Canticles 3:4, when the Bride finds the Beloved, she brings him home with her. Later, in Canticles 8:2, she says she would often do this if she were free to do it. There is always a place for him in her home. Perhaps that may have suggested to Ann the thought of the Shunammite woman who furnished a room for Elisha to occupy whenever he came by (2 Kings 4:10). Ann's soul is open to God's visitations always, and between times the sight of the furniture (i.e. presumably her beliefs and her knowledge of Scripture and her regular prayer-habits) assures her of her own constancy. Her soul is God's temple, where the devil can trespass but can find no lodging.

'The Lord thy God in the midst of thee is mighty' (Zephaniah 3:17). This verse follows upon a denunciation of slackness and corruption in Jerusalem, and is part of a prophecy of better things.

LETTER IV

This is the shortest of Ann's surviving letters, but it is full of matter.

'the sin of the mind': not harbouring thoughts of sinful acts, but the sin of not keeping the mind wholly centred upon God, of not loving God with the loyalty of a totally recollected mind. For this, as well as for sinful desires and actions, we need forgiveness and purification. This is an aspect of the doctrine of purification which would be likely to suggest itself more forcibly to an introvert than to an extravert soul. In what follows, Ann's words seem to mean that she herself has just seen it more clearly and forcefully than before. Hence for her a new intensity of longing to be purified, and love for the doctrine which promises purification through the blood. Only by ruthless chiselling (to change the metaphor) can she become a stone fit to stand in the temple of God.

'no need ever to change my garment, but a longing to be clean in my garment': i.e. not to shed the body, but to be pure even while in the body. Here is the first hint of a theme which comes increasingly to the fore in Ann's letters from now on, namely a weighing of the comparative advantages of life and death. In later letters Ann seems to come gradually to the conclusion that no purification as drastic as she desires is possible in this life, and therefore she looks forward to death for the sake of the full sanctification which only it can bring; though meanwhile she acknowledges the high gifts of grace which can be received even in this life. See Letter VIII.

'By this shall the iniquity of Jacob be purged' (Isaiah 27:9). The context is about God's judgments; those which fall upon Israel are purgatorial.

LETTER V

'where two seas meet' (*rhwng deufor-gyfarfod*). The word '*deufor-gyfarfod*' appears in the Welsh Bible in Acts 27:41, where '*ar le deufor-gyfarfod*' translates *eis topon dithalasson*. The word '*deufor-gyfarfod*' passed into Welsh usage to signify any place of stormy waters and conflicting currents, and metaphorically to signify troubled circumstances; but Ann would, of course, have been well aware of the word's occurrence in connection with the shipwreck in Acts.

'**while nature gets its own way**' ('*wrth i natur gael ei rhwysg*'). Perhaps a reference to Proverbs 29:15: '*Y wialen a cherydd a rydd ddoethineb: ond mab a gaffo ei rwysg ei hun, a gywilyddia ei fam.*' The Authorised Version has: 'The rod and reproof give wisdom: but a child left to himself bringeth his mother to shame.' The words 'left to himself' mean 'left without control' and correspond to the Welsh '*a gaffo ei rwysg ei hun*', which means 'allowed to govern himself' and so 'getting his own way'.

'**Go forth, O ye daughters of Zion ...**' (Canticles 3:11), which is mystically interpreted by reference to the Via Dolorosa. The day of Christ's espousals, the day of the gladness of his heart, when he wears the nuptial crown, is Good Friday, when he 'fulfilled the terms' and won his Bride. (See also the note on Hymn II, verse 4.) Ann here lays stress upon 'go forth'; we are to go outside ourselves and what is ours to contemplate Christ. Cf. Ruysbroeck's use of the summons to go forth to meet the Bridegroom (Matthew 25:6) in his *Adornment of the Spiritual Marriage.*

'**cieled houses**' – '*tai byrddiedig*', 'paneled houses': Haggai 1:4. The prophet reproaches the people for building themselves comfortable dwellings while the Temple stands unfinished. The implication here is that we are to leave our self-indulgences and face the overwhelming vision of the Crucified Incarnate. Note that here, as elsewhere, Ann's contemplation of the Crucified does not include dwelling on the detail of his sufferings. The astonishing truth of who he is drives all such considerations out of her mind.

LETTER VI

The copy of this letter in the John Hughes manuscript bears no date, but when he published it in the journal, *Y Traethodydd*, in 1846 he put '*Ebrill 1802*' ('April 1802') at the head of it. The end of the letter refers to John having recently been appointed a preacher, and of course he could recall the date by reference to that event. In the version of Ann's letters to him which he published in 1846, he so arranged them as to make this letter, with its note of congratulation to himself, the last of the series.

'I have been finding it very stormy for a long time now.' Here is the record of a minor spiritual crisis in Ann's life, which was substantially over when she wrote this letter, and must have occurred towards the end of 1801 or the beginning of 1802. It is perhaps significant that this letter, in which she reports her experience, is the only one in which she addresses John as her 'father in the Lord'. She was especially conscious at this moment of the need for spiritual counsel. Can we, from what she says, discern what had gone wrong? God spoke to her through Malachi, asking 'Where is my honour? where is my fear?' (Malachi 1:6) So she had been in some way depriving God of the honour due to him. In what way? Two possibilities come to mind. (1) Had she been too much involved with worldly interests or pleasures, and therefore doing dishonour to God 'by giving the first place to secondary things' (Letter V)? That might correlate with what she says later in this letter about the manifold distractions to which she is subject. Or (2) had she been practising some special austerity which she then came to think was presumptuous and tended to self-righteousness? That would agree with the implications of the passage from Malachi, where God rebukes his people for bringing him unworthy offerings, and it would fit with Ann's remark about being unable to 'feed on [God's] free mercy' in view of the path she was following. The reference to Psalm 23 would fit our first conjecture, i.e. 'God is my sufficiency, I need nothing else at all.' But if we follow on through the Psalm and through the way this section of the letter develops, it fits perhaps better with our second suggestion, i.e. 'It is God who leads me in the paths of righteousness, it is he who converts my soul' where I myself am powerless to return. God is 'wholly self-dependent in the matter of saving a sinner', and requires no contributions from us. As Ann says later in this letter, we can never glorify God more than by simply taking what he gives. This interpretation may seem to suggest that Ann had momentarily lost her hold on the doctrine of justification by faith; which is incredible. But the conclusion does not follow. It is quite possible in practice to believe in justification by faith and yet in sanctification by works. One may have followed the way for years and yet need to be told that one should wait upon God and not force the pace. This letter reads like the work of one who has recently been taught that lesson.

'grey hairs are spreading over her': Hosea 7:9, 'gray hairs are here and there upon him [i.e. Ephraim], yet he knoweth not'. John Hughes uses this text in his letters to Ruth Hughes dated 4 March and 27 May 1803. In the letter of 4 March he makes it the basis for a detailed analysis of the process of spiritual declension; and in the course of his exposition occurs a sentence about 'the spiritual stomach being unable to rightly savour the feasts of the gospel'. This looks as if John may have written his letter after having received the present letter from Ann, remembering some of her ideas and phrases but developing them in his own way. In the second letter to Ruth, dated 27 May 1803, he explains that, although a soul which has once been united to Christ cannot finally be lost, it can fall away very seriously in this life, often without noticing what is happening to it; and in this context he again refers to the text about grey hairs. It seems that a phrase thrown off in passing by Ann in this letter had set him off upon a line of serious analytical thinking.

'your new work'. John Hughes had just succeeded in being appointed as a preacher. 'Surely the Lord's anointed is before him' (1 Samuel 16:6): Ann here has changed the 'him' to 'me'. 'God seeth not as man seeth' (1 Samuel 16:7): the Welsh has 'God' where the Authorised Version has 'the Lord'. Samuel had been sent to find the Lord's anointed (Saul's destined successor) among Jesse's sons. When he saw the eldest, a fine upstanding figure of a man, he thought this must be the one, but it was made clear to him that it was not so. He saw seven of Jesse's sons with the same result. In the end they had to send for the youngest, David, who had been left in the fields looking after the sheep. Similarly the Methodist authorities had at first thought that John Hughes was not in the running, but in the end they had to accept him.

Additional note on Letter VI

There is a striking community of phrases and ideas between Ann's Letters VI and VII and the letter from John Hughes to Ruth Evans dated 4 March 1803. There are also a score of places in these three letters which appear to echo phrases from Ann's hymns, which is something unusual in this correspondence. While of course a single occurrence in a letter of a phrase which is also in a hymn proves nothing, what we have here is beyond mere accident and invites enquiry. Yet so little is known about the circumstances that any attempted explanation must be guesswork. Acknowledging and indeed emphasising that, we venture to offer our own guess.

We suggest that the spiritual upheaval which Ann reports in Letter VI was substantially over when she wrote the letter. She had seen what was wrong and had learned a lesson, and though it was a lesson of humiliation she was joyfully excited at having learned it. This excitement may have triggered off a creative process leading to the composition of a number of hymns at this time; that would be in accord with what we know of Ann's manner of composition. If Hymn VII and Hymn X are of this date, that will explain why there are two apparent echoes of Hymn VII and three of Hymn X in Letter VI. (Hymn VII contains the thought of glorifying God by accepting his free gift – the very thing which Ann has just learned she must do – and a reference to a wavering mind which goes after worldly distractions. Hymn X is especially striking. It contains a reference to the Church as Zion, with a lament that she is slackening in the fight; to God's name being obscured when his witnesses in the world are slain; and to God being wholly self-dependent in the matter of winning souls. All these are points in Letter VI.)

Some time after this, we suggest, John Hughes met Ann and Ruth and there was a discussion in which Ann's recent experience would be touched upon, and also her report, which Ruth could confirm, of slackness in the Pontrobert congregation. No doubt some of Ann's hymns would be called to mind, not only those recently written but others also. After this conversation John wrote a reasoned account of his views on certain points for Ruth, in his letter to her of 4 March 1803. In it he takes up some of Ann's points and develops them. Thus he takes her text from Hosea about grey hair spreading over Ephraim's head, and builds it up into an analysis of the process of spiritual declension. In the course of this exposition he adopts Ann's phrase in Letter VI about having a weak spiritual stomach, and the phrase from Hymn X about the Shekinah gradually departing, and the text from Hosea which Ann uses in Hymn XIII, 'What have I to do any more with idols?' A page or two further on he expands Ann's idea that the greatest honour we can pay to God is by venturing upon his mercy according to his plan in Christ, and goes on to an eloquent exposition of the paradoxes of salvation, in which there are distinct traces of Ann's Hymn XXII and Hymn II, and just possibly of Hymn VI. We quote parts of this passage in our notes on Hymns II and XXII.

Ann will, of course, have seen this letter from John to Ruth. After this will have come her Letter VII, in which she makes her clearest statement of the principle of doing honour to God's law precisely by accepting God's own act which has satisfied it, without trying to do anything of one's own. A phrase from Hymn XXII about being able to come to God 'without being slain', which John echoes in his letter to Ruth of 4 March 1803, recurs here too in Letter VII.

We repeat that this is all conjecture; but there are facts in the documents which tease the mind into venturing upon such conjectures.

LETTER VII

This whole letter, with the exception of a few lines at the beginning and the end, is missing from the John Hughes manuscript owing to a leaf having been torn out. John Hughes published the text of the letter in its entirety in *Y Traethodydd* in 1846; however since John allowed himself liberties in editing Ann's letters and hymns when he published them, there is every reason to believe that his published version of Letter VII contains a number of amendments. In 1972 the text of a manuscript copy found in one of John Hughes' other manuscripts was printed in the *Journal of the Historical Society of the Presbyterian Church of Wales*. It has been argued that this text may well be a copy of either the original letter or of the page torn out of the John Hughes manuscript, and therefore it is this text rather than John Hughes' edited text of 1846 which has been used here in translating the letter into English. It is a pity, in view of the importance of some things contained in this letter, that we cannot be sure we are dealing with Ann's own words. In the John Hughes manuscript this letter is placed seventh in order, being thus the last of Ann's letters to John. When he published the letters he moved it into third place, at the same time moving Letter III into sixth place. It is very hard to believe that this can be right. The content of the letter does not fit in particularly well between Letters II and IV; it suggests a greater maturity of experience and reflection, and what Ann says in the second paragraph follows on convincingly from Letter VI if our second interpretation of that letter be accepted. The remarkable parting formula which precedes the signature in this letter is almost identical with that in Letter VIII.

'I would be very glad to be prevented from ever venturing to offer to God's holy law less than that which has satisfied it.' This prayer of Ann's seems a natural sequel to our second suggested interpretation of the experience reported in Letter VI. 'That which has satisfied it' is of course Christ's offering on Calvary, and Ann reaffirms (what as an instructed evangelical she can never have forgotten) the all-sufficiency of this. It was wrong to try to gild the lily by unnecessary austerities of her own. But a further point: her renunciation of self-righteousness or self-sanctification is not made in any spirit of mere resignation, as if she were saying 'I wish I could offer something of my own to the law, but I will not try because I know it will be rejected.' On the contrary, she has been able to turn it into a glad act of self-effacement, as if to say 'I do not wish to put myself forward in any way at all, so that nothing may cloud the vision of the divine perfection in the law itself and in the only offering which has or ever could have satisfied it.' She goes on to rejoice in its intolerant perfection which strikes down all creaturely pretensions whatsoever. Ann herself knows she is safe because she has her Mediator, but she does not shrink from glancing for a moment at the plight of those who have none.

'Thy neck is like the tower of David; wherein there

hang a thousand shields.' Ann's use of Canticles 4:4 in this paragraph is an example of how she can shoot off from a biblical text, by image-association, into something which has nothing to do with that text. In the Song of Solomon the Bride's neck is likened to a tower, for the obvious reason of its shape; the 'shields' adorning it are earrings and pendants. Applying this to herself, Ann should conclude that she is a fort, handsome in appearance and stored with armour. What she actually says is that she is weaponless, and the tower becomes a source extraneous to herself, from which she can obtain armour.

LETTER VIII

This letter is not in the John Hughes manuscript. Alone of Ann's letters, it survives in the original. Comparison of this with the text published by John Hughes in 1846 shows what liberties he allowed himself as an editor.

In the first part of this letter Ann says she has been in grave error about the Holy Spirit. What was the error? It is true that in her writings she makes remarkably few explicit references to the Spirit; and there is no reason to doubt that the cause of this seeming neglect was what Ann here says it was: a failure to realise his personal nature and the consequently personal and intimate nature of our relations with him. When this dawned upon Ann she was shaken, as we see here, by the revelation of her past obtuseness and by the realisation of her inherent incapacity to do anything but grieve the Spirit. For of course it is not merely the holding of inadequate views as to his nature which grieves him, but the sinfulness which pervades us, and to which we so often and so easily yield, can be nothing but a continual grief to One indwelling us so intimately.

T. H. Parry-Williams (in an essay in the volume, *Cofio Ann Griffiths*) seems to be under the impression that grieving the Spirit is the same thing as committing blasphemy against him, that mysterious sin for which there is no forgiveness in this world or the next. Probably most of us have come across people whose lives have been shadowed by the obsessive dread of having committed this sin, and Parry-Williams thinks Ann was one of them. The two things however, grieving the Spirit and blaspheming against him, are mentioned in different contexts in Scripture and neither would fit into the context of the other. They are not at all the same thing. This ought not to need insisting upon. Ann suffered enough in her time from one thing and another, including fears as she says in Letters I and V, but there is no justification for burdening her with this particular morbid obsession. These very paragraphs show that she knew how to 'try the throne', and her gratitude for what she found there.

'**I give myself unto prayer**' (Psalm 109:4), and that answered the purpose of making them fall backwards. This seems to be an allusion to John 18:6, where the troop of armed men sent to arrest Jesus, on hearing him answer to his name, went backward and fell to the ground.

'**I will water it every moment**' (Isaiah 27:3). The full verse runs: 'I the Lord do keep it [i.e. my vineyard]; I will water it every moment: lest any hurt it, I will keep it night and day.'

'**the rock of the Word to set foot on to start**'. Is Ann thinking here of a mounting block? Only from what God gives can we set out. But we really can set out.

'**the law which is already on one's heart**'. The manuscript has '*ar ei calon*', which is grammatically impossible. For '*ei*' read '*ein*' ('our'). The English equivalent here would be 'one's'.

'**to enjoy God's likeness for ever**'. Cf. the last line of Hymn IX. It is worth mentioning that the whole spirit of that hymn has something in common with that of this section of the letter.

'Ruth wishes to be remembered kindly to you.' The recipient of this letter was probably Ruth's sister.

At the foot of the last page of the letter, Ann has written out the first verse of her hymn, '*Er mai cwbwl groes i natur*' (Hymn IV), but as one flowing sentence rather than in stanza form (which seems to reflect the general tendency in Ann's hymns towards long sentences trailing on through a whole stanza, rather than self-contained couplets). The presence of this verse is not evidence that it was written at the same time as the letter. She quotes it because it is appropriate to what she has been saying about her difficulties and perplexities. It is worth mentioning that the text of the verse as given here in Ann's own hand is identical with that in the John Hughes manuscript; this is a testimony to the accuracy of Ruth's memory.

Scriptural References and Allusions in the Hymns and Letters of Ann Griffiths

SCRIPTURAL REFERENCES AND ALLUSIONS IN THE HYMNS AND LETTERS OF ANN GRIFFITHS

by E. Wyn James

ONE OF THE most notable features of Ann Griffiths' work is its use of Scripture. In the discussion of the literary qualities of Ann's hymns in the introduction to their unpublished edition of her work, Hodges and Allchin argue that

> Ann at her best is a poet of imagery, especially paradoxical imagery, rather than of reflective thought. Those of her hymns which are widely known and loved are all in the imaginative mode, expressing also a certain exaltation of feeling.

They also emphasise that Ann Griffiths

> is first and foremost a poet of and for the Methodist community in which her life was spent. It was a community whose imagination was fed from one main source, and in which there grew up a common pattern of experience, a common vocabulary and a common mind on the things of the spirit.
>   Their principal source of imagery was the Bible, and the Bible to these people was not merely a quarry from which to draw material as needed, but a world in which they habitually lived.

However, while the Bible is a central text for Williams Pantycelyn and the other hymn-writers of the Methodist Revival, and while they all echo Scripture in their hymns, Ann's use of the Bible is particularly concentrated and complex. The resonances are more frequent and more tightly woven. Indeed, part of the intensity of expression which marks her work stems from the way in which it is packed full of references and allusions to various parts of Scripture. H. A. Hodges, in an unpublished discussion of Ann Griffiths' use of the Song of Solomon, notes that, whereas Isaac Watts in English and Williams Pantycelyn in Welsh wrote a number of hymns which were directly based on passages from the Song, Ann's treatment was different, using the Song as 'a source for words and images which [she] then weave[s] into [her] own devotional thinking'. She uses it, says Hodges, 'as one of the many sources for the rich web of imagery which evidently filled her mind and formed much of the substance of her thought'. The same could be said of her use of Scripture in general. Ann interweaves a range of biblical references in each of her hymns, reflecting the fact that she (like her fellow Methodists) regarded the whole of the Bible, both Old and New Testaments, as one rich tapestry worked by the same divine Author. As a result, she immersed herself in all parts of Scripture. Furthermore, she regarded the whole of Scripture as revolving around the person of Jesus Christ. To her, he is the key to every part of the Bible; to him it all refers, sometimes overtly, sometimes by means of allegory and typology.

Directly or indirectly, then, the language of all her hymns is based on that of the Bible, and the Bible is the source of the imagery she employs in making concrete her ideas and experiences. This plethora of scriptural references and allusions has led some to question the originality of her work. 'Her hymns, we are told [by such people],' say Hodges and Allchin,

Scriptural References and Allusions

'are a mere cento of biblical phrases and images, loosely strung together as they came into her mind.' Nothing could be further from the truth; for what we have in Ann Griffiths is a creative, meditative use of such imagery and sources. She selects her imagery skilfully and is so steeped in the language of the Bible as to be able to make it the language of her own deepest experiences. In this respect Ann Griffiths may be regarded as a 'classical' author. As Saunders Lewis maintains in his lecture, 'Ann Griffiths: A Literary Survey', in this volume:

> Some critics have said that all she did was to string together sentences from Scripture and that there is not much of her own in her work. Exactly the same charge could be brought against Virgil. There are hardly three lines together in all his works without a reminiscence of or a quotation from the work of earlier Greek or Latin poets. This is true of many poets of the first rank in Europe and China. In our own time Ezra Pound has taught this art to the poets of America. It is reflective poets, poets of the intellect, who have this gift.

Or to quote Hodges and Allchin once again:

> It is common form in Christianity for writers to draw upon a common store of ideas and phrases which is derived from the Bible and enriched by an ever-growing tradition. From a literary point of view, everything depends on *how* a writer draws upon this material, what selection he makes from it and how he develops and presents what he selects. It is here that the personal vision of the individual shows itself, not in going outside the communal tradition, but in a way of working within it.

One might add that the Bible is the backdrop against which Ann's spiritual experiences are played out. For example, all references to nature in her work are to the plants and animals of Scripture; the geography of her hymns is that of the Holy Land and the surrounding countries. One can see this clearly in the way Ann emphasises in her letters the importance of finding her spiritual condition reflected in God's Word and her great concern when that is not experienced. Similarly we see her fearing '*dychmygion*' ('imaginations') of all kinds, as she calls them, and striving to bring all her thoughts and emotions under the scrutiny of Scripture – '*y drych sanctaidd*' ('the holy mirror'), as she refers to the Bible in one of her letters. There were negative aspects to this, as the Bible kept a rein on her beliefs and experiences; but on the other hand, Scripture also played a positive role in creating and deepening her spiritual experiences as well as channelling and controlling them. This can be seen from the frequent references in her letters to the way a '*gair*' ('word') of Scripture would impress itself on her mind, bringing comfort and enlightenment as well as correction.

In a letter to A. M. Allchin in June 1967, H. A. Hodges wrote:

> We shall have to consider what to do about Bible references [i.e. in their proposed edition of Ann Griffiths' work]. I could not have made sense of some passages in the hymns without a concordance, which enabled me to track down Ann's sometimes obscure sources. It is only fair to the reader, and to ourselves, and to Ann, to give some of this information.

In the end, as can be seen from the following statement in the introduction to their planned edition of her work, they decided to proceed as follows:

> In this edition we have not attempted to elucidate every Biblical reference or allusion in the letters and hymns. To have done so would have made an impossibly bulky volume. We have tried

Scriptural References and Allusions

rather to give examples of the way in which Ann makes use of images and phrases taken from the Scriptures.

Such examples were discussed in H. A. Hodges' notes on her hymns and letters which are published in this volume for the first time. However, in order to facilitate a more extensive study, the list of scriptural references and allusions in Ann's work which appeared in my Gregynog edition of her work in 1998 has been included here. It should be explained that where a reference occurs in brackets, it denotes either that it is quite likely that this section of the Bible was in Ann's mind at the time, although one cannot be absolutely certain, or else that the wording of that portion of Scripture is echoed in Ann's work, but not its meaning. Ann Griffiths used the 'traditional' translation of the Bible into Welsh which was completed in 1588 and revised in 1620. Had she been writing in English, Ann would have used the Authorised Version of 1611. However, since the Welsh translation was made from the original biblical languages and not translated from the English, it differs sometimes from the Authorised Version in its rendering of a passage. It is important to remember, therefore, that there may be echoes of the Welsh Bible in Ann's work which have no equivalent in the corresponding passage in the English Authorised Version.

★   ★   ★

HYMN I

Hymn I:1: *l*.1: Revelation 3:8 (cf. 4:1); *l*.2: (Revelation 15:2); *l*.3: Psalm 68:18/Ephesians 4:8; *l*.4: Philippians 2:7; *ll*.5–6: Colossians 2:15; *l*.7: Psalm 68:18/Ephesians 4:8

Hymn I:2: *l*.1: (Jeremiah 31:25); *l*.2: Luke 1:44; (Isaiah

35:6, 10); *l*.3: Isaiah 42:21; *ll*.5–6: John 11:25; *l*.5: (Matthew 26:59/Mark 14:55; Luke 23:32); *l*.6: (1 Corinthians 15:4); *l*.7: (Isaiah 54:10; Ezekiel 37:26; Daniel 9:24; Colossians 1:20)

Hymn I:3: *l*.1: Ephesians 4:8–10; John 3:13; *l*.2: John 17:4, 19:28, 30; *l*.3: Psalm 24:7, 9; *l*.5: Psalm 24:7, 9; Isaiah 45:1; *l*.6: 1 Timothy 3:16; *l*.7: Proverbs 16:15; *ll*.7–8: Psalm 110:1

Hymn I:4: *ll*.1–2: Isaiah 43:2; *ll*.3–4: 1 Corinthians 7:35; *l*.7: Philippians 3:10; *l*.8: 1 Peter 1:19; (Luke 23:33)

HYMN II

Hymn II:1: *l*.1: (Exodus 29:41–43, 39:32–40:38; Hebrews 9); *l*.2: (Leviticus 17:11; Colossians 1:20; Hebrews 9:22); *l*.3: Numbers 35:9–28; *l*.4: Matthew 9:12/Mark 2:17/Luke 5:31; Hosea 14:4; *l*.5: Exodus 33:21; *l*.6: (Psalm 84:3; Song of Solomon 2:14); *l*.7: (Jeremiah 23:6); *l*.8: Proverbs 16:15

Hymn II:2: *l*.1: (Isaiah 64:6); *l*.2: 1 Timothy 1:15; *ll*.3–4: (Exodus 33:7–11); *l*.6: (Isaiah 25:6; Luke 14:16–24, 15:11–32); *l*.7: (2 Corinthians 3:5, 12:9); *l*.8: (Leviticus 3:1–17; Colossians 1:20)

Hymn II:3: *ll*.1–2: Esther 4:11, 5:1–2, 8:4; *l*.4: John 6:37; *l*.5: (Psalm 25:11); *l*.6: (Mark 5:22; Luke 7:44–48); *l*.7: (Psalm 51:2, 7; 1 Corinthians 6:11); *l*.8: Revelation 7:14

Hymn II:4: *ll*.1–4: Song of Solomon 3:6–11; *ll*.5–6: Revelation 3:14

HYMN III

Hymn III:1: *l*.1: (Hebrews 11:13; 1 Peter 2:11; Psalm 55:8); *l*.2: Daniel 10:5; *l*.3: (John 1:29; 1 Peter 1:19; Revelation 5:6; 1 Timothy 2:5; Hebrews 8:6, 9:11–15); *ll*.4–5: Exodus 28; Daniel 10:5; Revelation 1:13; *l*.5: Isaiah 11:5; Hebrews 2:17, 3:2; *ll*.6–7: Exodus 28:33–35; *l*.8: (Romans 3:25; 1 John 2:2)

Hymn III:2: *ll*.1–4: Ezekiel 47:3; *l*.5: Luke 20:36; *ll*.6–7: Ezekiel 47:5, 8; *l*.8: John 5:2–4

Scriptural References and Allusions

Hymn III:3: *ll*.2–4: 1 Timothy 3:16; *ll*.5–6: (1 Peter 2:21, 3:18); *ll*.7–8: Job 33:24; John 11:44; Acts 2:24

Hymn III:4: *ll*.1–2: (Hebrews 4:9); Revelation 14:13; Daniel 12:13; *l*.5: 2 Peter 1:11; *l*.6: John 14:2; (1 John 5:7); *l*.7: Isaiah 33:21; Ezekiel 47:5

HYMN IV

Hymn IV:1: *l*.4: Luke 9:29; (Psalm 42:5; Proverbs 16:15); *l*.6: Romans 5:3; *ll*.7–8: Psalm 107:7

Hymn IV:2: *l*.1: John 14:6; Judges 13:18; Isaiah 9:6; *l*.2: (Jeremiah 6:16; Deuteronomy 29:5); *l*.3: Hebrews 7:3; Isaiah 43:19; *ll*.3–4: Hebrews 10:20; *l*.4: (Isaiah 26:19; Luke 20:37–38; John 11:25; Romans 6:13); *l*.5: James 1:18; (Matthew 7:14); *ll*.7–8: Hebrews 10:20

Hymn IV:3: *l*.1: Job 28:7; *l*.2: (Proverbs 4:18; Isaiah 59:10; Romans 1:20); *l*.3: Psalm 107:4; *ll*.3–4: Hebrews 11:27; *l*.5: Romans 4:5; *l*.6: (Isaiah 26:19; Luke 20:37–38; John 11:25; Romans 6:13); *l*.7: (Proverbs 13:15; Hosea 14:9); *l*.8: (Romans 5:1; Ruth 2:2; Luke 1:30)

Hymn IV:4: *l*.1: (2 Timothy 1:9; Ephesians 1:4); *ll*.3–4: Genesis 3:15; *l*.5: Hebrews 8:6–7; *l*.6: (1 John 5:7); *ll*.7–8: Judges 9:13; (Numbers 15:5, 7, 10; Matthew 26:27–29/Mark 14:23–25)

HYMN V

Hymn V:1: *l*.1: (Daniel 1:3); *l*.2: (Hebrews 11:14–16); *l*.3: Exodus 1:14, 5:6–9; *l*.4: (2 Timothy 2:12; Revelation 20:4, 6); *l*.5: 2 Corinthians 5:7; (1 Corinthians 13:12–13); *ll*.5–6: (Galatians 5:5; Colossians 1:4–5, 23; 1 Thessalonians 1:3, 5:8; 1 Peter 1:21); *ll*.7–8: Revelation 5:9–10; *l*.8: 1 Peter 1:19, 2:9

Hymn V:2: *ll*.1–2: (Isaiah 2:18, 20; Hosea 14:8; Ezekiel 36:25–27); *l*.3: (Proverbs 3:3, 7:3; 2 Corinthians 3:2–3); *l*.4: 2 Corinthians 3:18; Romans 8:29; *l*.5: Revelation 4:11, 5:9, 12;

l.6: (Hosea 3:5; Matthew 21:37/Mark 12:6/Luke 20:13); *l*.7: (Judges 14:5–9, 14)

Hymn V:3: *ll*.1–2: Song of Solomon 1:12; *l*.2: Hosea 14:4; *l*.5: Matthew 5:29–30/Mark 9:43, 47; *l*.6: Isaiah 2:11; *ll*.7–8: Revelation 5; *l*.8: (Luke 1:31–33; Psalm 47:2, 95:3; Malachi 1:14)

Hymn V:4: *ll*.1–2: (Ezekiel 36:21–23); *l*.5: (Deuteronomy 23:21; Ecclesiastes 5:4–5); *ll*.6–7: 2 Timothy 2:1; *ll*.7–8: (Isaiah 45:2–3; Colossians 2:3; Matthew 13:44); *l*.8: (Revelation 12:11, 15:2)

Hymn V:5: *l*.1: (Psalm 17:15); *l*.2: (Ezekiel 26:21); *l*.5: (1 Corinthians 1:9; Philippians 3:10; 1 John 1:3); *ll*.5–6: Song of Solomon 1:3; *ll*.7–8: (Matthew 5:13; Mark 9:49; Leviticus 2:9, 13; 2 Corinthians 2:14–16); *l*.8: (Psalm 84:1; Song of Solomon 1:5, 16, 7:6; Romans 12:4–8; 1 Corinthians 12)

HYMN VI

Hymn VI:1: *ll*.1–2: (1 Peter 1:12); *ll*.2–5: (1 Timothy 3:16)

Hymn VI:2: *l*.4: (Psalm 55:22; 1 Peter 5:7); *ll*.5–6: Hebrews 4:15

Hymn VI:3: *l*.3: (2 Samuel 11:11); *l*.5: (Song of Solomon 1:12; Luke 22:29–30; 2 Samuel 9:13); *ll*.5–6: Proverbs 25:6–7; *l*.6: Luke 14:10; *l*.8: (1 Samuel 2:8/Psalm 113:7)

Hymn VI:4: *l*.2: Psalm 89:9; *l*.3: (Proverbs 8; 1 Corinthians 1:24, 30; Ezekiel 27:8); *l*.4: Psalm 89:8; *ll*.5–8: 1 Peter 3:20–22

HYMN VII

Hymn VII:1: *l*.1: (Psalm 39:3; Acts 18:25; Romans 12:11); *l*.3: (Romans 3:23; Luke 17:10); *l*.4: Psalm 19:7–8; Romans 7:12; (James 1:25); *l*.5: (Isaiah 42:21; Romans 2:23); *l*.6: (Romans 3:24; 1 Corinthians 2:12); *l*.8: (Exodus 12:22; 1 Corinthians 10:16; 1 John 1:7; Revelation 19:13)

Hymn VII:2: *l*.1: (Revelation 17:6); *l*.3: Jeremiah 2:20, 36;

Scriptural References and Allusions

*l.*7: (Romans 12:2; Philippians 3:10); *l.*8: Psalm 19:8; Romans 7:12; 1 John 3:2–5

HYMN VIII

Hymn VIII:1: *ll.*1–2: Daniel 3:19–25; *ll.*3–4: Job 23:10; (1 Peter 1:7; Zechariah 13:9; Malachi 3:3); *l.*5: Revelation 7:14; Daniel 11:35, 12:10; (Luke 22:31); *l.*7: Isaiah 32:2; *l.*8: Matthew 3:12/Luke 3:17

Hymn VIII:2: *l.*1: (Psalm 13:2); *l.*2: (Psalm 3:1); *l.*3: Psalm 118:12; *l.*5: Micha 7:6/Matthew 10:36; *l.*7: Hebrews 4:16; *l.*8: Hebrews 12:4

HYMN IX

Hymn IX:1: *l.*1: (Nehemiah 1:7; Ezekiel 20:40, 44); *l.*2: (Jeremiah 2:13; Hebrews 3:12); *l.*3: (Psalm 48:1); 2 Peter 1:17–18; *ll.*3–6: Isaiah 25:6–7; *l.*7: 2 Peter 1:16–18

Hymn IX:2: *l.*2: Isaiah 12:3; *ll.*5–7: Luke 12:36–37; (Matthew 25:1–13; Song of Solomon 5:2–6); *l.*8: Psalm 17:15; (2 Corinthians 3:18)

HYMN X

Hymn X:1: *ll.*1–2: Jeremiah 9:1; *l.*3: Song of Solomon 6:4, 10; *l.*5: Song of Solomon 5:15; (Revelation 10:1); *l.*7: 2 Corinthians 1:18–20; *l.*8: (Philippians 2:8)

Hymn X:2: *l.*1: (Jeremiah 2:2); *ll.*1–2: Song of Solomon 2:8–9, 8:14; *l.*3: (Exodus 17:8–16; Numbers 14:40–45; Deuteronomy 25:17–19; 1 Samuel 15:1–9, 30:1–20); *ll.*5–6: Song of Solomon 2:15; (Lamentations 5:18); *l.*7: (1 Samuel 4:21)

Hymn X:3: *l.*1: (Psalm 44:23; Exodus 14:31; Psalm 118:15–16); *l.*2: (Luke 1:72–73; Ezekiel 37:26; Isaiah 54:9–10); *ll.*4–5: Revelation 11:3–12; *l.*6: John 11:25; *l.*7: Revelation 2:17, 3:12; *ll.*7–8: (2 Corinthians 3:7–8)

Hymn X:4: *l*.1: Song of Solomon 1:3; *l*.4: (1 John 5:7); *l*.5: Hosea 13:14; *l*.6: (Numbers 23:19–20; Jeremiah 32:40); *l*.7: (Isaiah 53:11; Matthew 13:30; 1 Corinthians 3:9)

HYMN XI

Hymn XI:1: *l*.1: Psalm 84:6; *ll*.2–3: Exodus 17:6; Numbers 20:8–11; Psalm 78:16, 20; 1 Corinthians 10:4; John 19:34; *l*.4: (Daniel 12:10); Revelation 7:9, 14; *l*.5: (1 Peter 2:4–8; Revelation 21:11, 23–24); *l*.6: (1 Corinthians 1:30)

Hymn XI:2: *l*.1: (Psalm 143:6); *ll*.2–3: Revelation 22:2, 14; *l*.4: (Jeremiah 23:5–6; 1 Corinthians 1:30); Revelation 19:8; *l*.5: 2 Timothy 2:19; *l*.6: Genesis 3.7, Matthew 21.19/Mark 11:13

HYMN XII: *l*.1: Revelation 21:2, 9, 22:17; *l*.4: Song of Solomon 5:10

HYMN XIII

Hymn XIII:1: *l*.1: Zechariah 1:8; *l*.2: Revelation 4:11, 5:9, 12; *l*.3: 1 Corinthians 13:12; *l*.6: 1 John 3:2

Hymn XIII:2: *l*.1: Song of Solomon 2:1; *ll*.2–3: Song of Solomon 5:9–10; *l*.5: Matthew 11:19/Luke 7:34

Hymn XIII:3: *ll*.1–2: Hosea 14:8; *l*.4: Psalm 89:6; Isaiah 40:18, 25, 46:5; *ll*.5–6: John 15:9–10; (Judas 21)

HYMN XIV

Hymn XIV:1: *l*.3: James 1:18; (Psalm 119:32); *l*.4: Psalm 110:3; *l*.5: 1 Kings 8:10–11/2 Chronicles 5:13–14, 7:1–2; *ll*.5–6: 1 Kings 8:27/2 Chronicles 6:18, 2:6

Hymn XIV:2: *l*.3: (Song of Solomon 2:3); *l*.5: (Galatians 6:14); Matthew 10:38; Luke 14:27; Matthew 16:24/Mark 8:34/Luke 9:23; *l*.6: (Isaiah 54:5)

Scriptural References and Allusions

HYMN XV: *l*.4: (John 6:53–57); *ll*.5–6: 2 Corinthians 10:5; *l*.7: (Romans 12:2; Philippians 3:10); *l*.8: Proverbs 14:5, 25

HYMN XVI: *l*.1: (Malachi 1:7, 12; 1 Corinthians 10:21); *ll*.2–4: (Hebrews 10:1–3); *l*.3: (Genesis 7:23); *l*.5: Leviticus 25:8–13; *l*.6: Matthew 27:51/Mark 15:38/Luke 23:45; Hebrews 10:20; *l*.7: (1 Peter 2:24)

HYMN XVII: *ll*.1–4: Song of Solomon 1:5–6; *l*.6: Song of Solomon 1:5, (3:10)

HYMN XVIII: *ll*.1–2: Genesis 3; *l*.3: 2 Corinthians 13:11; *ll*.7–8: James 1:17

HYMN XIX

Hymn XIX:1: *ll*.1–2: John 17:3; *l*.2: 1 Thessalonians 1:9; *ll*.3–4: 2 Corinthians 10:3–5; *l*.5: (Luke 24:27; John 5:46, 20:31; Acts 4:4; 1 John 5:13); *l*.8: (Romans 3:25; 1 John 4:10)

Hymn XIX:2: *ll*.1–4: (Isaiah 6:1–5); *l*.2: Isaiah 2:11; *l*.4: Isaiah 57:15; *l*.5: (1 Timothy 2:5); *l*.6: (1 Peter 1:19, 2:4); *l*.7: (Numbers 5:6); *l*.8: (Romans 1:21)

HYMN XX

Hymn XX:1: *l*.2: 2 Corinthians 13:11; *l*.3: (Isaiah 8:13; Jeremiah 17:17); *l*.4: (Jeremiah 10:19); *l*.5: (Exodus 29:41–43, 39:32–40:38; Hebrews 9); *ll*.6–8: (Colossians 1:19–20)

Hymn XX:2: *l*.1: (John 6:55; 1 Corinthians 10:3–4); *l*.2: (2 Samuel 22:3; Psalm 61:3); *l*.4: (2 Samuel 22:3; Psalm 61:3; Proverbs 18:10); *l*.5: (Song of Solomon 4:4; Ephesians 6:11–13); *l*.7: Colossians 3:3

Hymn XX:3: *ll*.1–2: 2 Samuel 22:3; Psalm 61:2–3; (Deuteronomy 32:6, 31, 33:27; Psalm 89:26); *l*.2: (Psalm 31:3, 62:7); *l*.4: Isaiah 43:2; Psalm 66:12; *l*.5: 2 Corinthians 3:5; *l*.6: 2 Samuel 22:30/Psalm 18:29; *l*.7: (Lamentations 1:6)

HYMN XXI: *ll*.1–4: Song of Solomon 2:6/8:3; *ll*.5–8: Song of Solomon 2:7/3:5/8:4

HYMN XXII

Hymn XXII:1: *l*.1: (Luke 2:9–14; 1 Timothy 3:16; Hebrews 1:6); *l*.2: (Psalm 118:23/Matthew 21:42; Revelation 17:6); *ll*.3–4: (Colossians 1:16–17; Hebrews 1:1–4); *l*.4: (Romans 11:36; Hebrews 2:8–10); *l*.5: Luke 2:7, 12, 16; *l*.6: Matthew 8:20/Luke 9:58; *ll*.7–8: Luke 2:9–14; Hebrews 1:6

Hymn XXII:2: *l*.1: Exodus 19:18; *l*.2: Exodus 19:19; *ll*.3–4: Exodus 19:12–13, 24:4–11; (Isaiah 25:6–8; Ephesians 2:6; John 1:1–14); *l*.5: Colossians 1:19 (cf. 2:9); *l*.7: (Psalm 106:23; Ezekiel 22:30); *l*.8: Hebrews 7:27

Hymn XXII:3: *l*.1: 1 John 2:2, 4:10; Romans 3:25; Matthew 27:38/Mark 15:27–28; *l*.3: (Hosea 7:15); *l*.5: Zechariah 3:2; (Amos 4:11); *l*.6: Isaiah 42:21; *l*.7: Exodus 34:29; 2 Corinthians 3:7–11; Malachi 4:2; *ll*.7–8: (Romans 3:24–26)

Hymn XXII:4: *l*.1: Matthew 28:6; *l*.2: (Colossians 2:10); 1 Corinthians 14:33; *l*.3: Acts 17:28; *l*.5: (Isaiah 12:2; Exodus 15:2; Psalm 118:14; John 11:25, 14:6; Colossians 3:4); *ll*.6–7: (1 Timothy 3:16; 1 Peter 1:12); *l*.8: (Revelation 1:5–6, 5:11–13; Luke 2:13–14)

Hymn XXII:5: *l*.1: (Revelation 4:9); *l*.4: (Psalm 111:10); *l*.5: Hebrews 2:16–18, 4:15; *l*.7: Luke 2:16, 21, 27; 2 Corinthians 13:4; Luke 22:43; *l*.8: 1 Thessalonians 1:9

Hymn XXII:6: *l*.1: 1 Corinthians 15:42–43; Colossians 2:11; Romans 7:24; *l*.2: (2 Kings 2:11); *l*.4: (Luke 23:33); *l*.5: Hebrews 11:27; *l*.6: Revelation 2:8; *ll*.7–8: (Romans 8:35–39; Ephesians 4:13)

Hymn XXII:7: *l*.2: Romans 3:25; *l*.3: 2 Corinthians 10:5; Hebrews 9:3; Isaiah 25:7; *ll*.3–4: 2 Corinthians 3:13–18; *l*.4: Psalm 17:15; Romans 8:29; 1 Corinthians 15:49; *l*.5: Ephesians 3:9; *l*.6: (Romans 16:25); *l*.7: Psalm 2:12; *l*.8: (Psalm 78:9).

Scriptural References and Allusions

HYMN XXIII

Hymn XXIII:1: *l*.1: (Psalm 93:3–4); *l*.2: (Isaiah 43:2; 1 Corinthians 15:56); *l*.3: Hebrews 2:17, 3:1–2; *l*.4: (Matthew 14:31; Hebrews 6:17–20); *l*.5: (Romans 8:37; 1 Corinthians 15:57); *l*.6: (Isaiah 25:8; Hosea 13:14; 1 Corinthians 15:55; 1 John 5:4–5); *l*.7: (1 John 3:9, 5:18); *l*.8: Philippians 3:21; Romans 8:29–30; 2 Corinthians 3:18

Hymn XXIII:2: *l*.1: (1 Chronicles 16:15); *l*.2: (1 John 5:7); *l*.4: (Hebrews 2:16); *l*.6: Matthew 26:38; *l*.7: Revelation 14:1–3; *l*.8: (Hebrews 6:18–20, 9:3, 24, 10:19–20; Psalm 47:5, 66:1)

Hymn XXIII:3: *l*.1: Isaiah 49:10; Revelation 7:16; *l*.2: Luke 20:36; *l*.3: Isaiah 60:20; (Revelation 21:4); *ll*.3–4: Isaiah 35:10, 61:3; Jeremiah 31:13; *l*.4: Revelation 5:9; *l*.5: Revelation 22:1; *ll*.7–8: (Revelation 21:10–11, 23); *l*.8: 1 Peter 1:19; (Luke 23:33)

HYMN XXIV

Hymn XXIV:1: *ll*.1–3: Psalm 1:3; *ll*.1–4: Jeremiah 17:8, 13 (cf. Ezekiel 47:6–12; Song of Solomon 4:15)

Hymn XXIV:2: *l*.1: (Revelation 21:4); *ll*.1–2: (Exodus 3:7–8; Deuteronomy 8:7; cf. Song of Solomon 4:11, 12); *ll*.1–3: Numbers 13:23–27; *l*.4: Hebrews 11:16

Hymn XXIV:3: *l*.1: Exodus 3:13–15, 6:2–8; (Zechariah 14:9; Psalm 83:18); *l*.2: (Acts 13:32; Ephesians 3:6, 19); *l*.3: Isaiah 49:22; *l*.4: (Ephesians 3:8)

Hymn XXIV:4: *l*.1: (Isaiah 33:7); *l*.2: (Isaiah 25:6–8; Matthew 8:11, 22:1–14; Luke 14:15–24; Revelation 19:9); *l*.4: Ephesians 2:19

HYMN XXV: *l*.1: Song of Solomon 8:6; *l*.3: Jeremiah 2:2; *l*.4: (Matthew 24:12; Revelation 2:4, 3:15–16); *l*.5: Isaiah 33:5; *l*.6: (Proverbs 16:15; Psalm 21:6: 1 Corinthians 13:12); *ll*.7–8: (Psalm 131:2; Isaiah 28:9; 1 Corinthians 13:11)

HYMN XXVI: *ll*.1–4: Exodus 28:33–35; *l*.7: Hebrews 9:14; *l*.8: Matthew 3:17/Mark 1:11/Luke 3:22; Matthew 17:5; 2 Peter 1:17

HYMN XXVII: *ll*.1–2: Ruth 2:2–3, 7–9, 15–17; *l*.3: Exodus 19:18; (Exodus 24:17; Deuteronomy 4:11, 36, 33:2); *l*.4: Ruth 2:14 (cf. John 13:26; Hebrews 12:18–24); *l*.5: 1 Timothy 3:16; *l*.6: Exodus 24:4; *l*.7: (Hebrews 13:10–12); *l*.8: (Proverbs 2:3; Ephesians 1:18)

HYMN XXVIII: *l*.1: (Isaiah 12:3; Ezekiel 47:8–9); *l*.2: (1 Peter 2:9); *l*.3: (Ezekiel 47:12; Revelation 22:1–2); *l*.4: (John 4:14; Hosea 14:4; Revelation 21:6, 22:17); *ll*.4–5: Isaiah 55:1; *l*.5: Matthew 9:12–13/Mark 2:17/Luke 5:31–32; Genesis 3; *ll*.5–6: Isaiah 55:1; John 7:37–38; (2 Kings 5:10–14); *l*.7: Isaiah 9:7; Luke 1:33; *l*.8: John 5:2–4

HYMN XXIX: *l*.1: Isaiah 38:15; *l*.2 (Colossians 1:20); *l*.3: Hebrews 12:1; 1 Corinthians 9:24; *ll*.4–5: Exodus 14:13; 2 Chronicles 20:17; *l*.6: (Revelation 14:13)

HYMN XXX: *ll*.1–2: Proverbs 17:17; *l*.5: (Psalm 146:7; Isaiah 61:1; Luke 4:18; Matthew 9:12/Mark 2:17/Luke 5:31); *l*.6: Psalm 107:7; Jeremiah 50:5; *l*.8: 1 Peter 3:20

★ ★ ★

LETTER I
Ruth 2; Luke 6:1; Isaiah 32:2; Isaiah 26:20; Hebrews 4:14; Job 13:15; Genesis 8:21; Lamentations 4:1; Revelation 21:9; Romans 11:2; Psalm 75:8

Scriptural References and Allusions

LETTER II
Proverbs 18:24; John 21:15; Proverbs 23:23; Matthew 12:36; Luke 22:61; Philippians 3:9

LETTER III
Exodus 18:17–22; Song of Solomon 3:3–4, 5:7; 2 Kings 4:10; Isaiah 59:19; Psalm 87:3; Zephaniah 3:17

LETTER IV
Hebrews 12:24; 1 John 1:7; 1 Kings 6:7; Isaiah 27:9

LETTER V
Matthew 7:24–27; Isaiah 43:2; Acts 27:39–44; 2 Corinthians 4:18; Psalm 113:6; (Proverbs 29:15); Song of Solomon 3:11; Haggai 1:4; John 19:5; Revelation 2:18; Isaiah 42:21; Psalm 2:12; Hosea 2:7

LETTER VI
Titus 2:5; Malachi 1:6; Jeremiah 2:13; Psalm 23:1; Isaiah 45:22; Jeremiah 6:4; Hosea 7:9; Ruth 1:19; Esther 6:11; 1 Samuel 16:6–7, 11

LETTER VII
Revelation 3:8; Jeremiah 23:29; Hebrews 12:15; Romans 4:5; 2 Corinthians 5:19; Isaiah 55:2; Song of Solomon 4:4; Colossians 1:19; Song of Solomon 4:12; Ephesians 3:9; 1 Timothy 4:15; Hebrews 4:15; Lamentations 4:1; Lamentations 1:1; Hosea 7:9; Jeremiah 6:4; Song of Solomon 4:16

LETTER VIII
Ephesians 4:30; 1 Corinthians 6:19; Philippians 1:6; Matthew 26:41/Mark 14:38; James 5:16; 2 Corinthians 12:9; Psalm 109:4; John 18:6; Isaiah 27:3; Song of Solomon 1:8; Song of

Flame in the Mountains

Solomon 4:16; 2 Timothy 1:12; 2 Peter 1:14; Philippians 1:21; Philippians 1:23; Song of Solomon 2:9; 1 Corinthians 13:12; Zephaniah 3:17; 1 Corinthians 13:7